THRESHOLD COMPETITOR

THRESHOLD COMPETITOR

A MANAGEMENT SIMULATION

VERSION 3.0

Philip H. Anderson
David A. Beveridge
Timothy W. Scott
David L. Hofmeister

Upper Saddle River, **New Jersey** 07458

Editor-in-Chief: Jeff Shelstad
Managing Editor (Editorial): Jessica Sabloff
Editorial Assistant: Kevin Glynn
Media Project Manager: Michele Faranda
Senior Marketing Manager: Shannon Moore
Marketing Assistant: Christine Genneken
Managing Editor (Production): Judy Leale
Associate Director, Manufacturing: Vincent Scelta
Production Manager: Arnold Vila
Manufacturing Buyer: Diane Peirano
Cover Design: Bruce Kenselaar
Printer/Binder: Victor Graphics

Credits and acknowledgments borrowed from other sources and reproduced, with permission, in this textbook appear on appropriate pages within text.

Copyright © 2003, 1999, 1998 by Pearson Education, Inc., Upper Saddle River, New Jersey, 07458. All rights reserved. Printed in the United States of America. This publication is protected by Copyright and permission should be obtained from the publisher prior to any prohibited reproduction, storage in a retrieval system, or transmission in any form or by any means, electronic, mechanical, photocopying, recording, or likewise. For information regarding permission(s), write to: Rights and Permissions Department.

Pearson Education LTD.
Pearson Education Australia PTY, Limited
Pearson Education Singapore, Pte. Ltd
Pearson Education North Asia Ltd
Pearson Education, Canada, Ltd
Pearson Educación de Mexico, S.A. de C.V.
Pearson Education–Japan
Pearson Education Malaysia, Pte. Ltd

10 9 8 7 6 5 4 3 2 1
ISBN 0-13-101027-1

CONTENTS

Preface ix

Chapter 1 – Overview 1
   What Is *Threshold Competitor*? 1
   How the *Threshold Competitor* Simulation Works 1
   Threshold Competitor's Three Stages in a Decision-Round 2
      The Forecasting Stage 2
      The Processing Stage 2
      The Results Stage 3
   How to Approach the Simulation 4
   Purposes of *Threshold Competitor* 5
   Tips on Succeeding with *Threshold Competitor* 5
   How to Use This Manual 6

Chapter 2 – Review of Management Functions 8
   Planning 8
      Mission Statement 9
      Statement of Goals 10
      Strategies and Policies 11
      Other Planning Activities 11
   Organizing and Staffing 12
   Leading 12
   Controlling 13

Chapter 3 – The Threshold Team Competitor Business Environment 14
   Your Company's Products 14
   History of Your Company 14
   Current Status of Your Company 15
   Your Company's Marketplace 16

Chapter 4 – Installing the Threshold Team Competitor Software 18
   Introduction 18
   Installation Requirements 18
      Equipment Needed 18
      Internet Connection 18
      Valid Key Access Number 18
   Installing the *Threshold Competitor* Software 19
   Navigating Around *Threshold Competitor* 21

Chapter 5 – Working with the *Threshold Competitor* Program 22
   Chapter Overview 22
   Threshold Competitor Team and *Threshold Competitor Solo* Differences 22
      Processing Decisions 22
      Storing Your Company Data File – Floppy versus Hard Drive 22
      Starting the Programs 23
   Starting the *Threshold Competitor Solo* Program 23

Starting the *Threshold Competitor Team* Program 26
   Running the *Threshold Competitor Team* with Your Company Data File on a Floppy Disk 26
   Running the *Threshold Competitor Team* with Your Company Data File on the Hard Disk 27
Opening an Existing *Threshold Competitor* Data File 28
   Opening an Existing *Threshold Competitor Solo* Data File 28
   Opening an Existing *Threshold Competitor Team* Data File 30
Using the *Threshold Competitor* Program 30
   Entering a Decision 31
   Saving Your Decisions 32
   Correcting an Error 32
Moving the Cursor Around the Decisions Screens 32
   Using the Tab Key 32
   Using the Mouse 33
Moving from Screen to Screen 33
   Using the Menu Bar 33
   Using the [PgUp] and [PgDn] Keys 35
   Using *Threshold Competitor* "Hot" Keys 36
Menu Bar Operations 36
   The File Menu 36
   The Quarter Menu 40
   The Decisions Menu 41
   The Reports Menu 42
   The Info Menu 43
   The Print Menu 44
Seeing the *Forecasted* Results of Your Decisions 47
Processing the Decisions (Available Only for *Competitor Solo*) 48
Seeing the *Actual* Results of Earlier Quarters 48
Displaying Multiple Screens Simultaneously 48
Reprocess a Previous Quarter (Applies Only to *Competitor Team*) 49
Using *Threshold Competitor* on a Hard Disk 51
   Copying Files Between the Company Disk and the Hard Disk 51
Making a Backup Disk 52
Troubleshooting 52
   Complete System Failure 52
   Threshold Competitor Program Failure 53
   Threshold Competitor Company Disk Failure 53
   Viruses 53
   Data Entry Errors 53
A Step-by-Step Walk-Through 53

Chapter 6 – Making Decisions 54
Overview of Decisions 54
Preparing for Decisions: Your Business Plan 54
   Developing a Business Plan 54
Marketing Decisions 55
   Price 56
      Effect of Price on Sales 56
   Television Advertisements 56
   Newspaper Advertisements 56
   Magazine Advertisements 56

Sales Forecast Estimate 57
    Factors to Consider When Forecasting Sales 57
    Forecast Reports 58
    Diminishing Returns 58
    Substitute Products 58
    Marketing Decisions Limits 59
Market Research Decisions 59
    Price by Company 60
    Television, Newspaper, Magazine, and Product Quality Reports 60
    Units Sold by Company 61
    Future Sales Potential 61
    Cost of Market Research 61
Production Decisions 62
    Buy Raw Materials 63
    Spending on Product Quality 63
        Effect of Quality on Sales 63
    Number of Units to Produce 64
    Workers to Hire, Fire, or Lay Off 66
    Buy or Sell Plant Capacity 67
    Human Resource Development 67
Finance Decisions 68
    Short-Term Loans 69
    Mortgages 70
    Short-Term Investments 70
Management Dilemmas 71
Cost Parameters Report 72
Decisions Flow Chart 73
Some Decisions Guidelines 73

Chapter 7 – *Threshold Competitor* Reports 74
Decisions Reports 74
    Marketing Decisions Report 74
    Production / Finance Decisions Report 75
Operations Reports 76
    Inventory Report 76
    Labor Report 78
    Cost of Production Report 79
Marketing Reports 81
    Selling and Administrative Costs Report 81
    Marketing Research Report 82
Income Statement 83
Balance Sheet 85
    Assets 86
    Liabilities 87
    Owners' Equity 87
Cash Flow Statement 87
    Cash Receipts 87
    Cash Payments 88
    Net Cash Flow and Short-Term Loan 89

Industry Performance Reports 90
   The Four Performance Factors 91
   Calculation of Points Awarded 92
Information Reports 92
A Final Comment 93

Appendices 95

Appendix A – Quarter 0 Decisions 96
Appendix B – Quarter 0 Reports 97
Appendix C – Sample Market Research Report 102
Appendix D – Initial Cost Parameters 103
Appendix E – *Threshold Competitor* Limits and Time Lags 104
Appendix F – *Threshold Competitor* "Hot" Keys 105
Appendix G – Management Dilemmas 107
   1. Why Does It Have To Be Emily? 108
   2. Can You Steal Garbage? 109
   3. The Older Employee 111
   4. The Alcoholic Employee 112
   5. Wildcat Strike 113
   6. Substitute Raw Materials 114
   7. Where There's Smoke, There's Fire 115
   8. Did You Hear the One About…? 117
Appendix H – *Threshold Competitor* Industry Performance Reports 119
Appendix I – *Threshold Competitor* Flow Chart 120
Appendix J – A Step-by-Step Walk-Through 121
Appendix K – *Threshold Competitor* CompData Excel File 122
Appendix L – *Threshold Competitor* PerfData Excel File 123

Index 125

PREFACE

WHAT IS *THRESHOLD COMPETITOR TEAM* AND *THRESHOLD COMPETITOR SOLO*?

Threshold Competitor Team and *Threshold Competitor Solo* are computer-based models that simulate a small manufacturing company that produces two plastic molded products — Product 1 and Product 2. The manufacturing process consists of forming plastic raw materials (sheets of plastic) into the finished consumer products. The products are sold through retail markets to the general public. The two products are not substitutes for one another, nor are they complementary. This means that sales of one product do not effect sales of the other product.

In *Threshold Competitor Team*, you are part of a group organized to manage your company in competition with the other groups in your class. Each group will manage a separate company that will compete with the other groups in the same marketplace. In *Threshold Competitor Team*, the administrator uses the computer to process the decisions that teams make regarding the operation of their company after collecting the decisions from all the competing teams.

Threshold Competitor Solo is a play-alone version of the *Threshold Competitor Team*. It places you in competition with semi-intelligent companies managed by the computer rather than other groups in your class. While your competitors will act rationally, they are not all-knowing, perfect competitors.

In *Threshold Competitor Team* and *Threshold Competitor Solo*, you will:
- Decide your company mission, goals, policies, and strategies.
- Develop skills in planning, organizing, staffing, directing, and controlling a business.
- Make decisions in the areas of:
    1. Marketing, including market research and sales forecasts.
    2. Finance, including short-term and long-term loans.
    3. Manufacturing, including raw materials, production, scheduling, staffing, and inventory control.
- Have the opportunity to ask "what-if" questions by entering a sales estimate and seeing what the results of your decisions would be given this level of sales.
- See the results of your decisions and have an opportunity to correct mistakes in the following quarters of operation.

WHAT ARE THE COMPUTER SYSTEM REQUIREMENTS?

In order to operate the *Threshold Competitor* programs, you must have access to a personal computer system with the following characteristics:
- Windows 95, 98, 2000, ME, NT, or XP.
- 3 Megs of space on your hard disk.
- At least 1 disk drive.

Although optional, we advise that you use a printer so that you can generate printouts of your quarterly results. We also strongly recommend that you have a blank disk suitable for use with the PC to use to make backup copies of your *Threshold Competitor* company files. You should do this after each time that your decisions for a quarter are processed and you receive the results.

HOW DO *THRESHOLD COMPETITOR TEAM* AND *COMPETITOR SOLO* WORK?

You work on a personal computer, entering your decisions on two screens. You can review previous quarters' decisions and results either on the screen or on printouts as you work.

When your decisions for a quarter of *Threshold Competitor Team* and *Threshold Competitor Solo* operations are final, the decisions are processed either by your instructor (for *Competitor Team*) or by the computer (for *Competitor Solo*). The *Threshold Competitor Team* and *Threshold Competitor Solo* programs will determine the number of products each company sold and produce a series of operations, marketing, and financial reports for your company. The programs also rate the companies and rank them according to their performance on sales revenues, net income, return on assets, and accuracy in forecasting sales.

ACKNOWLEDGMENTS

We would like to thank the following people for their help and contributions to *Threshold Competitor Team* and *Threshold Competitor Solo*. As always, our families deserve thanks for their patience, as we took time from them to work on this project. To Sue, Lona, Emily, and Kelly — Thanks.

We also would like to thank the students at the University of St. Thomas and Minnesota State University, Mankato who participated in the class testing of *Solo Competitor*. A special thank you goes to Anne Cohen, a faculty member at the University of St. Thomas and Miles Smayling, a faculty member at Minnesota State University, Mankato who helped us in the testing process. Thanks also to Melissa Steffens, and Michelle Faranda of Prentice Hall, who gave their support for this project and provided great feedback on how to make this product the best possible we could produce.

A special note of thanks goes to Dave Hofmeister and Mike Thompson, our friends and colleagues from the first edition of *Threshold*. Dave designed and created the *Threshold* first edition software and started us down the road for a play-alone version of that simulation. Dave died suddenly of a heart attack in December 1993. We owe much to his dedication and determination to provide a product for you that would combine education, learning, and fun. Like Dave, Mike played a key role in developing the software for the first version of *Threshold*. Thanks, Mike, for helping us get the first edition of *Threshold* off the ground.

P.H.A.
D.A.B.
T.W.S.

CHAPTER 1

OVERVIEW

WHAT IS *THRESHOLD COMPETITOR*?

Threshold Competitor Team and Threshold Competitor Solo are computer-based models that simulate the business operations of a small manufacturing company. You or your team will make the decisions necessary to run that company. Chapter 4 describes your company and the products it sells. We designed *Threshold Competitor* to help you improve your skills in managing an enterprise. The simulation will also allow you to demonstrate your understanding of business concepts in a competitive, but safe environment. Working with this simulation is challenging, but manageable. We hope it will bring to life the topics you study in your management classes or read about in a management textbook, so that you can better see and understand the issues involved in formulating and implementing a management strategy. We also hope it helps you recognize the connections that exist among the management, marketing, and financial concepts used to manage a business. The chance to test your ideas is one of the best ways to learn about the field of management. Managers are inherently action oriented. *Threshold Competitor* provides you with the opportunity to put what you have learned into action.

In *Threshold Competitor Team*, you manage a company that competes against other companies run by students in your class. Each student-run company operates in the same marketplace and competes directly with other student-run companies. In *Threshold Competitor Team*, the administrator uses the computer to process decisions that students make regarding the operation of their companies after collecting decisions from all participants.

Threshold Competitor Solo is a play-alone version of *Threshold Competitor Team*. Rather than vying with other student-run companies, you compete against semi-intelligent companies managed by the computer. While these computer-run companies act rationally, they are not all-knowing, perfect competitors.

Your assignment is to manage the operations of your company, acting as the chief executive responsible for all aspects of the business. The decisions you make will include setting strategy for the company, determining the production and marketing of the products, financing the costs of the marketing and production operations, and the purchase of competitive information. Practicing with *Threshold Competitor Team* or *Threshold Competitor Solo* will sharpen your managerial skills.

You will compete with other companies selling similar products in your industry's marketplace. The computer will process your decisions and those of the other companies and provide reports regarding how well each company performed. The *Threshold Competitor* software uses the decisions you and your competitors make to determine how many units each company sells during a three-month period (i.e., quarter) and to provide operations, marketing, and financial reports for your company. You will manage your company for several quarters, analyzing the results of each quarter to help you make decisions for the next quarter's operations. What follows is a discussion of how the *Threshold Competitor* simulation works.

HOW THE *THRESHOLD COMPETITOR* SIMULATION WORKS

The *Threshold Competitor* program contains mathematical formulas and sets of rules. These formulas and rules allow the program to simulate, or imitate, the results that a business decision would have in the real world. So, for example, the *Threshold Competitor* program can determine how a much company's sales would be affected by the price that it sets for its product when compared with the prices of its competitors' products.

You will make approximately 30 decisions to manage each period of operation that you manage your *Threshold Competitor* company. Each period of operation represents one quarter (i.e., three months) of a calendar year. You begin managing *Threshold Competitor* operations in Quarter 1 (January – March) and continue to make decisions through succeeding quarters. Just as you would if you were managing an actual business enterprise, your goal is to manage your *Threshold Competitor* company as efficiently and effectively as possible. As you progress through each quarter of operation, you should work to improve your performance by analyzing your results, identifying your mistakes, and modifying your decisions to eliminate those mistakes.

THRESHOLD COMPETITOR'S THREE STAGES IN A DECISION-ROUND

There are three stages involved in working with the *Threshold Competitor* simulation. They are (1) the Forecasting Stage, (2) the Processing Stage, and (3) the Results Stage. In the Forecasting Stage, you enter decisions to test "what if" assumptions and then modify those decisions until you enter a set of decisions you think are the best. In the Processing Stage, the program assesses the decisions of all competitors to determine market share allocations for each company and the consequent profitability of each company. (In *Threshold Competitor Team*, other student-run teams supply competitors' decisions while in *Threshold Competitor Solo* the computer generates competitors' decisions.) In the Results Stage you respond to the results of the processing of your decisions, looking at your company's reports to assess your actual performance versus what you forecasted it to be during the Forecasting Stage. You then use your analysis in a new Forecasting Stage as you begin the next decision round.

The Forecasting Stage

In the Forecasting Stage, you will make decisions regarding (a) marketing (e.g., pricing, promotion, and quality of your products), (b) manufacturing (e.g., how many units of your products to produce), and (c) financing (e.g., requesting a loan to pay current bills). Once you have entered your decisions, you can look at *forecasted* reports for your company based on the decisions you just entered. You can view these *forecasted* reports using the Reports option on the Menu bar. (We explain how to do this in Chapter 3.) After analyzing these reports, you can enter new decisions to try to improve your *forecasted* results. Entering new decisions will allow you to test "what-if" assumptions and then to modify those decisions until you find the set of decisions you think are the best. You can enter new decisions as often as you like before you choose to process your entries. There is no limit to the number of times you can enter new decisions. The last set of decisions that you enter and save will be used in the Processing Stage.

The Processing Stage

Once you are satisfied with the decisions you have entered, your decisions must be processed before you can move to the next quarter of operation (e.g., from Quarter 1 to Quarter 2). In *Threshold Competitor Solo*, you simply instruct the computer to do this by selecting the "Process Industry" option under File on the Menu bar. Processing the industry commits you to the last set of decisions you entered. This means that once you process your decisions for a quarter, you cannot alter your decisions or the results for that quarter. Your next set of decisions will be for the next quarter of operation and will be based on the results of the quarter of operation you just completed. For example, once you process your Quarter 1 decisions, your next set of decisions will be for Quarter 2 regardless of how much you would like to change what you did in Quarter 1.

The processing stage of the *Team* version of *Threshold Competitor* is handled very differently from the *Solo* version. In the team version of *Threshold Competitor*, your decisions must be evaluated against other student-run companies. Consequently, you and all of your competitors must submit your decisions to the administrator for processing. The administrator can process the decisions for a quarter *only* after he or she has collected the decisions for *all* competitors. If the decisions for even one company are missing, the simulation cannot proceed. Once the simulation administrator has processed the decisions for a quarter they cannot be altered. Your administrator will return the results of your decisions and you will be ready to move on to the next quarter's operations.

Having to live with the decisions you have made is a part of organizational life. For example, the marketing team for Wal-Mart may use a model to test the effect of varying pricing strategies (e.g., higher price, but fewer unit sales) on profitability for the company. They will likely test many variations to the price versus sales trade-off. However, once they make the decision on the price of a product and the advertisement has run in the local newspaper, it is impossible to change the price (and the consequent sales results) for that advertisement. All Wal-Mart can do is to make a pricing change in *next* week's newspaper ad. So, once you choose to implement your decisions (i.e., process the quarter), you will also have to live with the consequences of those decisions for that quarter and make adjustments in your decisions for subsequent quarters.

In *Threshold Competitor Solo* your competition consists of 15 computer-managed companies operating in the marketplace. While the computer competitors act rationally, we designed *Threshold Competitor Solo* so that you can establish a competitive advantage in the industry. When working with *Threshold Competitor Solo* you will always manage Company #1. In *Threshold Competitor Team*, the number of teams in your industry will be determined by the simulation administrator and will depend upon the number of student participants. Your administrator will let you know which company you're managing (Company #1 or Company #2, etc.)

Having the computer manage the companies you compete with in *Threshold Competitor Solo* simplifies the procedure for processing your decisions. In *Threshold Competitor Solo* the computer makes the decisions for the competing companies. Consequently, whenever you have completed your decisions for your company, you can process the decisions yourself for all the companies in the industry. *Threshold Competitor Solo* eliminates the need for an administrator to collect and process the decisions of the companies operating in an industry. This allows you to play the game by yourself, at your own pace, not tied to anyone else's schedule. *Threshold Competitor Solo* allows you to work with the software without having to wait for decisions from the competing companies, nor wait for an administrator to process company decisions. In addition, if you perform poorly against the computer competitors, you can stop playing the current setup and start a new competition quickly and easily (discussed below).

The Results Stage

Once your decisions have been processed, the *Threshold Competitor* program will generate reports that show how well your company performed in competition with the other companies in your industry. The program will determine how many sales each company made based on their marketing efforts relative to the competition and will provide individual marketing, operations, and financial reports for each company. In *Threshold Competitor Team*, your administrator will return a disk or a file to you that will enable you to view your results. With *Threshold Competitor Solo* you can access your results immediately after you have processed your decisions.

You will use the results of the quarter just processed as the basis for your decisions for the next quarter of operation. For example, maybe in Quarter 1 your price for Product 1 was too high compared to your competitors. If this resulted in an increase of inventory for that product, your Quarter 2 operations will reflect the cost of carrying that extra inventory. It would be up to you to adjust your pricing of Product 1 in Quarter 2 to avoid repeating the problem in Quarter 3. In other words, you will use your analysis of the results of a quarter that was just processed to guide you as you make your adjustments in your decisions and forecasts for the next quarter of operations. So once you have processed a quarter and analyzed the results, you will return to the Forecasting Stage and repeat the three-stage sequence.

HOW TO APPROACH THE SIMULATION

Managing a business is a blend of art and science. This means the process of managing requires working with both the facts of the situation you are facing and with your intuition regarding how to succeed in that environment. Emphasizing one of these at the expense of the other makes you a less effective manager. Intuitive problem-solvers make decisions without considering all of the data available to them. They are more concerned with their "gut feelings" than with the realities they face. Ignoring these realities results in decisions that are ineffective in resolving problems. By contrast, problem-solvers who rely completely on facts tend not to consider the aspects of a problem that cannot be easily reduced to numbers. Certainly you cannot quantify everything that contributes to the resolution of a problem. This approach, then, also leaves out key components of a problem's solution. *Threshold Competitor* will give you a chance to develop and practice both kinds of managerial thinking. Although you must work with the detail of the numbers generated in your *Threshold Competitor* reports, you must also get a feel for the total simulated business environment created by *Threshold Competitor*. Learning to manage both of these dimensions of a problem will make you a more effective marketing manager, not only of your *Threshold Competitor* company, but also in your subsequent business experiences.

Both *Threshold Competitor Team* and *Threshold Competitor Solo* can be played alone or your instructor may choose to have you manage your company as part of a group. Many college participants dislike working in a group. They feel that it is not like work in "the real world." In fact, groups working with a *Threshold Competitor* company face almost exactly the same problems that a work group in any business organization has to face. Managers in a business organization do much of their work in teams. Working with a group of individuals requires learning how to manage competing ideas and egos while successfully accomplishing the group's goal. This is a common experience in modern organizations. It is also a necessary element in successfully managing the *Threshold Competitor* simulation. In business, as in the *Threshold Competitor* simulation, each participant's knowledge, motivation, determination, and time available, affects the success of the enterprise. Learning to work together cooperatively is a critical ingredient for success in any business enterprise. One of the keys for anyone to be successful in an enterprise is to learn how to use the talents of others. Managers that try to do it all by themselves, limit the growth and success of their business.

Backup Your Company Disk. We encourage you to make copies of your *Threshold Competitor* company disk. You should keep a backup copy in case the original disk is lost, damaged, or destroyed. We ***strongly recommend*** that you make a backup copy of your disk after every time you exit the program. The data stored on your disk is important.

PURPOSES OF *THRESHOLD COMPETITOR*

Working with *Threshold Competitor* will help you to:
- Experience problems and issues involved in managing a business.
- Understand the importance of a business plan in guiding business decisions, including:
  - The importance of developing a common vision and coordinating the marketing, operations, and financial areas of a business, and
  - The need for planning as you make tactical moves to react to changing conditions.
- Acquire experiences to aid your comprehension of issues presented in management courses.
- Understand the relationships between marketing, operations, and finance.
- Develop skills in planning, organizing, staffing, and controlling a business.
- Understand the relationships between financial statements such as the cash flow statement, the income statement, and the balance sheet, and their connections to the management reports.
- Experience the dynamics of marketing against constantly changing competitor positions and the need for market research.
- Understand the operational issues of production, inventory control, plant and workforce utilization, scheduling, and cost control of manufacturing operations.

TIPS ON SUCCEEDING WITH *THRESHOLD COMPETITOR*

The following are some tips to help you when you are working with the *Threshold Competitor* simulation:

- <u>Manage your time efficiently</u>. Learning how to manage time is a primary concern for any manager. It affects success in any business. There will never be enough time to do all that you would wish to do. Determine what issues to focus on (set priorities). Staying focused on these issues (efficiency) will have a significant impact on the effectiveness of the decisions you make. Working with *Threshold Competitor* gives you practice at managing this critical resource. Developing good time-management skills will increase your chances of success in your business career.

- <u>Manage your business; do not guess at your decisions</u>. You can either manage your company or guess when making decisions regarding the future. Managing the business involves having company goals, plus plans and strategies for meeting those goals. Use these goals, plans, and strategies to guide your decision-making. Guessing leads to making decisions randomly and without any consistency over time. This may be easier and more fun in the short run. You may even initially get better results than your competition. However, in the long run, if you make your decisions by guessing, you will not be able to outperform your competition. This is because you will not understand what you did that was correct and what you need to change to improve your position in subsequent quarters. Nor will you be sensitive to changes that your competitors are making or to changes in your economic environment. *Threshold Competitor* is the kind of project where effort is rewarded.

- <u>Learn from your failures as well as your successes</u>. Managers must always deal with their own and others' mistakes. When your decisions in *Threshold Competitor* do not give you the results you planned for, or they are not satisfactory for the long-term success of your company, analyze the results to see what you should do differently next time. A successful manager learns how to capitalize on success, recover from mistakes, and move forward to improve the company's position. You often can learn more from what you do wrong than from what you do right.

- <u>Do not worry if you are confused at first</u>. Participants are often confused when they begin working with the *Threshold Competitor* program. Remember, this is most likely a new form of learning experience for you. Working with a simulation requires *applying* your knowledge and skills to a business operation rather than *listening* to a lecture about the knowledge and skills needed to operate the business. It is a fundamental change to move from hearing to doing.

As with any new experience, it can be confusing and a bit overwhelming at first. However, after you make two or three sets of decisions, you should feel familiar with the rules of *Threshold Competitor* and become more comfortable with learning through active application rather than passive listening. Your willingness to invest the effort to learn your new environment will have a significant impact on your ability to outperform your competitors.

This exercise also replicates what you will experience in the world of business. Managers face a constantly changing business environment. Their ability to understand quickly new business situations significantly affects their personal and organizational success. You have only to think about the changes in computer technology you have witnessed over the past few years to recognize the importance of being able to adjust to changes around you.

HOW TO USE THIS MANUAL

Read this manual thoroughly, but do not try to memorize it. Instead, read the manual to get a sense of the business environment created by the simulation. Then, as you work on *Threshold Competitor*, refer to the appropriate sections of the manual for specific information. You will notice that the simulation's program contains much of the information supplied by this manual. For example, you can view the costs of operating the business through the Menu bar in the program. We will explain how to do this later in this manual.

When you get to Chapter 3, you will want to begin using the *Threshold Competitor* disk on your computer. Learning how to use the disk and keyboard to enter and record your decisions will make the rest of the manual easier to understand.

The appendixes have a number of forms and exhibits to help you manage your company. Look at them as you read the manual and refer to them later when you need the information.

The rest of the contents of this manual is outlined below.
- Chapter 2 reviews the fundamentals of management and shows how this simulation reflects these fundamentals.
- Chapter 3 describes the company you will manage and the business environment in which you will operate.
- Chapter 4 instructs you on how to load the *Threshold Competitor* program onto your computer.
- Chapter 5 introduces you to the simulation model created by the *Threshold Competitor* program. It gives you a quick, guided tour of the simulation. We explain how to access current cost information through the Menu bar in the *Threshold Competitor* program in this chapter.
- Chapter 6 discusses the decisions you will make and tells you how to enter them on the computer and onto your company disk.
- Chapter 7 describes the reports you will receive after each team makes decisions for each quarter of operation and after the computer has processed those decisions.
- Appendix A shows the decisions made in the last quarter of operations just prior to your team taking over the management of the company.
- Appendix B includes reports of the results of the decisions shown in Appendix A.

- Appendix C is an example of the market research reports you can purchase to help you in making decisions in future quarters, as you continue to manage your company.
- Appendix D provides a listing of the initial cost parameters for various elements in *Threshold Competitor*, such as advertising rates, costs for market research, and interest rates for loans and investments. This appendix also includes the worker productivity in Quarter 1 for each of the two products that your company produces. These costs and productivity levels will most certainly change during your management of your *Threshold Competitor* company. Current costs and productivity levels will be on your company disk. You will use the Cost Parameters option under the Info menu to see the current cost parameters for your company. We will explain this in Chapter 5.
- Appendix E gives you important limits on the decisions you can make in the management of your *Threshold Competitor* company. For example, it tells you the range of prices you are allowed to charge for your products. You can also view this information through the Menu bar in the *Threshold Competitor* programs. We will explain this in Chapter 5.
- Appendix F shows the screens to which you can move to directly using *Threshold Competitor*'s "hot" keys. These are a combination of the [CTRL], Shift, and Function (e.g., F1) keys. Directions for using these "hot" keys are given in Chapter 5.
- Appendix G describes some management dilemmas that your company may face during your management of the simulation. These dilemmas represent managerial problems outside your company's normal operations. How to make decisions regarding the *Threshold Competitor* management dilemmas is discussed in Chapter 6.
- Appendix H provides an example of an Industry Performance Report. It shows how each company performed in sales, income, return on sales, and sales forecasting when compared to the performance of the other companies in the simulation.
- Appendix I provides a flow chart of the decisions you will make and how they lead to forecast and actual reports you will use to manage your *Threshold Competitor* company.
- Appendix J gives a step-by-step walk-through for entering a set of decisions, reviewing the forecasted results, modifying the decision, processing the decisions, and then looking at the actual results. You can use this appendix with *Threshold Competitor Solo* to become familiar with how both of the *Threshold Competitor Team* and *Threshold Competitor Solo* simulations work.
- Appendixes L and M provide a description of the variables that are extracted using the "Create Company Spreadsheet" and "Create Performance Spreadsheet" options under the File menu. These two options allow you to extract data that you can use in an Excel worksheet to monitor your company's performance over time. We will discuss these two options in Chapter 5.

CHAPTER 2

REVIEW OF MANAGEMENT FUNCTIONS

The purpose of this chapter is to review the functions of management and show how each of these is involved in your management of the *Threshold Competitor* simulations.

Management is the process of establishing goals for an organization and then working effectively and efficiently to achieve those goals. Effective managers attain their goals. Efficient managers achieve those goals without wasting resources. For example, they manufacture the desired number of products at the lowest possible cost. Effectiveness is concerned with the accomplishment of goals. Efficiency is concerned with using the minimal amount of resources to accomplish those goals. An effective manager cares whether the goals are reached. An efficient manager is concerned with getting there for the least possible cost.

It is important for a manager to be both effective *and* efficient. For example, a manager might succeed at selling a desired quantity of a product (i.e., the manager was effective). However, if excessive overtime was needed in order to produce enough of the product to meet the high sales goal, the cost of manufacturing the product could also become excessive. The net result could be losses and a failed business. Similarly, a manager may succeed in cutting costs, but cut them so severely that the company fails to sell enough to be profitable. For example, reducing advertising will save on those expenses, but also will reduce sales, as fewer people are aware of what your products have to offer them. Drawing the proper balance between effectiveness and efficiency is the mark of a successful manager.

The functions of management are interrelated activities managers perform to achieve their chosen goals. Most textbooks say that managers plan, organize, staff, lead, and control. Each of these managerial functions can be further broken down into smaller parts. For example, planning has the following elements:
- Formulating objectives (what you want to achieve);
- Formulating strategies and policies (what behavior you will use to pursue your goals);
- Problem solving (developing alternative actions for overcoming obstacles to achieving your goals); and
- Decision making (choosing which alternatives to implement).

PLANNING

Planning is the most basic management function. It should be the first function you perform when you begin *Threshold Competitor*. Planning is deciding in advance what to do, how to do it, when to do it, who is to do it, and where it will be done. Planning comes first because you cannot, for example, determine the financial needs for your company's activities until you know what you want to accomplish. The financing (i.e., money) needed to manage a large-scale company is considerably different from that needed to operate a small, niche player in the industry.

Planning is costly in its use of resources, especially time. Often participants do not like to plan, arguing that things change too fast to make planning worth the effort. Although excessive planning can be inefficient, making decisions without a plan is also inefficient when the company has to correct mistakes made because it had no clear sense of direction. For example, a company must know whether it wants to offer a high-quality/high-priced product or a low-quality/low-priced product *before* it can determine decisions regarding production volume and advertising. You must balance the benefits and costs associated with formulating and operating a plan. Remember also that planning is an ongoing process, not a one-time event. Just because you develop a plan at the beginning of the simulation does not mean planning activities are finished. You will need to adjust your goals and policies in response to your competitors' actions and to unforeseen changes in your environment. This means your company should periodically reevaluate its plan and make adjustments to reflect current conditions.

Mission Statement

The first step in the planning process for *Threshold Competitor*, as it should be for any company, is the development of a company mission. A mission statement describes the purpose of the organization. It states why your company is in business and what kind of company it wants to be. Identifying a mission is critical to guiding your business successfully. Without this focus to guide your decisionmaking, you may drift in how you approach your marketplace. As a consequence, the competitors who have a clearer mission will enjoy more success than you. They will know who their customer is and be ahead of you in determining what that customer wants.

The focus of a mission statement should be on the marketplace in which the company plans to operate. Who are the customers that it wants to serve? What customer need does the company intend to fulfill? And how will the company satisfy that need better than its competitors? The core of a mission statement should not be about making a profit, but about satisfying a customer need. This does not mean that making a profit is not important. A company wants and needs to be as profitable as possible if it is to maintain a long-term existence. If a company cannot sustain a profitable operation, it will eventually go out of business. If it cannot achieve a level of profit that allows it to invest in the future, it will lose its ability to compete in the marketplace over time as others invest in product enhancements and cost-effective equipment. Consequently, knowing where a company wants to go becomes key to knowing where, and in what, to invest the profits of today's operations. Further, understanding what customer needs you are trying to satisfy is critical to knowing how to allocate the company's limited resources.

Which of these, satisfying a customer need or making a profit, is the principal purpose of a business? Which of these should come first? That is the classic chicken-egg conundrum. Clearly, you must attend to both. Our belief is that you should start with the desire to satisfy a need, recognizing that if you do not maintain a profitable organization, your ability to satisfy that need will be short lived. If a company does not make a profit, it cannot continue to satisfy its customers' needs, no matter how much its customers may want what the company is offering them. Consequently, we contend that a company has an obligation to make a profit so that it can continue to satisfy the needs of its customers and pay its employees a fair wage.

The debate may be less on whether making a profit is acceptable, but more on how much profit a company should make. At what point does a company begin to "gouge" its customers and to violate its social responsibility as a corporate citizen? That debate is not the focus of this manual, but you may choose to reflect on the ability of a competitive market to "control" excess profit taking by companies in that market as you participate in the *Threshold Competitor* simulation exercise.

A mission statement should not consist simply of a series of platitudes that carry little operational meaning, such as "to maximize profits." The mission statement needs to go beyond statements of profitability in order to give the organization identity and focus, both for yourself and for your potential customers. Because you will know very little about your company and its market environment when you begin, your mission statement will be relatively vague compared to that of a real organization. However, you do need to determine, in a broad sense, what role your company will play within its industry. How will you compete with the other companies in the simulation? For example, do you want to be a discount-priced/high-volume producer or a premium-priced/low-volume producer? What will be your competitive edge? How will customers distinguish your company from your competitors' companies? What will you do better than your competition? Perhaps most importantly, why will consumers want to buy your product rather than your competitors'? A sample mission statement is provided in Exhibit 2.1.

Exhibit 2.1

SAMPLE MISSION STATEMENT

Our mission is to provide quality-sensitive customers with technologically-advanced, premium-priced products. Our quality focus will extend beyond our products to our employees. We will provide them with a high quality of work life by conducting developmental training programs and maintaining a rewarding compensation structure.

Statement of Goals

Once you determine your company's mission, you must decide what goals you want it to achieve in order to accomplish that mission. State your goals in terms that provide you with a clear sense of direction. A goal such as "to increase profits" is too vague to be very useful. Goals should also refer to a single, specific topic that is measurable, such as a sales goal or a cost of manufacturing goal. Unless you are able to measure your progress toward a goal, you will be unable to perform the managerial function of control. Control, which we discuss later in this chapter, involves deciding whether changes are necessary in order to reach your goals. Finally, goals should be challenging but achievable. If you set goals too low, the company will not advance as fast as it could. At the same time, if goals are unreasonably high, people will give up rather than strive to achieve them.

In addition, you must take into account the relationship among the goals. A good set of goals will avoid putting the organization in a position where accomplishing one goal has negative consequences for another goal. For example, a 25% market share may require a high promotional effort to achieve that target, making it difficult to also achieve an ROS goal of 15%. In this example, the high volume goal may be inconsistent with the profit goal. Exhibit 2.2 shows some sample goals.

Exhibit 2.2

SAMPLE COMPANY GOALS

1. Maintain market share of 10% for both products.
2. Rank in the top 20% of the industry on product quality.
3. Eliminate lost sales due to insufficient inventory levels.
4. Keep manufacturing cost of goods sold below $42.00 for Product 2.
5. Achieve 5% return on sales on a yearly basis.

Sometimes the shorter-term objectives of a firm will differ from their longer-term goals. For example, a company may sacrifice some profits in the short term and attempt to build market share in the hopes of achieving a market position that will permit earning above average profits in the long run. An illustration of this approach would be a company that greatly increased its advertising in the short term in the belief that the increased visibility would create a superior market position and increased profits in the longer run. However, managers must be cautious about doing this since no company can afford to disregard profits for too long.

Strategies and Policies

Once you have set your goals, you must plan how you will achieve them. This involves determining strategies, policies, procedures, and budgets. Strategies identify general courses of action for achieving your goals. Some examples of strategy statements are shown in Exhibit 2.3. Policies specify desired, acceptable behavior within your organization and serve as the basis for controlling behavior. Procedures and budgets describe the detailed actions you will take and the financial limits within which you will work.

Exhibit 2.3

SAMPLE STRATEGY STATEMENTS

1. Utilize premium pricing and above-average advertising to discriminate our product from our competitors' and to finance continued product development.
2. Maintain price levels $1.00 above the industry average.
3. Invest 7% of sales revenues for Product 1 in quality improvements for that product.
4. Maintain safety stock levels at 12% of forecasted sales.
5. Maintain work-force levels sufficient to avoid any overtime charges.

Other Planning Activities

Besides developing these broad plans, you will need to make specific plans in the functional areas of the simulation. For example, *Threshold Competitor* requires financial planning. You will need to borrow and repay money needed to operate and perhaps expand the business. In both *Threshold Competitor Team* and *Competitor Solo*, companies pay out cash immediately for marketing and production expenses. You must pay advertisers and employees at the same time that you use their services. At the same time, each *Threshold Competitor* company sells its products on credit, allowing customers to receive the product now, but pay for it later. It takes two quarters to collect all the cash owed for items sold. This delay in receiving payment for your sales, while having to pay immediately for the cost of producing and marketing your product, complicates the need for cash. Your financial planning must take into account the need to pay for the cost of generating sales before you can collect on those sales.

You also are responsible for planning production levels, marketing strategies, and market research activities. Production planning involves forecasting material and labor needs, and determining production levels, product quality, and investments in plant expansion. When planning your marketing strategy, you will need to determine how much of the market you intend to capture and what mix of pricing, advertising, and product quality you will use to capture it. You must also decide what market research information you need in order to stay aware of market conditions; that is, your competitors' actions and predicted future consumer demand levels for products in your industry. Chapter 6 discusses these decisions in more detail.

ORGANIZING AND STAFFING

Threshold Competitor Team was designed with the expectation that you will manage your company as one member of a group. *Threshold Competitor Solo* was designed so that you can work alone as you progress from one quarter to the next. However, you could also work as one member of a group to manage your company as it competes with the 15 other *Threshold Competitor Solo* companies.

If you are a member of a group managing your company, you must decide how to organize your group so that you can effectively and efficiently work together to achieve your company's goals. You should begin by establishing a structure for managing the company. To do this, first develop an organizational chart and a hierarchy of command that clarifies the relationships between the activities needed to manage your company. For example, you may choose to have positions in marketing, operations, and finance; all with a reporting responsibility to a Chief Executive Officer (CEO) who will resolve disputes between individuals in those positions. Next, establish the necessary personal and professional relationships between team members. Remember, you are all entering into this exercise as peers. You would be well advised to discuss, in advance, how you will manage your dual roles of peers (social - friendship) and *Threshold Competitor* managers (organizational - work). Then determine the qualifications for each position and the corresponding responsibilities. Finally, the team should staff the company by determining who should fill the positions. Notice that the positions and their duties are determined before the group decides which member will staff which position. This will help you determine whether you need to acquire additional skills beyond those that the group currently possesses to effectively manage your company. For example, there may be no one in your group with experience in finance. This will require some outside learning by the person assigned to that position, so that he or she can perform the necessary duties of a finance manager. This, too, is no different from what occurs in a business organization. Companies hire people for their ability to learn to manage the responsibilities assigned to them, not just for what they know when they join the organization.

Even if you are managing your company alone, you should determine what kind of activities you will need to perform and what skills you need to perform these activities well. For example, if you decide you lack skills in finance, you should invest some time in learning how to interpret financial ratios and how you can use them to help guide your business decisions.

LEADING

If you are going to be managing your *Threshold Competitor* company as a member of a team, you must decide how you will influence your team members to accomplish desired goals. How should the team divide responsibilities among its members? Are you going to have a management hierarchy or are you going to operate as a cooperative of equals?

Most likely the members of your team will have a mix of attitudes and abilities. This diversity means that most teams will face some motivational problems as these differences surface during the simulation. Team members may have differing perceptions on what constitutes an acceptable level of effort. One individual may only be willing to put in the effort necessary to receive a "C" for the exercise, whereas others may want to work at a higher level of effort. The team will have to decide how to deal with an unmotivated or undermotivated group member. The experience of having to work with real problems in motivation is valuable and underlines the fact that not all people choose to perform at the level you want or expect. This is the simulation's equivalent of the leadership function. In real businesses, leaders direct, delegate, coordinate, motivate, manage personal differences, and manage change. You will have to work with all of these issues if you are part of a team that is managing your company.

Leading is not always performed in a hierarchical sense. Many organizations rely on teams consisting of individuals from various departments across the company to manage a specific project to its successful completion. Companies also expect employees to work "horizontally" across the organization to accomplish their assigned responsibilities. For example, in order for a marketing person to be effective, he or she must have the cooperation of individuals in the operations area of the business. Failure to manage this relationship will eventually lead to failures in the marketing area.

Further, organizations depend not just on their formal leaders to direct, motivate, and coordinate a group's activities. Informal leaders also play a critical role in an organization's success. Regardless of who is in charge of your group, you are all responsible for leading it to a successful experience with *Threshold Competitor*. Managing peers is a critical skill for success in any organization.

CONTROLLING

Finally, you must deal with issues of control. You must establish a reporting system that determines what information is necessary to manage your company. You must also develop performance standards. This means you need to determine what indicates good performance by your company. By monitoring these indicators, you can determine when you need to improve your performance on key duties. Since you cannot measure everything, you need to select indicators that are critical to your company's success. Watch these indicators to determine how much your company's actual performance differs from the performance you desire. For example, you may determine that controlling manufacturing costs is a key to the success of your business. You must then also decide what is the desired manufacturing cost you would like to maintain and what is the maximum cost you can incur without becoming unprofitable. Knowing these numbers will allow you to determine whether you need to take corrective action and where to focus your efforts, should the need arise.

Whether the differences between actual and desired performance require corrective action or not depends on the level of importance you have given to the indicator and the degree of accuracy desired. If the differences are small, it may not be worthwhile to take action to correct your performance. For example, suppose you have a goal of no stockouts of Product 1, but also want to control inventory costs. In order to achieve that goal, you have set a target of maintaining a safety stock of 1,000 units of finished goods inventory for Product 1 and stated that a deviation of 500 from that target is acceptable. If you incur an ending inventory of 1,250, you will not have to take any special actions during the next quarter. However, if your ending inventory for Product 1 rises to 1,800 units, corrective action is necessary. You will have to adjust its activities in order to get its operations back within acceptable performance limits. The ability to identify critical indicators, determine a means for monitoring them, and then adjust decisions to bring the company back in line can easily separate the winners from the also-rans.

CHAPTER 3

THE *THRESHOLD COMPETITOR* BUSINESS ENVIRONMENT

This chapter will provide a description of the *Threshold Competitor* business environment. It will describe your company's history leading up to you taking managerial control. It will also describe your company's products and its manufacturing capacity, as well as the marketplace in which it operates.

In the *Threshold Competitor* simulation, all companies start from an identical position. This means each company has the same amount of cash and other assets, as well as the same amount of debt and owners' equity. In addition, each company also has the same inventory, plant capacity, number of production employees, and the same company history. After the first quarter, all of that will change as a consequence of the decisions you make. The *Threshold Competitor Team* companies all manufacture the same kinds of products, and compete against each other for customers. So, after the first quarter, companies will have different market shares and will be in different financial positions. Whether your company develops a stronger position relative to the other companies in your industry will depend on your ability to manage your company better than the competing companies.

This chapter describes your company's history and the nature of its business. As you read, keep in mind that you are reading the description of the current position of the company you will manage, regardless of the company number. If you are working with the *Threshold Competitor Solo* simulation, you will always manage Company 1. If you are working with the *Threshold Competitor Team* simulation, you will be assigned to either Company 1, Company 2, Company 3, and so on up to the maximum number of companies operating in your industry.

YOUR COMPANY'S PRODUCTS

In the *Threshold Competitor* simulations, you will operate a small manufacturing firm that produces two plastic molded products — Product 1 and Product 2. The manufacturing process consists of forming plastic raw materials (sheets of plastic) into the finished consumer product. You will sell these products through retail markets to the general public. The two products are not substitutes for one another, nor are they complementary. This means that sales of one product do not affect sales of the other product.

Given the inherent durability of your products, the likelihood of immediate repeat purchases by a customer is small. This means if a customer has just purchased one of your products in Quarter 1, that customer is not likely to purchase another one in Quarter 2. Consequently, you should assume that sales for a particular quarter will come from new customers that you have attracted to your product based on that quarter's marketing efforts and product characteristics. You should not assume that customers will buy your product because of past experiences with that product. In addition, your company is too new to the market to expect brand satisfaction with one of your products to boost the sales of your other product. In short, you have to earn each quarter's sales that quarter. Brand loyalty is not part of your sales environment.

HISTORY OF YOUR COMPANY

David and Emily Anderscott were the original developers of this business. They and a small group of investors provided the financing needed to establish the company. Your company is privately held because the investors chose not to offer stock for sale to the general public. Neither David, Emily, nor any other owner/investor has any interest in managing the firm. They consider themselves to be financiers rather than managers. Consequently, they have decided to hire someone from outside the firm to run the business and have selected you for the job. You will have a free hand in managing the company as you best see fit. However, the firm's owners expect high performance and will receive quarterly reports that will compare your performance with the other companies operating in your industry. If you fail to achieve the success the owners of your company want, they will undoubtedly take action to protect their investment.

Your firm's owners do not freely distribute information about their investments. As a consequence, management reports for two quarters ago, when the company was created, are not available to you. You will receive only the reports for last quarter, Quarter 0, which was the first quarter the company was in operation. These reports are shown in Appendix B. The owners have informed you that, before Quarter 0 (that is, two quarters ago), they were busy setting up the company. They purchased a plant with 11,100 units of production capacity for $499,500. They also hired 45 production workers and purchased 6,500 units of raw materials for Product 1 and 5,500 units of raw material for Product 2 during that quarter. This allowed them to have the necessary plant, labor, and materials for their company to be in operation in Quarter 0. (The results of all these actions are reflected in the Appendix B, "Quarter 0 Reports.") In order to finance these activities, the owners put up $249,500 of their money and obtained a mortgage for $250,000 to purchase their plant. A short-term loan paid for that period's purchase of raw materials, the cost of hiring the workers, and general office expenses.

CURRENT STATUS OF YOUR COMPANY

Your company's manufacturing plant is capable of producing 11,100 units of finished product during each quarter of operation (i.e., three months of operation or one quarter of a year). Your production equipment can produce both product lines interchangeably. This allows you to produce both products in the same plant. You are limited in how much you can produce in a particular quarter by three factors: (a) the supply of raw material in inventory for each product, (b) the company's total manufacturing capacity, and (c) the number of production workers on staff to meet those needed for the production level you desire. The plant can produce any combination of your two products. This means that in any one quarter you could, for example, produce 5,000 units of Product 1 and 6,100 units of Product 2. Or you could produce 4,100 of one product and 7,000 of the other. As long as you have the needed raw materials and production labor force, you can produce any combination of the two products that total 11,100.

You can also produce a limited amount of product at overtime rates. The maximum overtime production allowed is 50% above your normal plant capacity. At your current capacity of 11,100 units, that means the maximum production using maximum overtime would be 16,650 units (11,100 + 5,550).

You will incur overtime charges if you choose to produce more than your workers can manufacture given their current productivity levels. Your production employees are first assigned to produce the desired volume of Product 1. Once the appropriate number of workers have been assigned to Product 1 (based on their current productivity level for producing Product 1), the remaining workers are assigned to produce Product 2. If you have an insufficient number of workers to produce the total number of units you have entered when making your decisions, you will incur an overtime charge. Overtime charges are double the labor rate for each unit produced at overtime. Chapter 6 ("Making Decisions") discusses the calculation of overtime charges under the heading of "Number of Units to Produce."

You can also choose to produce less than the total production capacity of your plant. While this decision increases the cost of making each unit because of fixed costs associated with owning your plant, you may decide it is in the best long-term interests of your company to produce below the plant's total possible manufacturing capacity. This is usually the consequence of the company having product inventory levels you have determined to be excessive.

There is a regular turnover in your production work force as they quit to accept employment elsewhere. You will lose 10% of the workers you employ each quarter. This will occur after the current quarter's production operations have been completed but before the next quarter's operations begin. For example, if you started Quarter 2 with 35 workers, three would quit at the end of that quarter. Consequently, you would have 32 workers available to produce your products in Quarter 3. This means you will have a shrinking labor pool unless you hire workers to replace those that are lost to turnover.

There is also a 10% probability of losing one extra production worker to turnover each quarter. Because the low level of unemployment in the area provides many job opportunities, you will not be able to change the turnover conditions in your company.

Currently, you have only one source of supply for your raw plastic materials. This company has been a steady supplier. The owners have mandated that you deal exclusively with this supplier.

At present, the owners limit you to selling your product in one market area and in the current single geographical territory. How much you are able to sell in this territory will depend on how much effort you put into marketing your products compared to your competitors' efforts to sell their products. You must spend your money wisely and determine what mix of the marketing strategies will produce the best results.

You may borrow from the *Threshold Competitor* simulation bank for short-term periods in order to finance the normal operation of your business. After you have made your other decisions for a particular quarter, you can request a short-term loan to cover the cash shortages you expect. You can also borrow money from the *Threshold Competitor* bank to help finance an expansion of the production capacity of your manufacturing plant. You can borrow the money needed for this capital expenditure as a long-term mortgage.

YOUR COMPANY'S MARKETPLACE

Each company in the *Threshold Competitor* simulation sells the same two products. Initially, there is no difference in product quality between your products and your competitors' products. However, the investment you make in product quality may create a differentiation in the consumer's mind. This will depend on what you spend improving product quality compared to what your competitors spend in this area. If you and your competitors all spend similar amounts, the customers may recognize that you have a high-quality product, but see it as no different than your competitors' high-quality product. In other words, how much you invest in quality on a relative basis is as important as how much that you do spend on an absolute basis.

Fluctuations in the simulation's economic indicator, which gives some indication of the economy's health, can affect the demand for your products. A rising indicator signals a healthy economy. It indicates that business might be better than the market forecasts you can purchase from economic forecasters through the market research options on the Marketing and Market Research decisions screen. However, changes in the economy may not affect demand for all products equally. Your ability to analyze the market's reaction to your marketing efforts, and the efforts of your competitors, will affect your ability to market your products efficiently and effectively.

The customers in your company's marketplace, although value conscious, will not invest large amounts of time trying to find the company that offers the best value for its products. It may be tempting to pursue a strategy where you limit your company's marketing efforts, attempting to benefit from product awareness created by other companies' marketing efforts. However, potential customers may not recognize how good your product is if your promotional efforts lag too far behind your competitors'. Advertising creates awareness of your product. Too little effort in this area and customers will not remember your brand name as they head out to make their purchase.

Further, if all companies adopt a low product promotion strategy, customers will stop buying this type of product at all and will begin buying substitute goods from companies outside your industry. Total industry demand will suffer. In the *Threshold Competitor* environment, a weak marketing effort may be doubly disastrous. Not only will one company suffer from a weak effort, but the whole industry may decline as well. All companies in the industry will then face an overcapacity problem (manufacturing capacity in excess of demand for the product) that in turn will create other problems.

The next two chapters will give detailed descriptions about how the *Threshold Competitor Team* and *Competitor Solo* simulations software work. They will also explain the marketing, production, and financial decisions you will have to make each quarter as you manage your business.

CHAPTER 4

INSTALLING THE *THRESHOLD COMPETITOR* SOFTWARE

INTRODUCTION

In this chapter we will specify the computer requirements for using *Threshold Competitor*. We will also tell you how to install the *Threshold Competitor* software onto your computer's hard drive. This software consists of *Threshold Competitor* program files and certain Windows setup files. Once you have installed these files onto a computer, you will not have to reinstall them on that particular computer.

INSTALLATION REQUIREMENTS

In order to install the *Threshold Competitor* program on a computer, you will need a computer with a Microsoft Windows operating system. The *Threshold Competitor* programs do not work on computers that use the Apple operating system. You must also have an Internet connection and a valid key access number. This number is located with the CD at the back of this manual. We discuss each of these installation requirements below.

Equipment Needed

In order to install and then operate the *Threshold Competitor* programs, you must have access to a personal computer system with the following characteristics:
- Windows 95, 98, 2000, ME, NT, or XP.
- 3 Megs of space on your hard disk.
- At least 1 disk drive.

Although optional, we advise that you use a printer so that you can generate printouts of your quarterly results. We also strongly recommend that you have a blank disk suitable for use with the PC to use to make backup copies of your *Threshold Competitor* administrator files. You should do this after each time that your decisions for a quarter are processed and you receive the results.

Internet Connection

To install the *Threshold Competitor* programs on a computer, you must be connected to the Internet. This requirement is only for the installation process. You do not need to be connected to the Internet to work with the *Threshold Competitor* programs after they have been installed successfully.

Valid Access Code Number

The installation program for *Threshold Competitor* requires that you enter the access code number that is found on the flap behind the CD-ROM envelope in the back of this manual. During the installation process, the program will display a screen where you will register and validate the installation of your software. ***If this access number has been used previously, it is invalid. You will NOT be able to use it to install the programs!*** You are limited to installing the *Threshold Competitor* programs on **only one** computer for each manual and CD that you purchase. After you register, your access number, it will no longer be valid. **Make sure that you install the programs on the computer you intend to use with the *Threshold Competitor* program before you begin the installation process**. Once you have installed the *Threshold Competitor* programs on a particular computer, you will have to purchase another manual and CD if you wish to install the programs on a different computer.

INSTALLING THE *THRESHOLD COMPETITOR* SOFTWARE

Before you can start the *Threshold Competitor* programs, along with these programs, you must install certain Windows files that the programs need that are not in your Windows Systems directory. After you have completed the installation process, just follow the instructions in Chapter 5 for *starting* the *Threshold Team Competitor* or *Threshold Solo Competitor* program. To *install* the *Threshold Competitor* Windows files and programs, follow these steps:

1. Load Windows. Open your Windows 95, 98, 2000, ME, NT, or XP program. (Note that this program will not work with Windows 3.1 operating systems.)

2. Close any open applications. Before beginning to install the *Threshold Competitor* Windows files, close any applications that are already open or that are opened as part of your Windows startup options. For example, if Microsoft Office automatically loads during your startup of Windows, you will need to close its applications. Closing all applications will prevent conflicts that might arise between files for the *Threshold Competitor* program that are being installed and Windows Systems files currently in use. Do this by closing the applications that are open in the Task Bar displayed across the bottom of your monitor. If your computer automatically loads the MS Office Task Bar (typically found along the side of the monitor or across the top), make sure you close this as well if you experience any difficulties in installing the software.

3. Connect to the Internet. If you use a dial-up modem to connect with the Internet, do this now. If you are continuously connected to the Internet through a cable modem or DSL access, go to Step 4. This is only necessary for the installation of the *Threshold Competitor* programs. You do not need to be connected to the Internet to use the programs.

4. Insert the *Threshold Competitor* CD into your computer. Click on the Start button and select the **Run** option. Type **f:setup** (*note*: the CD drive for your computer may have a designation other than "f". If your CD drive is *not* "f", substitute the appropriate letter) and click on OK or select the Browse button and find the CD drive that way. A message will appear on your monitor to remind you to close all open applications. Select "Cancel" if you have any open applications; otherwise select "Next."

5. Choose Destination Location. Next you will be asked to choose the location where your *Threshold Competitor* program files will be stored. The default folder is C:\Program Files\ThreshC. Unless you need to change this location, select the "Next" button and go to Step 7. If you want to change the folder where you store your program files, go to Step 6.

6. Creating a new directory for storing the program files. If you want to create a directory (i.e., folder) with a different name to hold your *Threshold Competitor* program files, select the "Browse" button. A screen like Exhibit 4.1 will appear on the monitor. If you do not have a mouse connected to your computer, press the Tab key until you reach this button and then press [ENTER]. Enter the directory name you prefer. You can use any combination of letters and numbers up to a maximum of eight (8) characters. Remember to follow the Windows protocol when creating the location of the new directory. Make sure you have specified the drive where you want to locate the directory, plus the directory's name. For example, if you want to name the directory ThreshC2 and have it located in Drive C, you would enter **C:\ThreshC2**.

20 Chapter 4, Installing the *Threshold Competitor* Software

Exhibit 4.1

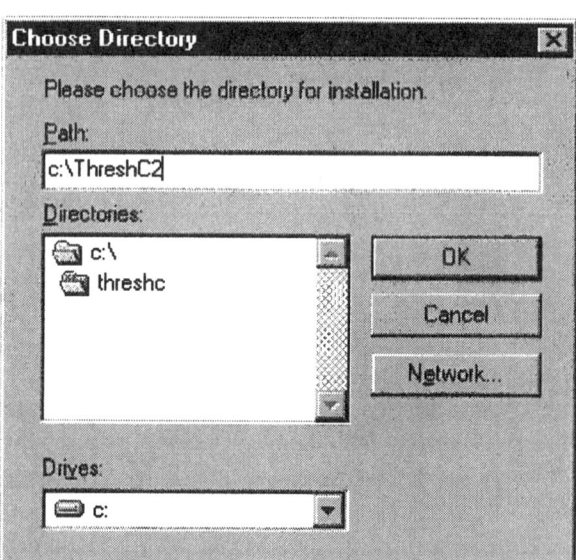

7. Select Program Folder. You will be given the option to change the name of the Program Folder in which the program icons will be stored. Leave this as the default "*Threshold Competitor*."

8. Start Copying Files. A screen will appear on the monitor to allow you to verify your prior entries. Select the "Next" button to start copying the files to your computer. Wait while the files are installed. The setup program will install the Windows files needed by *Threshold Competitor* that may not be in your Windows Systems directory.

9. Register *Threshold Competitor*. As we discussed at the beginning of this chapter, you **must** enter a **valid** access code number before you can use the *Threshold Competitor* programs. After the installation program has finished copying the *Threshold Competitor* programs to your computer, a screen for registering the programs will be displayed on your monitor. Enter the access code number found on the flap behind the CD-ROM envelope in the back of this manual. Next enter the additional information requested and then click on the "Register" button.
   a. If the dialog box tells you that this is not a valid number, or that the number was previously used, you have most likely purchased a used manual. Each access code number is valid for **only one** installation of the software. Return the manual and CD to the bookstore where you purchased it and exchange it for a new manual. Alternatively, you can phone Prentice Hall at 1-800-282-0693 to purchase a new access code number.
   b. If you get an error message when you click on the "Register" button, see your institution's system administrator to ensure that Microsoft Internet Explorer is installed on your computer and properly configured to access the internet. This is only necessary for registering the *Threshold Competitor* programs. You do not need to use Internet Explorer or the Internet to operate these programs.

10. Location of the *Threshold Competitor* icon. As *Threshold Competitor* completes its setup process, it will inform you that it has created icons for the *Threshold Competitor Team* and *Threshold Competitor Solo* programs. You can access the *Threshold Competitor* icon through the "Start" button. To do this, select the "Start" button. A dialogue box will appear on your monitor. Select the icon labeled "Programs." Another dialogue box will appear on your monitor listing the various programs available on that computer. Select the *Threshold Competitor* option. Then select the *Threshold*

Competitor Team Company or *Threshold Competitor Solo* Company icon to start the desired program.

11. Create a *Threshold Competitor Team* Company Disk. Use Windows Explorer or My Computer to copy the Cthr.cts file to a blank, formatted floppy disk. Unless you changed the default folder for storing the files during Step #6 (above), this file resides in the ThreshC folder in the Program Files folder on Drive C of your computer. You will use this company disk when working with the *Threshold Competitor Team* program. We will discuss this in Chapter 5.

NAVIGATING AROUND *THRESHOLD COMPETITOR*

To work with *Threshold Competitor*, you need to be able to move within a screen and among the multiple screens. If you are familiar with working in a Windows environment, the *Threshold Competitor* program utilizes standard Windows protocol for keystroke entries. This means the Tab key moves you to the next entry point, the Shift key + Tab key moves you backward to the preceding entry point, and so forth. You can also use a mouse if one is connected to your computer. You can use these two methods in combination with each other, switching back and forth as often as you like. You will use this Windows protocol to move around a screen and make entries. These commands will also allow you to access the Menu bar on your screen. You will use the Menu bar to move among the multiple *Threshold Competitor* screens.

In the next chapter we explain in detail how to work with the *Threshold Competitor* programs. If you are ready to begin working with the program, turn to Chapter 5 now.

CHAPTER 5

WORKING WITH THE *THRESHOLD COMPETITOR* PROGRAMS

CHAPTER OVERVIEW

This chapter will introduce you to the *Threshold Competitor* programs. It will explain how to:
- Work with the *Threshold Competitor* program, either with or without a mouse.
- Make entries on the two decisions screens.
- Move from one screen to another screen using (a) the [PgDn] and [PgUp] keys, (b) the Menu bar displayed across the top of every screen, or (c) the *Threshold Competitor* "hot" keys.
- Use the Menu bar to perform various operations.

After reading this chapter, you should be familiar with the mechanics of working with the *Threshold Competitor* software. In the next chapter, we discuss the decisions you will make to manage your *Threshold Competitor* company.

Whether you will be using the team or the solo version of *Threshold Competitor* we recommend that you use *Threshold Competitor Solo* as a tool to learn the fundamentals of working with the *Threshold Competitor* program. Use *Threshold Competitor Solo* to try out each step as you read about it. Do not worry about what decisions you enter. Any of the decisions you enter now can be changed later. If you cannot get access to a computer as you read this chapter, you will still be able to understand the information presented here. Read the text and look at the sample screens in the text to see what you will see on the computer monitor. Then try everything out on a computer as soon as possible.

THRESHOLD COMPETITOR TEAM AND *THRESHOLD COMPETITOR SOLO* DIFFERENCES

As explained in Chapter 1, the *Threshold Competitor Team* and *Threshold Competitor Solo* are two versions of the same program. The decisions you enter and the reports created by the programs are identical. In the *Competitor Team* program, your competition will be companies managed by other simulation participants. In the *Competitor Solo* program, your competition will be 15 companies managed by the computer. While the decisions and the reports associated with the two programs are the same, there are some differences between them that we will highlight now. We will discuss them in more detail later in this chapter.

Processing Decisions

Threshold Competitor Team and *Threshold Competitor Solo* programs differ in how the decisions you enter are processed. If you need to refresh your memory on this issue, reread the section in Chapter 1 on how the two programs work. When you get to the section in this chapter that deals with processing, we will discuss the differences between *Competitor Team* and *Competitor Solo* in detail.

Storing Your Company Data File – Floppy versus Hard Drive

Both *Threshold Competitor Team* and *Competitor Solo* require that you create and save a company data file for storing your decisions. For both the *Team* and *Solo* versions of *Threshold Competitor* you can choose to run the simulation with either a floppy disk or your computer's hard disk. Which to use depends on the format desired by your simulation administrator and on how often you will be submitting your *Threshold Competitor* work. Most administrators will ask you to submit decisions for the team version of

Threshold Competitor on a disk. If you will be submitting your work frequently or are uncomfortable with your ability to copy files from the hard disk to a floppy disk, we recommend that you use a floppy disk for storing your company data file. Otherwise use the hard disk, as it provides faster processing of a quarter's decisions. **It is imperative that you remember where you store (i.e., save) your company data file. If you exit the program and forget where the file is located, you will be unable to access the information you need to process future decisions. (If you are playing *Threshold Competitor Solo*, you will have to start from the beginning the next time you work with the program!)**

Starting the Programs

Because there are separate programs for *Threshold Competitor Team* and *Threshold Competitor Solo*, the procedure for starting each program is different. With the exceptions of how to start the programs and how to process your decision entries, *Threshold Competitor Team* and *Threshold Competitor Solo* are identical in their operation.

Remember that you need to have previously loaded the *Threshold Competitor* Windows files on *the machine on which you are working* before you are able to use the *Threshold Competitor* programs. If you have not done this, you will get an error message similar to that shown in Exhibit 5.1. Go to Chapter 2 and follow the directions for loading the *Threshold Competitor* programs onto this computer.

Exhibit 5.1

STARTING THE *THRESHOLD COMPETITOR SOLO* PROGRAM

1. To start the *Threshold Competitor* program, select the "Start" button. A dialogue box will appear on your monitor. Select the "Programs" option. Another dialogue box will appear on your monitor listing the various programs available on that computer. Select the *Threshold Competitor* option. Then select the *Competitor Solo* Company icon to start the program.

2. Wait while the computer loads *Competitor Solo*. You will see the opening title screen for *Threshold Competitor Solo*. Press any key to begin working with the program.

3. The screen shown in Exhibit 5.2 will appear. Select the "Create New Industry" button and click OK.

Exhibit 5.2

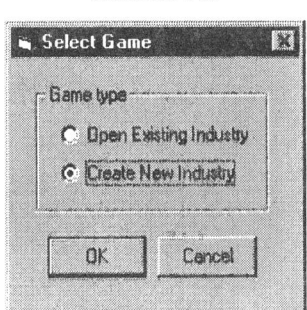

4. You will now see a dialog box that will prompt you for your company name and password. The dialog box is shown in Exhibit 5.3.

Exhibit 5.3

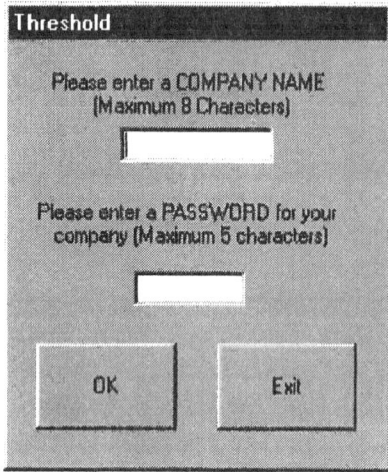

Enter a company name and password and select the OK button. Exhibit 5.4 describes issues you should consider when choosing your company name and password.

Exhibit 5.4

Entering a Company Name. Think of a name that you would like to call your company. This name can be any combination of letters or numbers up to a maximum of eight (8) characters. In this example, we will use the company name "demo". There is no relationship between your company name and the success or failure of your company, so select any name that you desire. Type in this name and press the Tab key. This action will move the cursor to the cell for entering a password for your *Threshold Competitor* disk.

Entering a Password. Think of a password for your company that you can remember easily. Your password can have a maximum of five (5) characters. It is advisable not to select a password others are likely to guess such as a nickname or the name of a family member. Type in your password. Then press the Tab key until the OK button is highlighted and press [ENTER] or click on the OK button if you are using a mouse.

Thereafter, you will have to enter this password whenever you start the *Threshold Competitor Solo* program. If the correct password is not entered, the program will not proceed. If you forget your password, you will have to take your company disk to your administrator to have it read. If you desire, you can change your company's password and your company name later in the simulation exercise. We explain how to make these changes later in this chapter under "Menu Bar Operations."

Make sure you protect your password and your *Threshold Competitor* company data file. If other players find your company data file in a computer and know your password, you give them access to all your company's records. You would no more want to do this than to give them printouts of your company reports. You do not want them to benefit from your hard work.

5. Next, you must select the location for your company's data file. This location will determine where (a) the data file will be stored (i.e., saved) after you create it and (b) where you will find an existing company data file that you created earlier. We discuss how to create an existing company data file

next. Later we explain how to retrieve an existing company data file that contains results from decisions you made during an earlier working session. The default location for saving your *Threshold Competitor Solo* file is the directory in which you stored the program files (usually ThreshC) when you installed *Threshold Competitor*. (See Chapter 2.) Exhibit 5.5 shows how this screen looks.

Exhibit 5.5

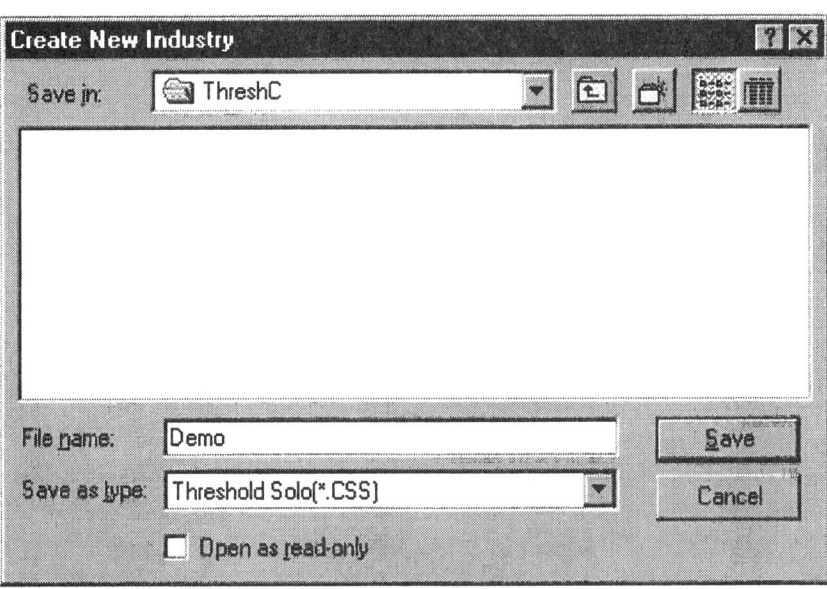

If you wish to run *Threshold Competitor Solo* from your hard drive, you may accept this default location. However, if you would rather run *Threshold Competitor Solo* from a floppy disk, you must change this default designation to the floppy drive. (There is a discussion of the advantages and disadvantages of using the hard drive versus the floppy above, see **Storing Your Company Data File – Floppy versus Hard Drive**). If you wish to save your company data file on a floppy disk, you must first insert a blank, formatted disk in your floppy drive (Drive A or B). Make sure that you put your name on the disk. You can now switch the destination of your *Threshold Competitor Solo* company data file to your floppy drive (Drive A or B) by selecting the ▼, then choosing A (or B). *Note: If you designate the floppy drive without having a formatted disk in the drive, a box will appear stating that your floppy drive is not accessible, the device is not ready.*

6. Select "Save" and your company data files will be stored on your chosen location and you will see a screen like that shown in Exhibit 5.6. (Note: The *Threshold Competitor Solo* program names your company data file by adding a ".CSS" extension [Competitor Solo Student] to the name you chose when you saved the file. In this example, the company data file is DEMO.CSS. When you work with a *Competitor Team* program it will add a "CTS" extension [Competitor Team Student] to your company data file name.) If you have chosen to save your *Threshold Competitor Solo* company data file on a floppy, this saving operation will take from 20 to 30 seconds, depending on the speed of your computer. This is because the program has to create a large file on your company disk. This long delay occurs only when you *create* a new game. Once this file has been created, it will take only a few seconds to load your company data file when you next start the program. Once the program has loaded the company data file, you will be able to enter decisions and view your company's results.

Exhibit 5.6

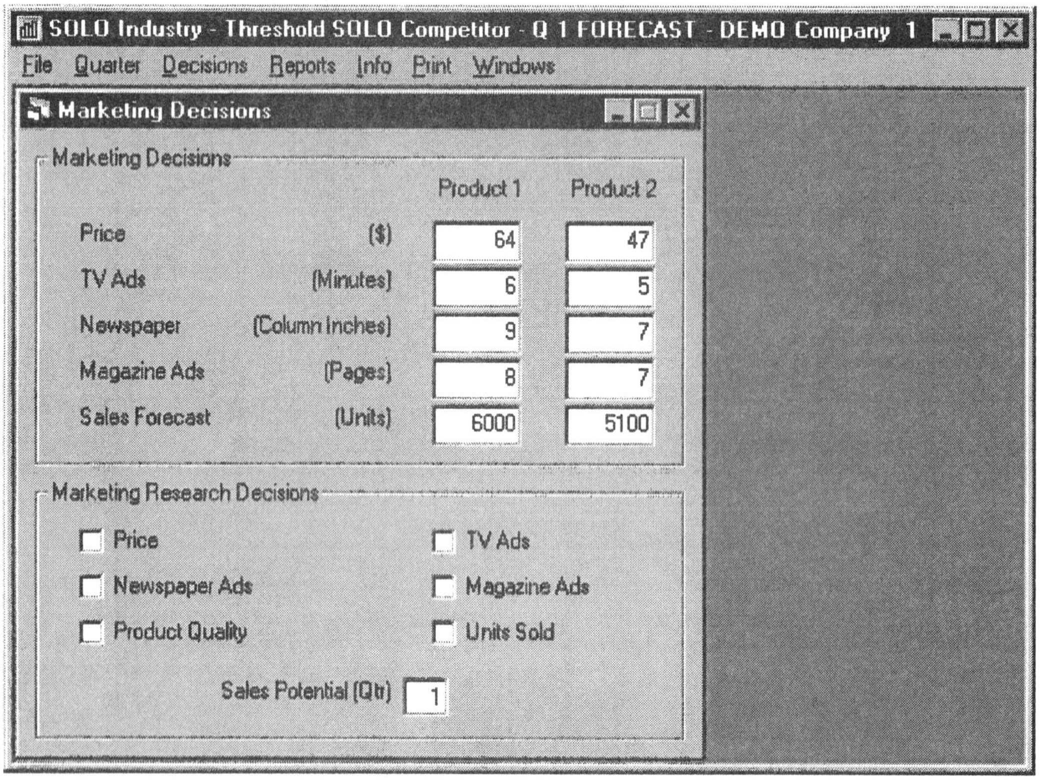

![Exhibit 5.6: Screenshot of SOLO Industry - Threshold SOLO Competitor - Q 1 FORECAST - DEMO Company 1, showing Marketing Decisions window with the following values:

Marketing Decisions:
		Product 1	Product 2
Price	($)	64	47
TV Ads	(Minutes)	6	5
Newspaper	(Column Inches)	9	7
Magazine Ads	(Pages)	8	7
Sales Forecast	(Units)	6000	5100

Marketing Research Decisions (checkboxes, all unchecked): Price, TV Ads, Newspaper Ads, Magazine Ads, Product Quality, Units Sold. Sales Potential (Qtr): 1]

STARTING THE *THRESHOLD COMPETITOR TEAM* PROGRAM

Remember, you need to have previously loaded the *Threshold Competitor* Windows files on *the machine on which you are working* before you are able to use the *Threshold Competitor* programs. If you have not done this, you will get an error message similar to that shown in Exhibit 5.1. Go to Chapter 2 and follow the directions for loading the *Threshold Competitor* programs onto this computer.

Running the *Threshold Competitor Team* with Your Company Data File on a Floppy Disk

If you are participating in the team version of *Threshold Competitor*, your simulation administrator will provide you with the data file (usually on a floppy disk) that you need for starting the simulation. If your company data file is on a floppy disk, insert your disk in Drive A (or Drive B, if that is your floppy drive). It is easiest if you insert your disk into the floppy drive *before* you start the *Threshold Competitor* program.

Next, start the *Threshold Competitor* program by selecting the "Start" button. A dialogue box will appear on your monitor. Select the "Programs" option. Another dialogue box will appear on your monitor listing the various programs available on that computer. Select the *Threshold Competitor* option. Then select the *Competitor Team* Company icon to start the program.

Wait while the computer loads *Threshold Competitor Team*. You will see the opening title screen for *Threshold Competitor Team*. Press any key to begin working with the program. If your company disk was in your floppy drive when you started *Threshold Competitor*, you will see a dialog box like that shown in Exhibit 5.7. Click OK and the *Threshold Competitor* program will start.

Exhibit 5.7

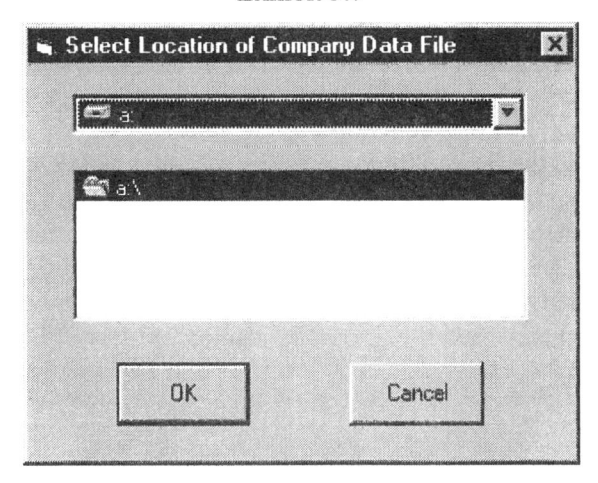

NOTE: If your company disk was not in the floppy drive when you started the program, the dialog box shown in Exhibit 5.8 will appear. To run *Threshold Competitor Team* from the floppy drive, you must insert your company disk in the floppy drive (Drive A or B) and then select the floppy drive by clicking on the ▼, then choosing A (or B). When you see the dialog box shown in Exhibit 5.7, click OK and the *Threshold Competitor Team* program will start.

Exhibit 5.8

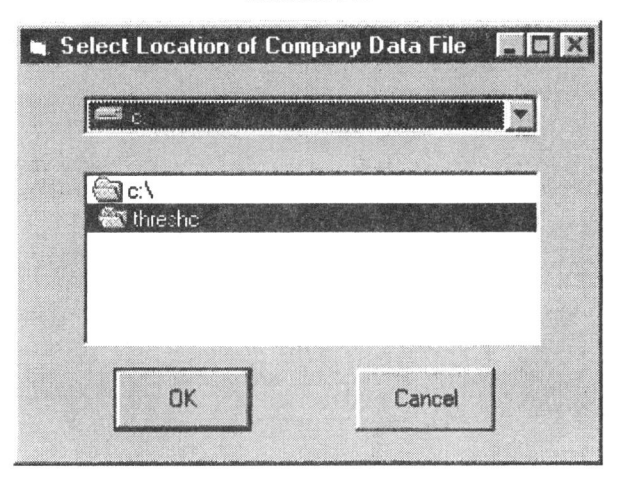

The first time you start the *Threshold Competitor Team* program, a screen will appear asking you to provide a company name and password. See Exhibit 5.3 above for the dialog box and Exhibit 5.4 for advice on choosing a company name and password. Once you have entered your company name and password you will see a screen like that shown in Exhibit 5.6.

Running the *Threshold Competitor Team* with Your Company Data File on the Hard Disk

If you wish to run *Threshold Competitor Team* from the hard drive of your computer, you must copy your company data file into a folder on the hard drive. This copying operation is most easily accomplished using Windows Explorer. If you are unfamiliar with the procedure for copying files, we strongly recommend that you operate *Threshold Competitor Team* using the floppy disk option described above.

Once you have your company data file in a folder on the hard drive, start the *Threshold Competitor* program by selecting the "Start" button. A dialogue box will appear on your monitor. Select the

28 Chapter 5, Working with the *Threshold Competitor* Programs

"Programs" option. Another dialogue box will appear on your monitor listing the various programs available on that computer. Select the *Threshold Competitor* option. Then select the *Competitor Team* Company icon to start the program. Wait while the computer loads *Competitor Team*. You will see the opening title screen for *Threshold Competitor Team*. Press any key to begin working with the program.

It is easiest if there is *no* disk in the floppy drive when you start the *Threshold Competitor* program. If the floppy drive is empty, the program will automatically look for your company data file in the same folder (i.e., directory) in which you stored your *Threshold Competitor* program during the setup process. If you decide to store your company data file in a different location on the hard drive, you must select that folder by clicking on the ▼ and then choosing the proper location. Exhibit 5.9 shows how the dialog box would look if you had stored your company data file in a folder named "Example".

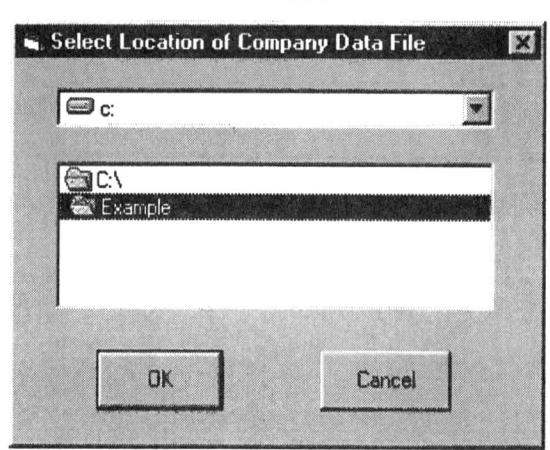

Exhibit 5.9

Note: If you start *Threshold Competitor Team* with a disk in the floppy drive, you will see a dialog box like that shown in Exhibit 5.7. You will have to switch to the location of your company data file by clicking on the ▼, and selecting the appropriate folder.

Once you have designated the folder containing your company data file, click OK. The first time you start the *Threshold Competitor* program, a screen will appear asking you to provide a company name and password. See Exhibit 5.3 above for the dialog box and Exhibit 5.4 for advice on choosing a company name and password. Once you have entered your company name and password you will see a screen like that shown in Exhibit 5.6.

OPENING AN EXISTING *THRESHOLD COMPETITOR* DATA FILE

Since the procedure for locating an existing company data file is a bit different for *Threshold Competitor Solo* than for *Threshold Competitor Team*, we'll discuss each separately.

Opening an Existing *Threshold Competitor Solo* Data File

Once the program for *Threshold Competitor* has loaded and you have moved past the opening title screen, the screen shown in Exhibit 5.2 will appear. Select "Open Existing Industry" and click OK. The program will automatically look for the company data file in the same folder (i.e., directory) in which you stored your *Threshold Competitor* programs during the setup process – usually ThreshC. If you stored your data file in this folder, your company data file name will appear in the dialog box. Select the data file and click on the "Open" button.

If your company data file is stored in a different location, you will have to switch to that location by clicking on the ▼, and selecting the appropriate folder. For example, if your company data file is named "Demo" and is stored on a floppy disk, you would click on the ▼, select the A (or B) drive, highlight "Demo", and click open. You would then see a screen like that shown in Exhibit 5.10.

Exhibit 5.10

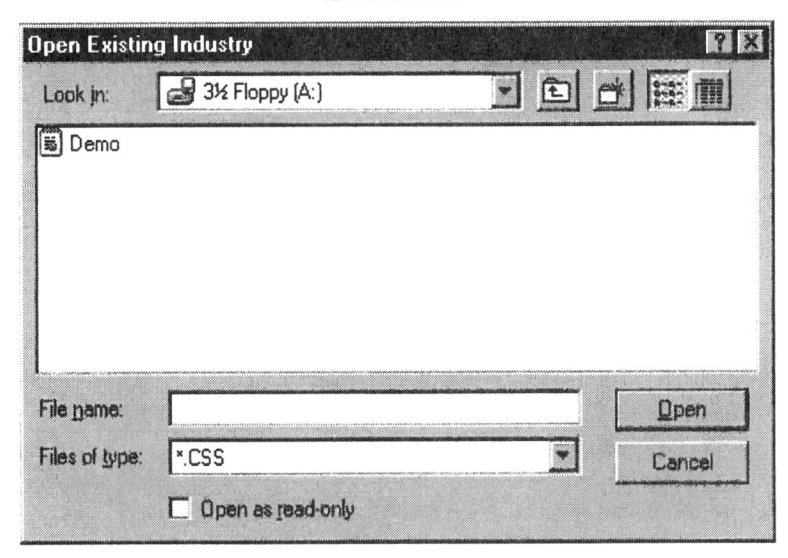

When you have completed this task, you will be prompted for your password. (See Exhibit 5.11.) Note that you are not asked for your company name, as was the case when you entered the program the first time. When you enter you enter your password and click OK, you will see a screen similar to that shown in Exhibit 5.6.

Exhibit 5.11

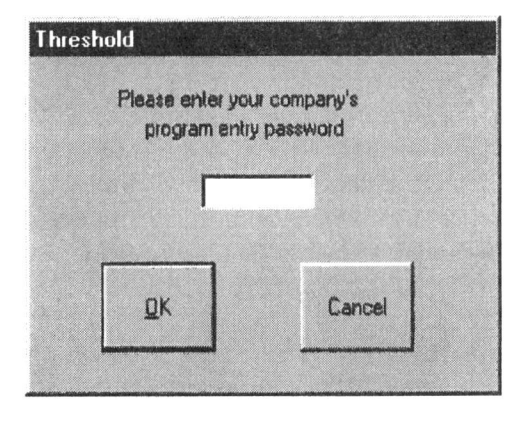

If you are at an incorrect location using *Threshold Competitor Solo* (and the program is unable to find the data file, for example DEMO.CSS) the program will create an entirely new *Competitor Solo* company data file and **you will have to begin the game from the beginning!** (It will create this company data file either on the disk in Drive A, or in the folder that contains the program file – usually C:\ThreshC). You need to know the location of your most current company data file, if you intend to use it again. **Do not forget where you save your most current company data file.**

Opening an <u>Existing</u> *Threshold Competitor Team* Data File

Once the program for *Threshold Competitor* has loaded and you have moved past the opening title screen, you must specify the location of your company data file. If you have a disk in your floppy drive when you load the program *Threshold Competitor Team* will assume that you are operating the simulation from a floppy disk and you will see a screen like that shown in Exhibit 5.12.

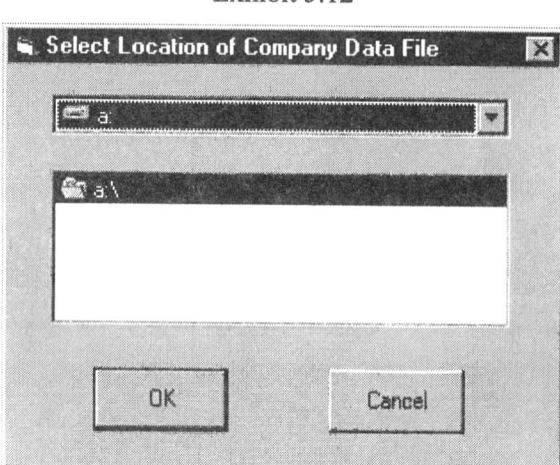

Exhibit 5.12

If company data file is on the floppy, simply click on OK and you will be prompted for your company password. (See Exhibit 5.11.) If your company data file is stored in another location, click on the ▼, and select the appropriate folder.

If there is no disk in the floppy drive when you start *Threshold Competitor Team*, the program will default to the hard disk folder where the program is stored – usually ThreshC. If this is where you stored the data file, select OK. If you saved the file elsewhere on your hard drive, you must first change to that location and then select OK.

If you are working with *Threshold Competitor Team* and you select a location that does not contain your *Threshold Competitor* company's data file (CTHR.CTS), the program will assume that you are just starting the simulation and will prompt you to enter your company name and password. You need to know the location of your most current company data file, if you intend to use it again. **Do not forget where you save your most current company data file.**

USING THE *THRESHOLD COMPETITOR* PROGRAM

Once you have loaded the *Threshold Competitor Solo* or *Threshold Competitor Team* you will see the opening title screen. Press any key and the screen asking for your password will come up. Once you have entered your password you will see a screen that looks like Exhibit 5.6, shown above. If you are working at the computer, this is what you should see now.

This is the first of two screens that your team will use to enter its decisions for Quarter 1 and subsequent quarters as you move through the simulation exercise. What follows is a preview of *Threshold Competitor* that describes how to enter decisions, move around a decision screen, and move from one screen to another screen.

Both *Threshold Competitor Team* and *Threshold Competitor Solo* have two screens you will use to enter your decisions regarding the operation of your business. These are the Marketing & Market Research Decisions screen (see Exhibit 5.6) and the Production & Finance Decisions screen (see Exhibit 5.13).

Exhibit 5.13

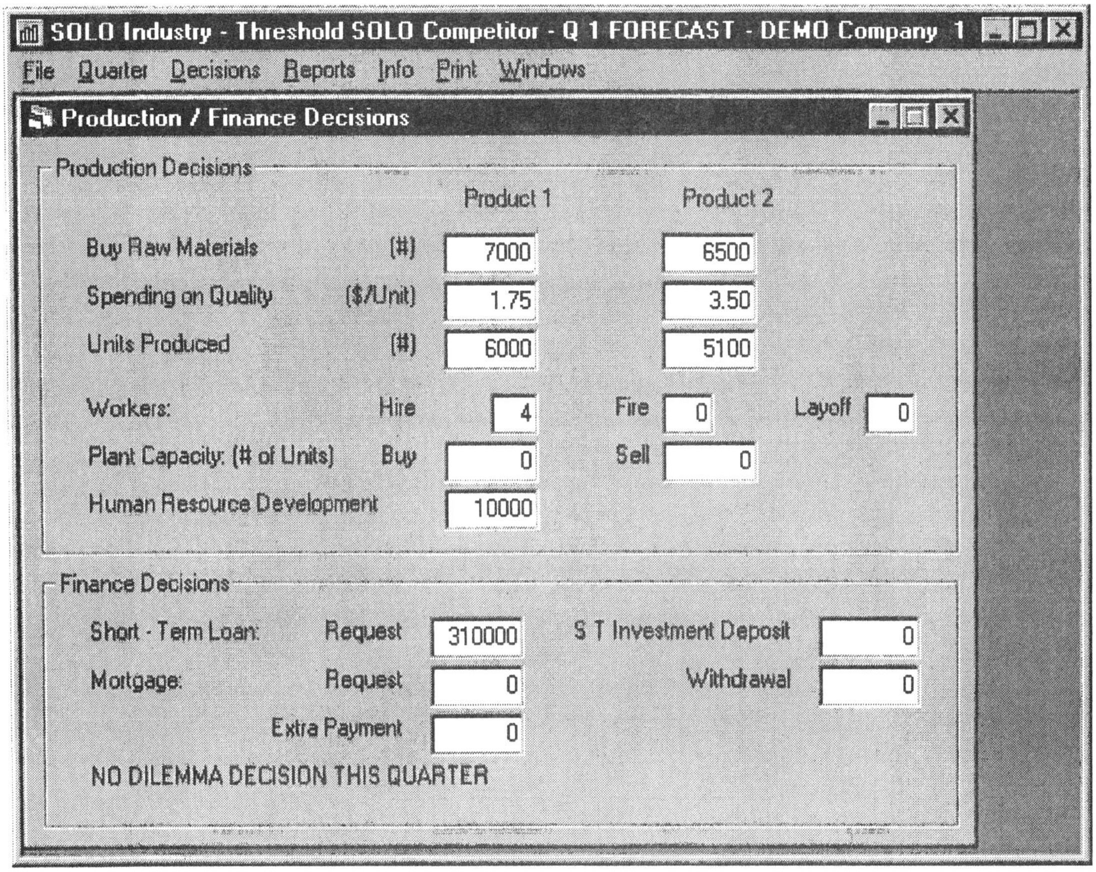
SOLO Industry - Threshold SOLO Competitor - Q 1 FORECAST - DEMO Company 1
File Quarter Decisions Reports Info Print Windows
Production / Finance Decisions
Production Decisions
Product 1
Product 2
Buy Raw Materials (#)
7000
6500
Spending on Quality ($/Unit)
1.75
3.50
Units Produced (#)
6000
5100
Workers: Hire
4
Fire
0
Layoff
0
Plant Capacity: (# of Units) Buy
0
Sell
0
Human Resource Development
10000
Finance Decisions
Short - Term Loan: Request
310000
S T Investment Deposit
0
Mortgage: Request
0
Withdrawal
0
Extra Payment
0
NO DILEMMA DECISION THIS QUARTER

In addition to these two decision screens, there are a number of screens that display reports showing the results of the decisions you made. The two decisions screens will have a flashing cursor to guide you in entering your decisions. You cannot make entries on any of the report screens. Consequently, there is no need to move the cursor around those screens.

Entering a Decision

The *Threshold Competitor* program will only allow you to make certain entries in specific locations. This is to prevent you from making entry mistakes. If you attempt an invalid entry (e.g., a number that exceeds the decision limits or entering a letter where a number is required), the *Threshold Competitor* program will indicate this by displaying an error message on the screen. You can access information on the costs for various decisions through the Info heading on the Menu bar, or by using certain *Threshold Competitor* "hot" keys. We will explain just how to view this information later in this chapter. You can also find the acceptable limits for *Threshold Competitor* decisions in Appendix E of this manual.

Saving Your Decisions

The *Threshold Competitor* program **automatically** saves any entries you make whenever you exit the program. This means the only way you will not save the entries you make onto your *Threshold Competitor* disk is if you either shut off the computer or remove the disk before exiting the program. As will be explained later, you can always change any entries you have made and saved onto your disk up to the time the quarter's decisions are processed. Once your decisions for a quarter have been processed, you can no longer change them.

Correcting an Error

If you make a mistake or want to change something you have typed, simply move to the number you want to change using either the Tab key or the mouse. Type in your new decision and press the Tab key. This will replace the old number with your new number.

MOVING THE CURSOR AROUND THE DECISIONS SCREENS

You can move the cursor around the two decision screens by either of two methods. One method is to use the Tab key. The second method is to use the mouse, if one is connected to your computer. You can use each of these methods in combination with the other method. This means you can make one move using the mouse and the next move using the Tab key. You can switch back and forth between these two methods of moving around a decisions screen as often as you like. Each of the two methods is described briefly in the following two sections.

Using the Tab Key

When the decision screen first appears, a flashing cursor will appear next to the first decision you must make — the price of Product 1. Use the Tab key to move from decision to decision on the screen. Pressing the Tab key alone will move you "forward" to the next decision entry cell. Pressing and holding the Shift key and then pressing the Tab key will move you "backward" to the preceding decision entry cell. When you reach the last decision on the screen, pressing the Tab key will take you back to the first decision on the screen. You can enter the individual decisions in any order you choose. What matters is the last set of numbers showing on the screen after you have finished entering your decisions.

If you do not want to change the number shown on the screen, press the Tab key to move to the next decision you must make. This will automatically enter the number displayed on the screen. If you wish to make a change, simply type in your new number (or letter) and press the Tab key. This will enter your new number (or letter) and move you to the next decision. Notice that when you tab to a new cell, the whole cell is highlighted. If you press the Backspace key, the whole number is erased. You must then enter a new number and press the Tab key, or the *Threshold Competitor* program will automatically enter a zero for that decision.

If you press an Arrow key while the number is highlighted, the highlighting will disappear, but the number will remain. You can then use the Arrow key to move to a digit within the number and make a change to the existing number without having to change the whole number. For example, you could change a sales forecast number from 6,100 to 6,150. To *insert* a digit into an existing number, use the Arrow key to move to the insertion point, type in the new digit, use the Delete or the Backspace key to remove any unwanted digit(s), and press the Tab key. To *type over* a particular digit, use the Arrow key to move to the digit you want to replace, press the Insert key, then type in the new digit and tab to the next decision cell. Notice how the shape of the flashing cursor changes after you press the Insert key. Once you have pressed the Insert key, you will be able to type over existing numbers until you press the Insert key again and the flashing cursor returns to its original shape.

Using the Mouse

Use the mouse to move around a decisions screen the same as you would when working in any Windows environment. Simply move the mouse indicator to the decision number you want to change and click the left mouse button. The number you selected will become highlighted. Type in the number you desire and either press the Tab key or click onto a new number. Repeat this process until you have made all the changes you desire to the decisions showing on the screen.

Clicking twice on a number will allow you to edit the existing number on the screen. The first click highlights the number. The second click positions the cursor in the number so that you can type in a digit and delete unwanted digits using the Backspace or Delete keys. As with working without a mouse, pressing the Insert key allows you to type over existing numbers.

You will need to enter information on only two screens — the two decisions screens. If you are at the computer, try entering some information on the Marketing and Market Research Decisions screen now. None of the numbers you enter at this time will become permanent. Even during the simulation exercise, no decision is permanent until you process the quarter's decisions. This means the only numbers that matter are the *last* ones entered before your quarter's decisions are processed. So feel free to experiment now. Chapter 6 explains each of the decisions you will enter on the four decisions screens.

MOVING FROM SCREEN TO SCREEN

Threshold Competitor has a number of screens that you can view and/or print out when working on the exercise. These are: (a) the decisions screens, on which you enter your decisions, (b) the reports screens, where you can see the results of decisions you have made, and (c) the information screens, which provide you with information on various parts of *Threshold Competitor*, such as the costs of your operations.

There are three methods that you can use for moving from screen to screen. One method is to use the Menu bar displayed across the top of the *Threshold Competitor* screens. The second method is to use a combination of the [PgUp] and [PgDn] keys. The third method is to use the *Threshold Competitor* "hot" keys to move directly to a decision, report, or information screen. We will now discuss each of the three methods, in turn.

Using the Menu Bar

You can access each of the reports/screens listed above through the Menu bar. The Menu bar is always shown across the top of your screen, regardless of what particular screen you are viewing. There are seven headings listed on the Menu bar. They are File, Quarter, Decisions, Reports, Info, Print, and Windows. Under each of these headings are a number of options that you can use. For example, as shown in Exhibit 5.14, under the File heading you have the option to (a) Open Existing Industry, (b) Create New Industry, (c) Create Backup Company File, (d) Process Industry, (e) Create Company Spreadsheet, (f) Create Performance Spreadsheet, (g) Select Quarter, (h) Change Password, (i) Change Company Name, and (j) Save & Exit. We will discuss each of these options, in detail, later.

Exhibit 5.14

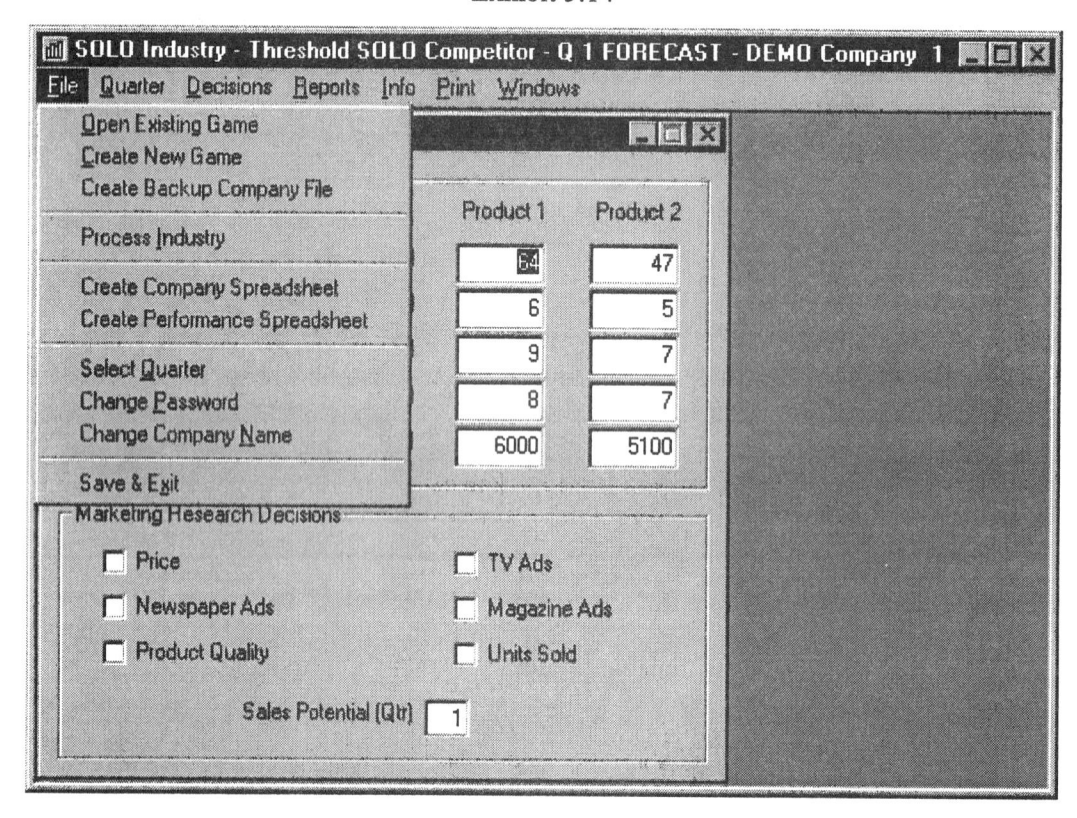

There are two methods you can use to access each of the headings on the Menu bar and the options associated with each heading. One method is to use a mouse; the other is to use a combination of the [ALT] and Arrow keys. As with the decision screens, you can use each of these methods in combination with the other method. We describe both methods for accessing the Menu bar next.

Using the Mouse. To access a heading on the Menu bar using the mouse, simply click on the heading with which you want to work. The options available for that heading are automatically displayed. To select an option, just click on it with the mouse.

Using the [ALT] and Arrow Keys. To access the Menu bar, press the [ALT] key. Notice that the heading labeled as "File" becomes highlighted. Notice also that the first letter in each of the other headings is underlined. Press the → and ← arrow keys to move to the other headings on the Menu bar. You can also move directly to a heading by pressing the letter that is underlined for each option.

To access the options under each heading, press the ↓ (i.e., down) arrow key. A list of options available under that heading will appear on your screen. To select one of these options, press the down arrow key until your desired option is highlighted and press [ENTER]. Alternatively, each one of the options will have a letter that is underlined. Pressing that letter on your keyboard will also select that option. Each of the options available through the Menu bar headings will be discussed later in this chapter. For now, concentrate on the mechanics of moving from screen to screen using the Menu bar.

Notice that once the options for a particular heading have been displayed, pressing an Arrow key to move to the next heading will automatically display the options for that heading. The options for the headings will continue to remain displayed until you press either the [ALT] key again or the ESC key.

Using the [PgUp] and [PgDn] Keys

To move from screen to screen using the [PgUp] and [PgDn] keys, press:
- [PgUp]   to move back to the previous screen.
- [PgDn]   to move to the next screen.

Press [PgDn] to see the next screen. You should now see the second decisions screen, the Product 2 Decisions screen (Exhibit 5.13).

The Report Screens. Press [PgDn] again. This time you will see the first of the reports screens, the Products Cost Report (see Exhibit 5.15). We will explain this and the other reports screens in Chapter 7. Continue pressing [PgDn] to see the rest of the reports. The reports appear in the following sequence:
- Inventory Report
- Labor Report
- Cost of Production Report
- Selling and Administrative Costs Report
- Income Statement
- Balance Sheet
- Cash Flow Statement
- Market Research Report
- Quarter Performance Report (Actual results only. Not shown for Forecast reports.)
- Game-to-Date Performance Report (Actual results only. Not shown for Forecast reports.)
- Marketing & Finance Limits and Time Lags Report
- Production Limits and Time Lags Report
- Cost Parameters Report
- Bulletin

Exhibit 5.15

RAW MATERIAL	Product 1		Product 2	
INVENTORY REPORT	Units	Value	Units	Value
Beginning Balance	500	4000	400	4800
Units Received	7000	56000	6500	78000
Total Available	7500	60000	6900	82800
Used in Production	6000	48000	5100	61200
Ending Balance	1500	12000	1800	21600
Raw Matl Warehouse Costs	500	500	400	800
Total Product Cost		48500		62000

FINISHED GOODS	Product 1			Product 2		
INVENTORY REPORT	Units	$/Unit	Value	Units	$/Unit	Value
Beginning Balance	0	0.00	0	0	0.00	0
Production	6000	37.59	225526	5100	40.45	206304
Units to Sell	6000	37.59	225526	5100	40.45	206304
Units Sold	6000	37.59	225526	5100	40.45	206304
Ending Balance	0	0.00	0	0	0.00	0
FG Warehouse	0	2.50	0	0	1.50	0
Lost Sales	0	64.00	0	0	47.00	0

If you are working on the computer, try pressing [PgDn] and [PgUp] a number of times until you are familiar with their operation.

Using *Threshold Competitor* "Hot" Keys

In addition to using a combination of the [PgUp] and [PgDn] keys or the Menu bar, the *Threshold Competitor* program also has a number of "hot" keys that let you to move from one screen directly to another screen, regardless of where you are in the program. For example, pressing the F1 key moves you directly to the Marketing and Marketing Research Decision screen. You can also use "hot" keys to move directly to any of the reports. To do this, press and hold the [CTRL] key, then press the letter or function key listed under the Reports Menu option. For example, if you press and hold the [CTRL] key and press C, the Cash Flow Statement will appear on the monitor.

Appendix F provides a listing of these special "hot" keys for *Threshold Competitor*. These "hot" keys are also listed with their associated reports or screens when you access the options under the heading on the Menu bar. The Menu bar appears at the top of all screens when you use the *Threshold Competitor* program.

This means you are not limited to using the [PgUp] and [PgDn] keys or the Menu bar to move from one screen to another screen. However, if you have pressed the [ALT] key and highlighted the Menu bar, the "hot" keys are disabled. They will not work while you are using the Menu bar options. Pressing [ESC] will take you out of the Menu bar and enable the "hot" keys for your use. Learning to use the *Threshold Competitor* "hot" keys allows you to move quickly around the program and can shorten the time necessary to make a decision.

You now should know how to move around the decisions screens and to move from one screen to another. Next we will describe what each of the options under the Menu bar headings can do.

MENU BAR OPERATIONS

As mentioned earlier, the Menu bar contains seven headings: File, Quarter, Decisions, Reports, Info, Print, and Windows. Using the Menu bar will allow you to work with your *Threshold Competitor* files. You will be able to enter decisions for managing your company, view reports on your company's operation, access information regarding *Threshold Competitor*, and print out any, or all, of the screens you can view. Each of these is discussed below.

The File Menu

You can perform ten different operations using the File menu (see Exhibit 5.14). These are: Open Existing Industry, Create New Industry, Create Backup Company File, Process Industry, Create Company Spreadsheet, Create Performance Spreadsheet, Select Quarter, Change Password, Change Company Name, and Save & Exit. Each of these will be discussed in order.

Open Existing Industry (Available only for *Competitor Solo*). Selecting this option allows you to open a file for a *Threshold Competitor Solo* industry that was created earlier. This could be a file that you created and then saved to work with at a later time. It could also be one created by someone else, such as your instructor or a teammate. Exhibit 5.10 shows the screen that will appear on your monitor when you select this option. We discussed using this option earlier under "Opening an Existing *Threshold Competitor* Data File". Go back to that section for directions on how to use this option.

Create New Industry (Available only for *Threshold Competitor Solo*). Selecting this option will begin a new game at Quarter 1 with a new setup. Exhibit 5.3 shows the screen that will appear on your monitor when you select this option. We discussed using this option earlier under "Starting the *Threshold Competitor Solo* Program" at the beginning of this chapter. Go back to that section for directions on how to use this option.

Create Backup Company File. This option allows you to save your company data file to another disk for safekeeping. It is important to maintain a backup of your company's data file to protect against unexpected damage of loss of your company disk.

When you select this option, a dialog box similar to the one in Exhibit 5.16 will appear on your monitor. To save your company data file on a floppy disk, make sure you have a disk with at least 100KB of free space in the floppy drive. Next, if the "Save in" box does not show the floppy drive as the save location, click on the ▼, choose A (or B) and then click on the Save button. **NOTE: if you are working with *Threshold Competitor Team*, do *NOT* change the file name!** You must leave it with the default "CTHR.CTS" file name! If you change the file name, your company data file will not be able to be read by the administrator's program.

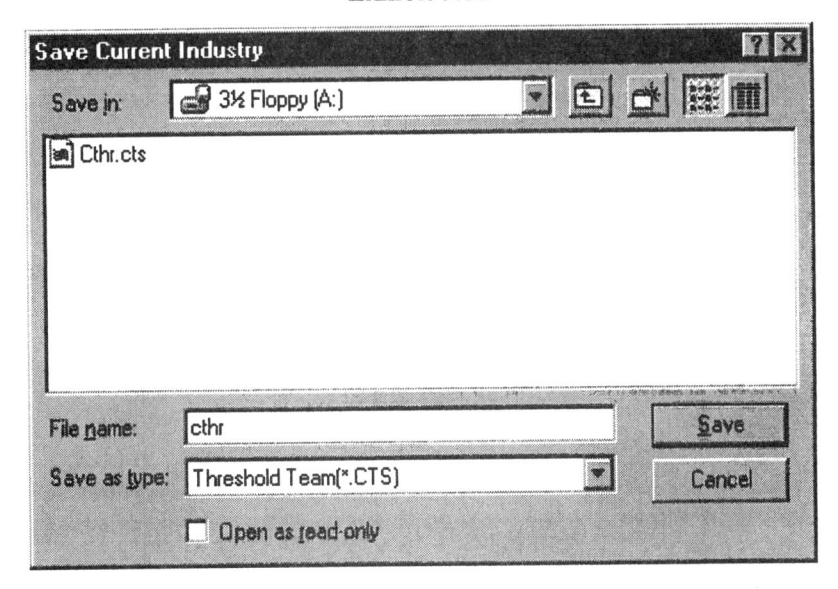

Exhibit 5.16

Process Industry (Available only for *Threshold Competitor Solo*). After making your forecasts, you can process your decisions for Quarter 1 by selecting the Process Industry option. If you are satisfied with your decisions and want to proceed to the next quarter (e.g., Quarter 2), click on "Yes" when the dialogue box appears on your monitor (see Exhibit 5.17). Once you say "Yes," the program will process Quarter 1's decisions and move forward to Quarter 2.

Exhibit 5.17

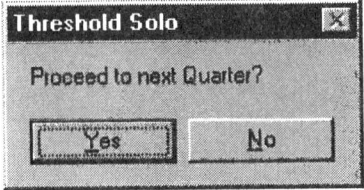

To view or print your Actual Results and Standings for Quarter 1, choose the Select Quarter option under the File heading, as was discussed earlier. Next, enter a "1" in the dialogue box that appears on your monitor. When you finish reviewing your results and are ready to proceed to Quarter 2 to enter decisions, choose the Select Quarter option and enter a "2." Repeat this process for each subsequent quarter of play. You can also change to a different quarter by using the Quarter Menu, which we will discuss later.

Create Company Spreadsheet. This option creates a data file (CompData.csv) of selected data from your company's reports that you can open with Excel. The file will contain the chosen data from all the quarter that have been processed. It does not include the current quarter for which you are making decisions and forecasting results. You can use the data in this file to track your company's performance over time. You can also choose to create graphs using the data that will provide a visual record of your company's performance. (Note that if you attempt to create a data file before you have processed the first quarter of decisions, you will receive a message informing you "You cannot use this function until after Quarter 1 is processed".) See Appendix K for the definition of the headers used in the Excel spreadsheet.

When you select this option, a dialog box like that in Exhibit 5.18 will appear on your monitor stating where the file was stored. If you are working with *Competitor Team*, the file will be saved in the same location as your *Threshold Competitor* company data file. If you are working with *Threshold Competitor Solo*, the file will be saved in the same location where your *Threshold Competitor* program file (ThreshC, unless you changed the default location during the setup process.).

Exhibit 5.18

Create Performance Spreadsheet. This option creates a data file (PerfData.csv) of selected data from the Quarterly and Game-to-Date Performance reports you receive after a quarter has been processed. As with the CompData.csv file, you can open the PerfData.csv with Excel. The data in this file will allow you to compare your company's performance against the other companies' performance over time. (Note that if you attempt to create a data file before you have processed the first quarter of decisions, you will receive a message informing you "You cannot use this function until after Quarter 1 is processed".) See Appendix L for the definition of the headers used in the Excel spreadsheet.

When you select this option, a dialog box like that in Exhibit 5.19 will appear on your monitor stating where the file was stored. As with the CompData.csv file, if you are working with *Competitor Team*, the file will be saved in the same location as your *Threshold Competitor* company data file. If you are working with *Competitor Solo*, the file will be saved in the same location where your *Threshold Competitor* program file (ThreshC, unless you changed the default location during the setup process.).

Exhibit 5.19

Select Quarter. The Select Quarter option allows you to change from the current quarter in which you are operating and select an earlier quarter of company operations. This will allow you to access earlier company reports and to view or print that information. The *Threshold Competitor* program retains all of your company's history on your company's disk. You will have the ability to view, and print, any or all of your company's reports from Quarter 1 through the current quarter of operation. However, this option will not allow you to return to an earlier quarter and change the decisions you made earlier.

To select a particular quarter, choose the Select Quarter option. Exhibit 5.20 shows the screen that will appear on your monitor. Enter the number of the quarter desired and select OK. If you select a quarter that has already been processed, the two *decision* screens will not be displayed since these decisions already have been made and cannot be changed. (However, you *can* see those decisions by examining the "Marketing Decisions" and the "Production/Finance Decisions" reports under the Reports menu option. If you select a quarter beyond the current quarter (e.g., Quarter 3 when you are making decisions for Quarter 2), you will receive an error message on the screen.

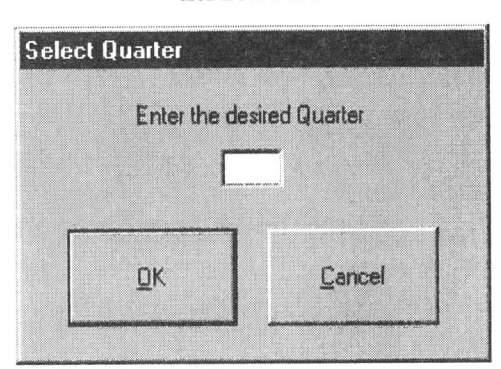

Exhibit 5.20

Take note: When you process a quarter, you must use this option (or the Quarter menu option, discussed below) to view and/or print your results for the quarter that was just processed. The *Threshold Competitor* program automatically loads your company files for the next quarter of operation, *not for the quarter that has just been processed*. This means after Quarter 2 has been processed, Quarter 3 will appear on the screen when you load the *Threshold Competitor* program. To see the results of your Quarter 2 decisions *and any market research information you have purchased*, you have to choose the Select Quarter option and enter a "2" as the desired quarter number. You can then choose to view or print these results. Once you are ready to begin entering Quarter 3 decisions, choose the Select Quarter option again and enter a "3" as the quarter number.

Change Password. The first time you entered the *Threshold Competitor* program, you gave your company a password to prevent unwanted access to your company's reports that are stored on your disk. You may decide, for security reasons, to change your disk's password. This option allows you to make that change. You can change your password as often as you wish, but be careful. Frequent changes can lead to confusion. If you forget your password you will not be able to access the files on your disk, nor make decisions for the upcoming quarter of operation. If this happens, see your administrator for help.

To change your password, select the Change Password option. Exhibit 5.21 shows the screen that will appear on your monitor. Enter a new password you will remember and press [ENTER] or click on OK. Again, it is usually advisable not to select as a password the name of a family member or a nickname that others are likely to guess.

Exhibit 5.21

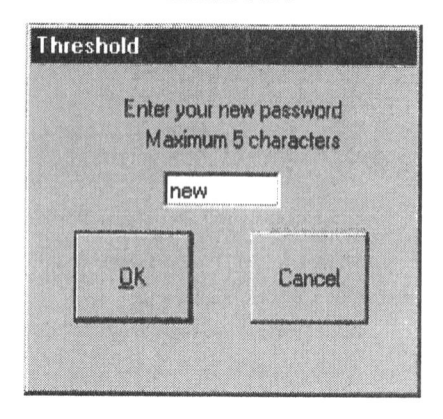

Change Company Name. As with the password, the first time you entered the *Threshold Competitor* program, you also gave your company a name that was saved onto your disk. As stated earlier, there is no relationship between your company name and the success or failure of your company. However, if you wish to change your company name at any time during the simulation exercise, use this option to do so. To do this, select the Change Company Name option. Exhibit 5.22 shows the screen that will appear on your monitor. Type in your new company name and press [ENTER] or click on OK.

Exhibit 5.22

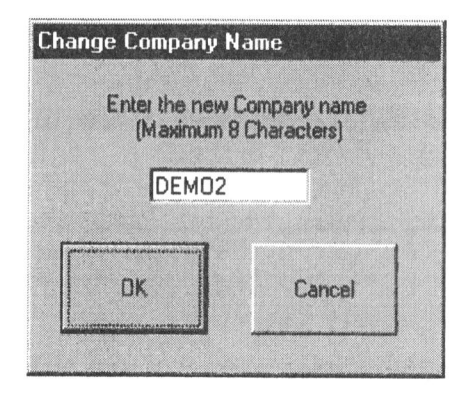

Save & Exit. Selecting this option will take you out of the *Threshold Competitor Team* and *Threshold Competitor Solo* program and return you to Windows. To do this, simply select the Save & Exit option and press [ENTER]. You can also exit the program by selecting the File heading and then pressing X. **Whenever you exit the *Threshold Competitor* program, the last numbers that were on the screens will be saved automatically.** If you started the *Threshold Competitor* program using your company disk, your decisions will be saved onto that disk. If you started the *Threshold Competitor* program using the hard drive, you will have to copy your company's data file from the hard drive to the company disk when you turn your decisions in to your administrator. Read how to do this under the "Using *Threshold Competitor* on a Hard Disk" section later in this chapter.

The Quarter Menu

The Quarter Menu is an alternative method from the Select Quarter option (described above) to change from one quarter of operation to a different quarter. As with the Select Quarter option, you can use this menu to access earlier company reports and to view or print out that information.

To use this method, select the Quarter menu option. A number of buttons with numbers will appear under the Quarter heading as is shown in Exhibit 5.23. Select the button number for the quarter you wish to view. There will only be buttons for the quarters that you are able to access. So if you are forecasting for Quarter 4, there will not be buttons for 5, 6, or higher. This is because those quarters have not yet been processed and consequently there are not yet reports to view for those quarters.

Exhibit 5.23

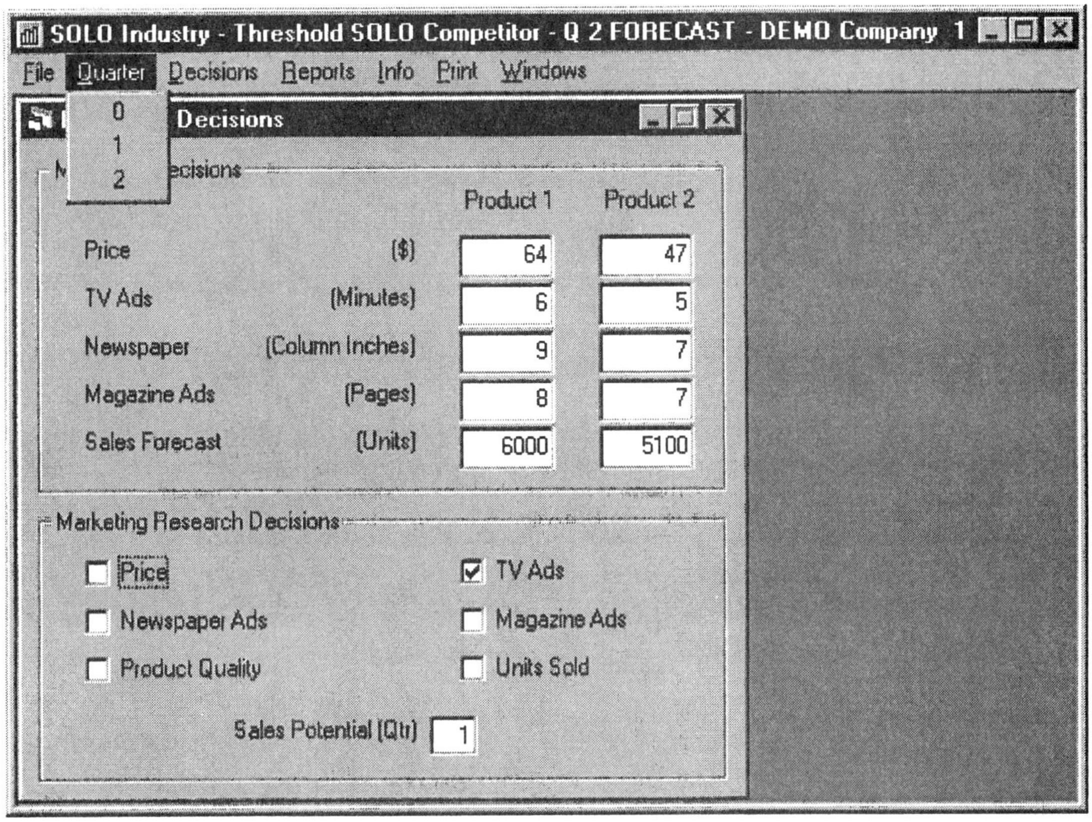

The Decisions Menu

The Decisions menu option provides you with access to the two screens on which you will enter your decisions for managing your company's operations (see Exhibit 5.24). Each of these will be discussed in order. Remember, you can access the decisions screens using either the Menu bar or *Threshold Competitor* "hot" keys. Press the F1 function key to move to the decisions screen for Marketing and Marketing Research. Press F2 to move to the decisions screen for Production and Finance.

Exhibit 5.24

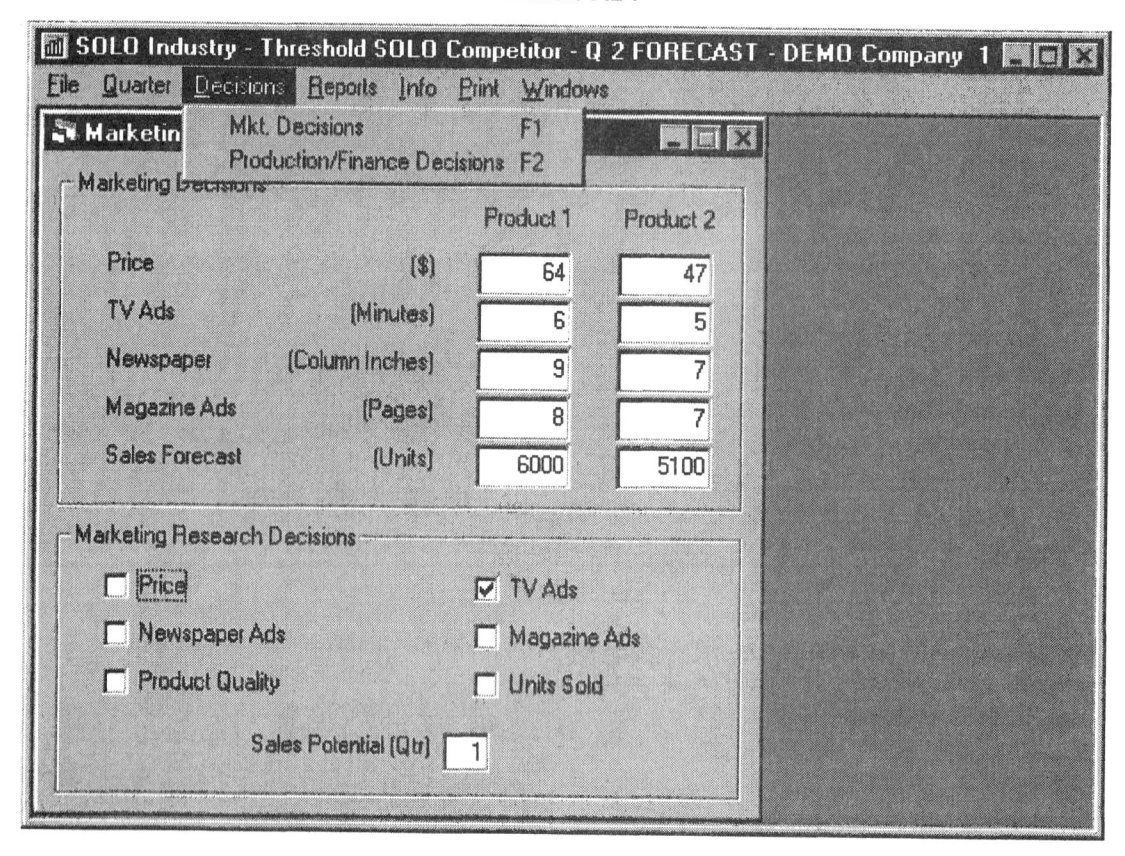

[Screenshot of SOLO Industry - Threshold SOLO Competitor - Q 2 FORECAST - DEMO Company 1, showing Marketing Decisions screen with:

Marketing Decisions:
		Product 1	Product 2
Price	($)	64	47
TV Ads	(Minutes)	6	5
Newspaper	(Column Inches)	9	7
Magazine Ads	(Pages)	8	7
Sales Forecast	(Units)	6000	5100

Marketing Research Decisions:
- Price (unchecked)
- Newspaper Ads (unchecked)
- Product Quality (unchecked)
- TV Ads (checked)
- Magazine Ads (unchecked)
- Units Sold (unchecked)
- Sales Potential (Qtr): 1]

Marketing and Market Research. This screen allows you to enter your decisions regarding pricing, and advertising for the two products your company is marketing. It also allows you to purchase market research about your competitors' marketing activities and the forecasted industry-wide demand for each of the products in future quarters. You will also use this screen to enter your forecasts for the sales volume that you expect to achieve for each of your two products for the current quarter of operation.

Production and Finance. This screen allows you to enter your decisions regarding the production of your two products. This involves the ordering of raw materials, staffing of workers, setting production volumes, investing in the quality of your product (which affects customer perception of your product), investing in training programs for your production workers, and adjusting plant capacity to meet production needs. You will also request the financing needed to pay for your marketing and production activities. In some quarters of operation, you may be confronted with a management dilemma that will require a decision from you. On those occasions, you will enter that decision on this screen.

The Reports Menu

The Reports menu allows you to access the reports detailing your company's operation. Exhibit 5.25 shows the reports that you can view using this option. When accessing these reports after loading *Threshold Competitor*, the program will display the reports for the most current quarter of operation. If you want to view an earlier quarter, you must first use either the Select Quarter option under the File menu heading or the Quarter menu, as were discussed earlier. We will discuss each of the reports used in *Threshold Competitor* in Chapter 7.

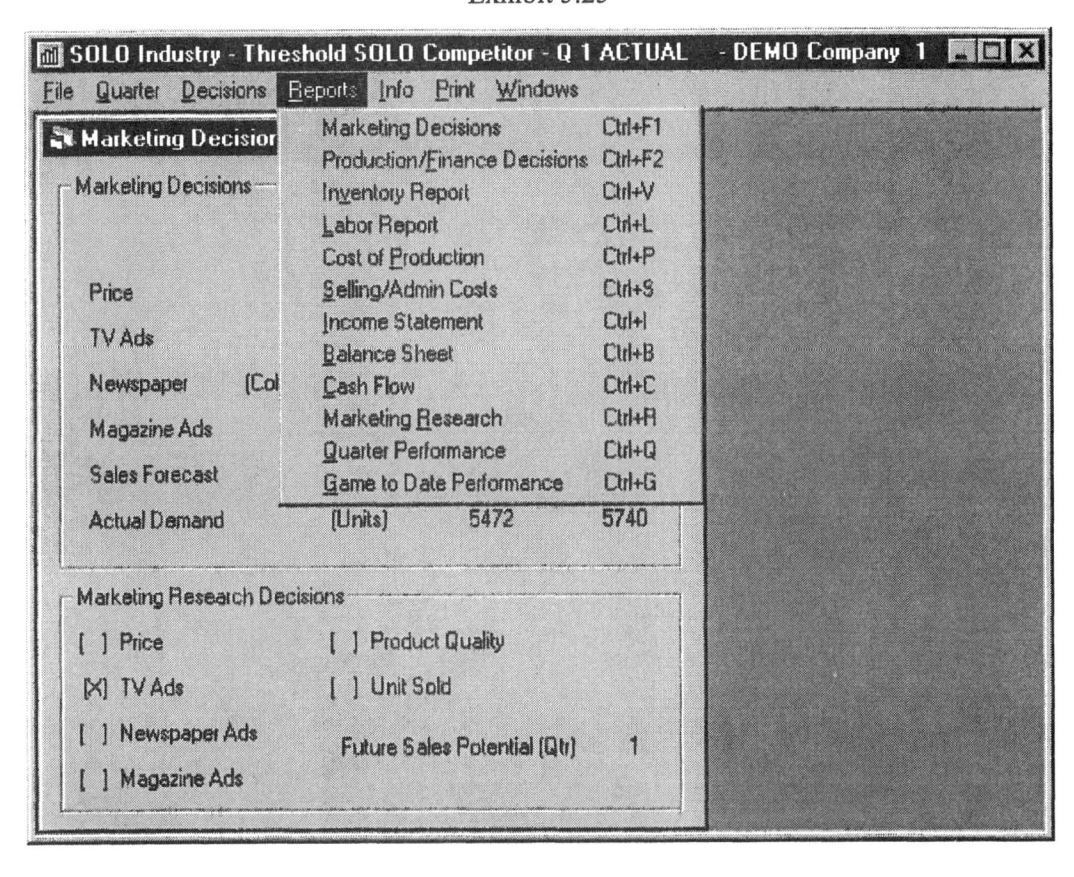

Exhibit 5.25

The Info Menu

The Info menu provides you with access to the decision entry limits and costs involved in managing your *Threshold Competitor* company (see Exhibit 5.26). You can also access the Bulletin through the Info heading. We will discuss each of these options next.

Marketing and Finance Limits Report. Use this option to display the acceptable limits for decision entries relating to marketing and finance. These include limits such as price ranges and maximum advertising levels. The screen also shows whether the decision will take effect in the current quarter (i.e., immediately) or in the following quarter (i.e., a one-quarter lag). You can also access the Marketing and Finance Limits screen using a "hot" key by pressing and holding the Shift key and then pressing F1. An example of this report is shown in Appendix E.

Production Limits Report. You can use this option to display the acceptable limits for decision entries relating to production. These include, for example, limits on Human Resource expenditures and the purchase of raw materials. As with the Marketing and Finance Limits screen, it also shows whether the decision will take effect in the current quarter (i.e., immediately) or in the following quarter (i.e., one-quarter lag). You can also access the Production and Finance Limits screen using a "hot" key by pressing and holding the Shift key and then pressing F2. An example of this report is shown in Appendix E.

Cost Parameters Report. Selecting this option will provide you with a listing of the costs for various items associated with operating your *Threshold Competitor* company. These include, for example, the costs for advertising, workers' wages, and interest rates. You can also access the Cost Parameters screen using a "hot" key by pressing the F3 function key. The costs displayed on your monitor are the costs

44 Chapter 5, Working with the *Threshold Competitor* Programs

related to the quarter you are viewing. That is, if you are viewing Quarter 5, pressing F3 will show you the Cost Parameters screen for Quarter 5. These costs can change as you progress through the simulation. Therefore, you should check the cost report for the quarter for which you are making decisions to see if any changes have occurred. To view the costs for earlier quarters, use the Select Quarter option under the File menu to choose the quarter you want to inspect. Then look at the cost report for that quarter. An example of a Cost Parameters Report is shown in Appendix D.

Exhibit 5.26

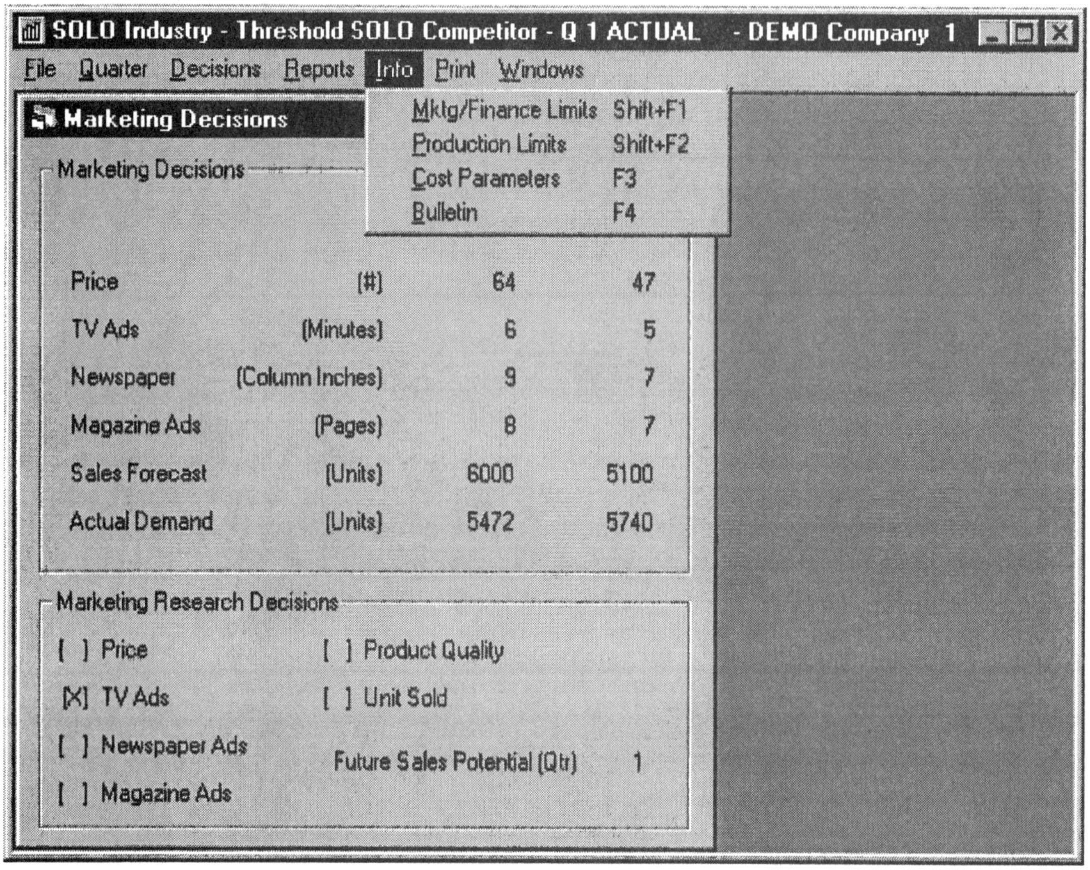

Bulletin. The Bulletin may have a message that your administrator wants to pass on to you. In *Threshold Competitor Team*, this message can change after your administrator processes company decisions. In *Threshold Competitor Solo*, this message can change after you submit your company data file to your administrator for review. So do not forget to check the bulletin after each time your administrator returns your *Threshold Competitor* data file to you. It is your responsibility to be aware of the information provided in the Bulletin. You can also access the Bulletin screen using the F4 "hot" key.

The Print Menu

The Print menu allows you to print any screen that appears on your monitor. You can choose to print an individual screen, a selection of screens, or all screens using this menu (see Exhibit 5.27). You can use this menu either (a) to print the screens you have selected to a printer connected to your computer or (b) to create a file containing the print image. We will explain how to do each of these next.

Exhibit 5.27

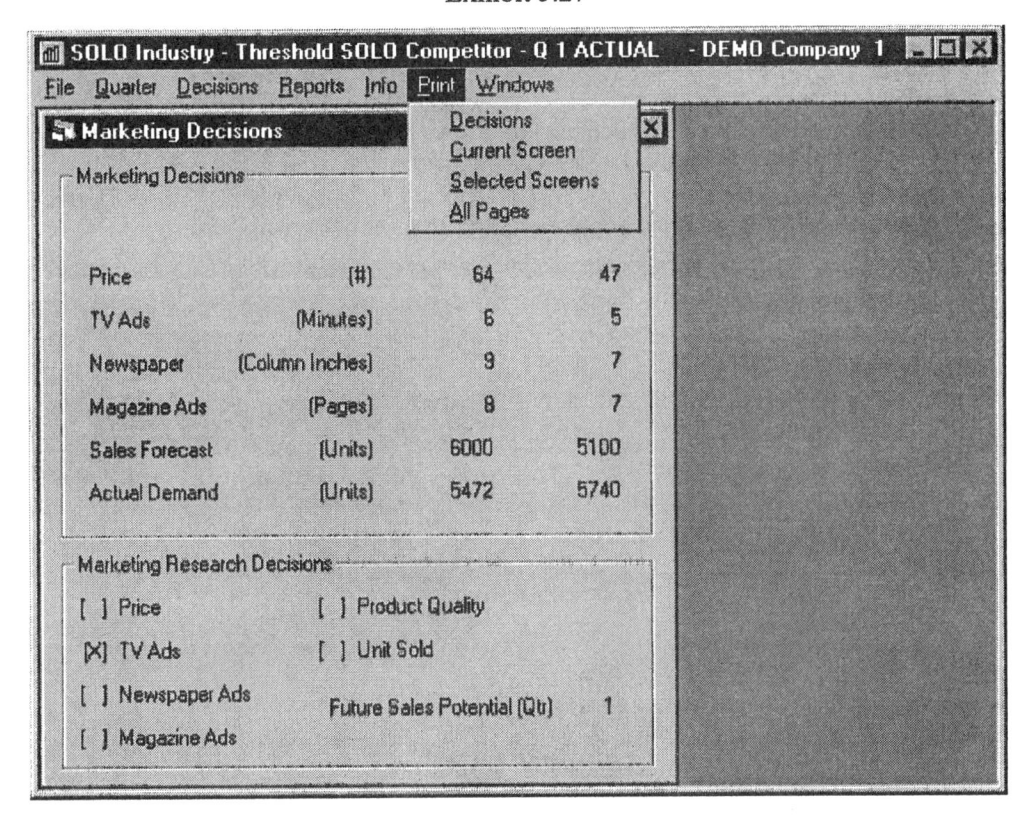

Print to a Printer. To print your selection of screens to a printer, select the screens you wish to print using one of the print options described below. After making your selection, a print dialogue box similar to that shown in Exhibit 5.28 will appear on your monitor. This dialogue box allows you to decide where you want to "print" the screens. If you want to send them to the printer connected to your computer, use the Tab key to move to the OK button and then press [ENTER] or use the mouse to select the OK button, to begin the printing of the screens.

Exhibit 5.28

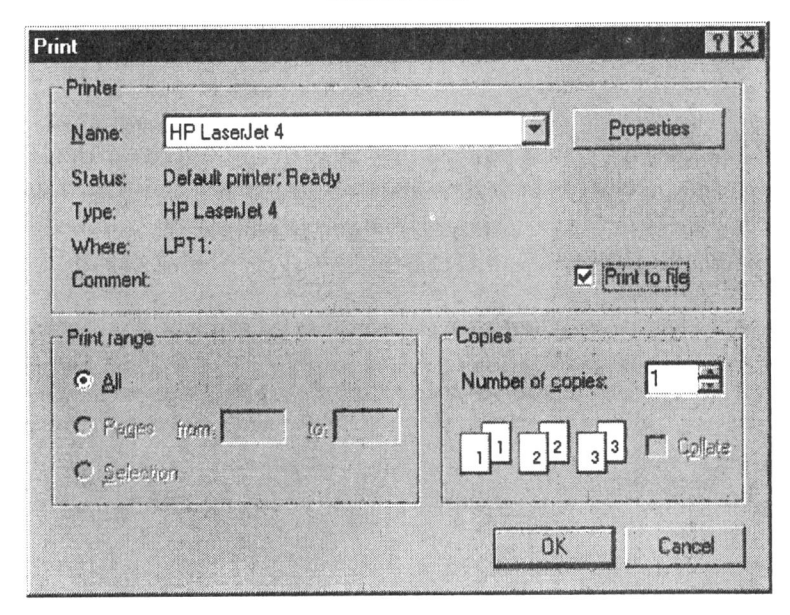

46   Chapter 5, Working with the *Threshold Competitor* Programs

Print to a File. You also have the option of printing the screens to a file instead of a printer. You could then transfer the file electronically to a teammate at another location using a modem. If you want to select this option, use the mouse to "check" (✓) the Print to File option in the lower left corner of the dialogue box as is shown in Exhibit 5.28. Alternatively, you can use the Tab key to move the cursor to the box, then press the space bar to check the box. Then select the OK button.

Another dialogue box will appear on your monitor prompting you to name the file and select the location where you want to save the file (see Exhibit 5.29). A default file name will appear in the upper left corner. If you wish to change the file name, select a file name that describes the contents of the file. File names can be up to eight characters long. To store that file on your *Threshold Competitor* company disk located in Drive A, select the "**a:**" drive option and press the Tab key to move to the OK button or use the mouse to click on OK.

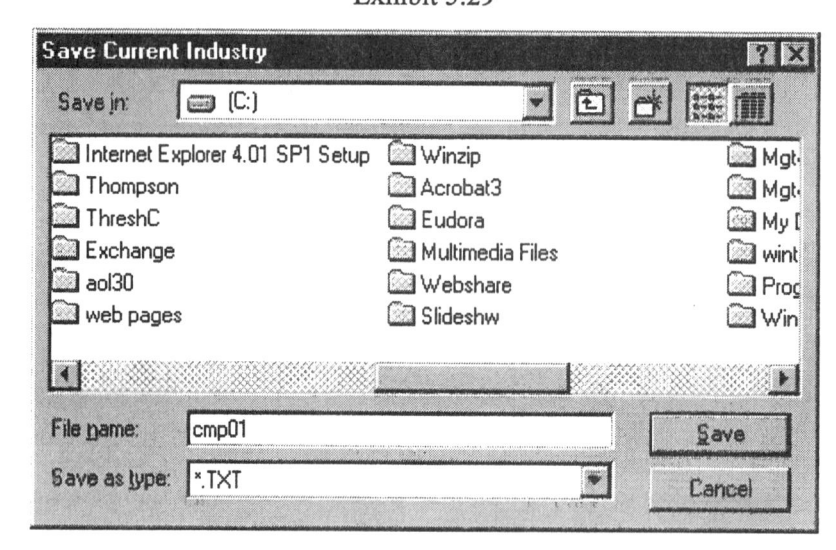

Exhibit 5.29

Print Decisions. Selecting this option will print the two decision screens: Marketing and Market Research and Production and Finance. To print these two screens, select the Print heading using the mouse or the Tab key, then select the Decisions option. Select the OK button to print the screens. To save the screens as a file, check (✓) the Print to File option box, then select the OK button and follow the directions given in the "Print to a File" section, above.

Print Current Screen. This option lets you print the last screen you were viewing before selecting this option. As with the Print Decisions option, a print dialogue screen will appear on your monitor so you can decide where you want to print the screen (see Exhibit 5.28). Select the OK button to print the screen. To save the screen as a file, check (✓) the Print to File option box, then select the OK button and follow the directions given in the "Print to a File" section, above.

Print Selected Screens. This option allows you to print only the report screens you desire. After selecting this option, a screen will appear with a listing of the reports you can choose to print (see Exhibit 5.30). Use the mouse to click on the report(s) you desire (e.g., the Income Statement) or use the Tab key to move to the screen you want printed and then press the space bar to select that screen. When you have selected all the screens desired, use the Tab key to move to the OK button and press [ENTER] or click on OK using the mouse. Select the OK button to print the screen. To save the screens as a file, check (✓) the Print to File option box, then select the OK button and follow the directions given in the "Print to a File" section, above.

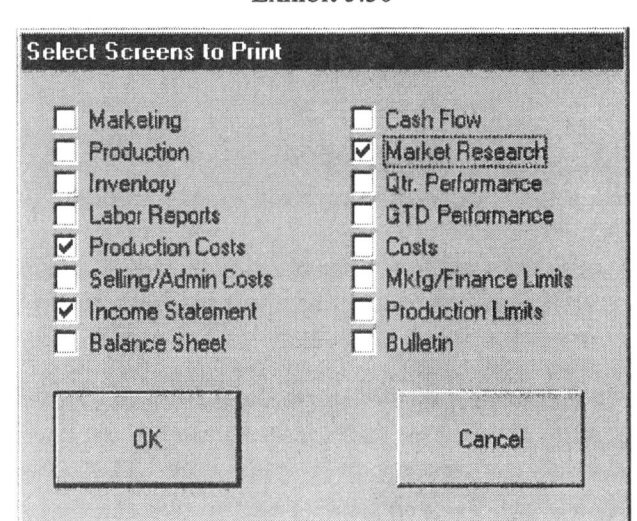

Exhibit 5.30

[Dialog box: Select Screens to Print — checkboxes for Marketing, Production, Inventory, Labor Reports, ✓ Production Costs, Selling/Admin Costs, ✓ Income Statement, Balance Sheet, Cash Flow, ✓ Market Research, Qtr. Performance, GTD Performance, Costs, Mktg/Finance Limits, Production Limits, Bulletin; OK and Cancel buttons]

Print All Pages. This option will automatically print all of the *Threshold Competitor* screens. As with the Print Decisions option, a print dialogue screen will appear on your monitor so you can decide where you want to print the two screens (see Exhibit 5.28). Select the OK button to print the screen. To save the screen as a file, check (✓) the Print to File option box, then select the OK button and follow the directions given in the "Print to a File" section, above.

SEEING THE *FORECASTED* RESULTS OF YOUR DECISIONS

Once you have entered decisions, you can view the *forecasted* reports for your company. These are not your "actual" results, like those that will be on your disk after you have processed your decisions. Instead, these reports are based on the sales forecast that you entered on the Marketing and Market Research decisions screen. So, if you said, for example, that you will sell 6,000 units of Product 1 at a price of $40 each, you will see in the reports that you sold 6,000 units and made $240,000 in sales. However, when the *Competitor Team* or *Competitor Solo* program actually processes your decisions, your sales may look very different! For example, if you sell only 5,000 units because of aggressive pricing by your competitors, your sales revenues for Product 1 would be only $200,000. This reduction in sales revenues could move you from a profit to a loss for that quarter's operation. In other words, your forecast reports are only as accurate as your sales forecasts. If you are overly optimistic in your sales forecasts, your reports will reflect this optimism and may show profits that will be nonexistent after you process your company's decisions. The program will not warn you that your forecasts are inaccurate. It will only process your forecasts, not judge them. It is up to you to enter realistic sales forecasts. Chapter 6 discusses making a sales forecast in more detail.

You can view the reports to see what will be the effects of your decisions, *assuming that your forecast is accurate*. You can look through the reports using any one of the methods for moving around the screens that was described earlier. Notice that before you process your decisions, the reports are labeled as "Forecast" reports. After you process your *Threshold Competitor Team* and *Threshold Competitor Solo* decisions the reports will be labeled as "Actual" reports. The "Actual" reports are the ones that matter. These are the reports that will be used to determine your standing relative to your competition and that you will use to determine your decisions for your company's next quarter of operation.

PROCESSING THE DECISIONS (AVAILABLE ONLY FOR *COMPETITOR SOLO*).

After you have entered decisions, reviewed your anticipated performance by looking at forecasted results, and modified any decisions you wish, you are ready to process those decisions. We described the processing stage of working with *Threshold Competitor* in Chapter 1. Instructions for processing *Solo Competitor* are also provided earlier in this chapter. Processing the decisions will move you from the quarter in which you are now operating (e.g., Quarter 1) to the next quarter (e.g., Quarter 2).

SEEING THE *ACTUAL* RESULTS OF QUARTERS THAT HAVE BEEN PROCESSED

As discussed earlier, when you load the *Threshold Competitor* program, it automatically advances to the next quarter for which you must make decisions. This means that if you want to view or print the actual (vs. forecasted) results for the quarters of your company's operations that have been processed, you will have to use the Select Quarter option under the File menu, or the Quarter menu, to index the program back to an earlier quarter. So, for example, after your decisions for Quarter 2 have been processed, your *Threshold Competitor* program will automatically set up for your company's Quarter 3 decisions. To see how your company performed in Quarter 2 and to see the market research information you purchased, select the Quarter menu and choose the "2" that drops down from the menu heading. You will then be able to view or print the actual results of your decisions and the market research information for Quarter 2. When you are ready to begin entering your Quarter 3 decisions, select the Quarter menu again and choose the "3" to return to the Quarter 3 screens. To view the actual results for Quarter 1, you would repeat this process choosing the "1" from the Quarter menu options.

DISPLAYING MULTIPLE SCREENS SIMULTANEOUSLY

Threshold Competitor is designed to allow you to display multiple screens on your monitor at the same time. This lets you enter decisions on one screen and simultaneously see the effect of that decision on one, or more, report screens. For example, Exhibit 5.31 shows that you can display all, or a portion, of the Marketing Decisions, Income Statement, and Cash Flow screens at one time. In order to see more than one screen at a time, you will have to move them from where they are initially displayed on the monitor. To do this, open the screen with which you want to work (e.g., Income Statement). Next, position the mouse arrow (↖) in the title bar of that screen. Press and hold the left mouse button and drag the screen to the location on the monitor where you want to move it. Once you have the screen in the desired position, release the mouse button. This is standard Windows protocol for moving screens on a monitor. If you have questions on how to do this, consult a Windows manual for additional guidance.

As shown in Exhibit 5.31, you can have screens overlap each other. If you want to see the full screen of one that is partially covered, just click on any portion to the screen that is exposed and it will be displayed above all other screens showing on the monitor.

Simultaneously displaying multiple screens will help you to test quickly different decision entries. For example, you can change the price and forecasted sales volume, and see the effect on net income without having to leave the Marketing decisions screen and switch to the Income Statement screen. Using the multiple screen capabilities of the *Threshold Competitor* program allows you to fine-tune your decisions quickly and efficiently.

Exhibit 5.31

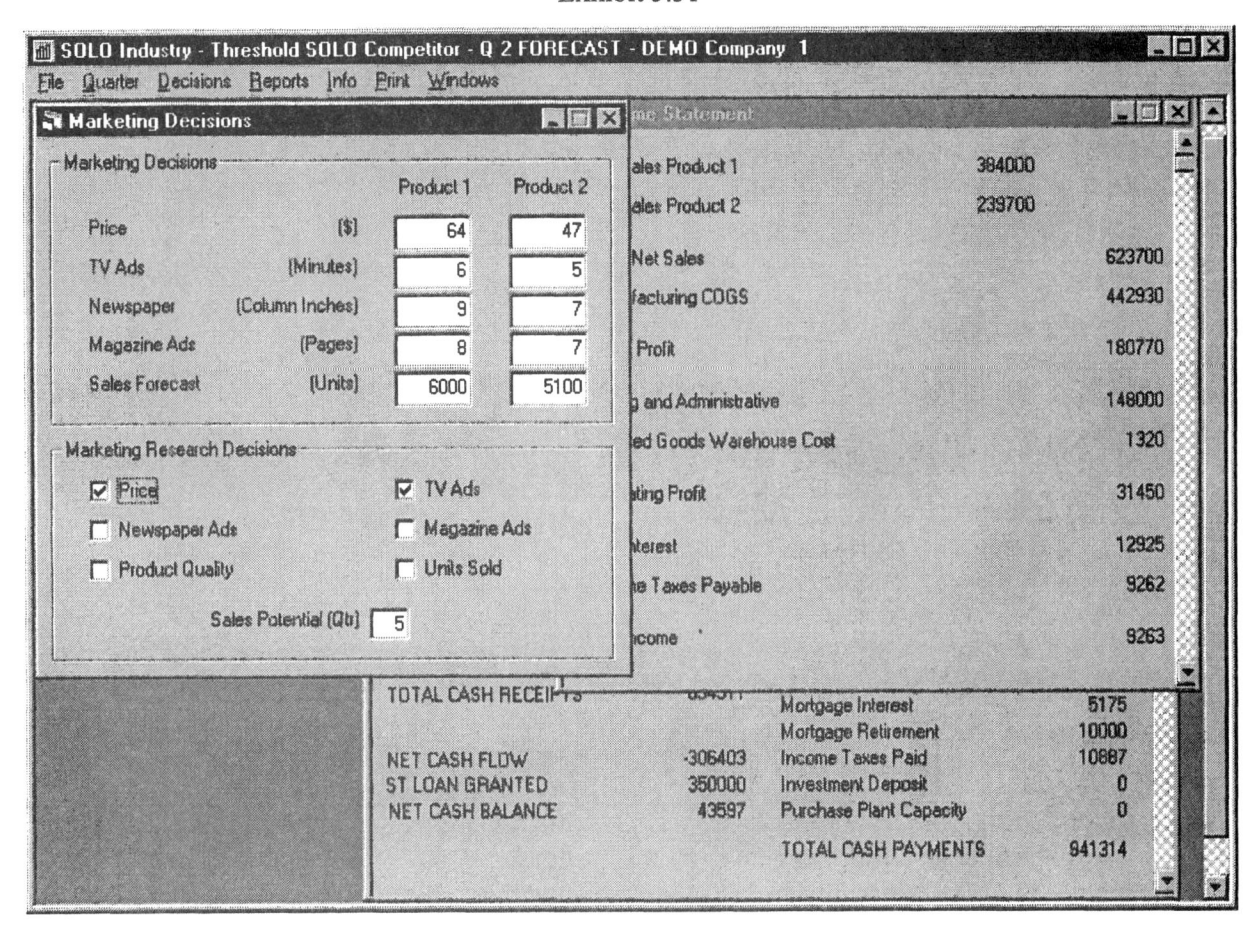

REPROCESS A PREVIOUS QUARTER (APPLIES ONLY TO *COMPETITOR TEAM*)

This option is similar to the Start New Game option for *Threshold Competitor Solo*, described earlier. But in *Threshold Competitor Team*, your administrator will decide when it will be used. This option is used only in very rare instances where it is necessary to make changes in decisions that have already been processed. If your administrator instructs you to repeat a previous quarter, use the Select Quarter option under the File menu heading. Enter the quarter number told to you by your administrator that is going to be re-processed. Next, select the Decisions menu heading. Notice that there is now a third option under that heading: "Change Decisions." Exhibit 5.32 shows an example of what this screen will look like.

50 Chapter 5, Working with the *Threshold Competitor* Programs

Exhibit 5.32

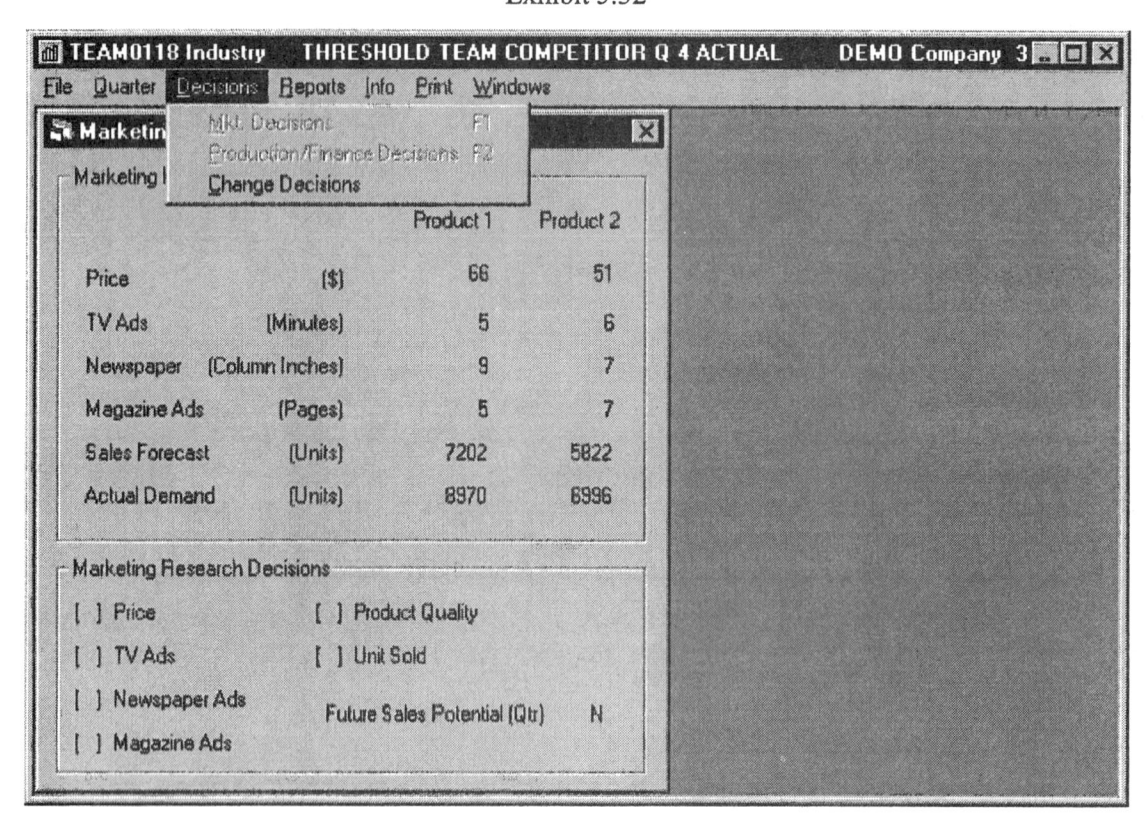

When you select that option, *Threshold Competitor Team* will ask for a password (see Exhibit 5.33). Enter the password your administrator has given you. You will then be able to enter new decisions for that quarter.

Exhibit 5.33

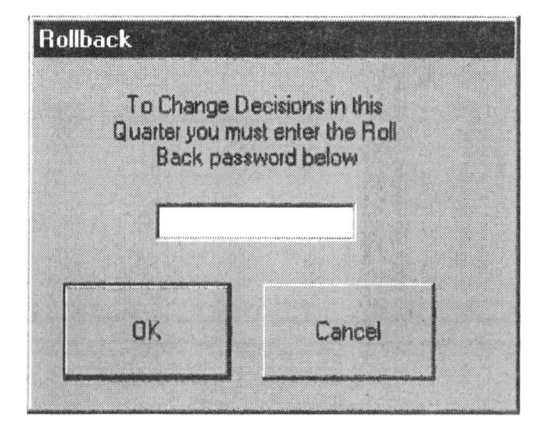

If you enter the wrong password, a dialogue box will appear on your monitor telling you that you entered the wrong password (see Exhibit 5.34). If you do not enter the correct password, you will not be allowed to enter decisions for that quarter.

Exhibit 5.34

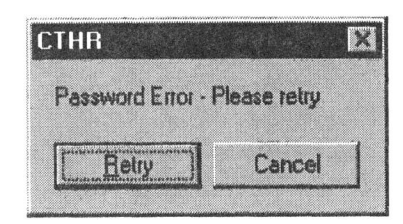

Do not attempt to make changes on your own without the administrator's approval. Even if you succeed in doing so, the records your administrator keeps in the administrator's files will override your changes, put your company records in turmoil, and make successful completion of the simulation extremely difficult.

USING *THRESHOLD COMPETITOR* ON A HARD DISK

As mentioned earlier in this chapter, you can work with *Threshold Competitor* using your computer's hard disk rather than on your company's floppy disk, if you so desire. If you use the hard disk, it is very likely that you will have to move files back and forth between the hard disk and a floppy.

Copying Files Between the Company Disk and the Hard Disk

If you plan to work with *Threshold Competitor* using your hard disk, you will need to use Windows Explorer to copy files. If you are unfamiliar with how to copy files using this Windows program, we *strongly* recommend that you do *not* use the hard disk to work with *Threshold Competitor*. We believe you would be much wiser to operate the *Threshold Competitor* program off of the company disk. The cost of copying an incorrect file to or from either the hard disk or the company disk is severe. The benefits do not outweigh the hazards involved. We suggest that you practice working with Windows Explorer in circumstances where mistakes are of less consequence.

If you choose to work off of your hard disk, use the following directions to copy the proper files to and from the hard disk and your company disk.

For *Threshold Team Competitor*.
- To copy files from the company disk to the hard disk:
  Copy the CTHR.CTS file from your company disk in Drive A to the ThreshC directory created on your C Drive during your Windows setup.
- To copy files from the hard disk to the company disk:
  Copy the CTHR.CTS file from the ThreshC directory created on your C Drive during your Windows setup to your company disk in Drive A.

For *Threshold Competitor Solo*.
- To copy files from the company disk to the hard disk:
  Copy the company file that you created and saved when you started the simulation from your company disk in Drive A to the ThreshC directory created on your C Drive during your Windows setup.
- To copy files from the hard disk to the company disk:
  Copy your company file from the ThreshC directory created on your C Drive during your Windows setup to your company disk in Drive A.

NOTE: The name of the file you must copy was established when you saved the file at the start of the simulation. The name of the file is the name you chose, with a ".CSS" extension. The file name used in the example in this chapter is DEMO.CSS.

Make sure you do not accidentally forget to transfer your files from your hard disk to your *Threshold Competitor Solo* company disk before you submit the disk to your administrator. *You* are responsible for the accuracy of the decisions you turn in to your administrator, *not* the administrator! If you forget to transfer your files to your company disk, you will have to live with the consequences of this mistake, which could be severe. Just as in business, you have to be responsible for your mistakes.

MAKING A BACKUP DISK

You should always keep a backup of your *Threshold Competitor* company disk, or company data file if using the hard disk, to protect against unexpected damage or loss of your company's data. **It is your responsibility to protect your company's assets! This includes your *Threshold Competitor* data!** Just because you are careful does not mean nothing can, or will, go wrong. Bad luck does happen. It is up to you to protect against it.

Failure to maintain a backup of your company disk or company data file can have severe consequences. It is extremely important to make backups regularly. This will protect you in case your main disk is damaged in any way. Remember Murphy's Law: "If something can go wrong, it will, and usually at the worst time possible."

If Using a Company (Floppy) Disk. Make a backup copy of your *Threshold Competitor* company disk by using the Windows Explorer program. Click on My Computer and highlight the icon labeled "3½ floppy [A:]." Then select the Copy Disk option from under the File heading and follow the directions.

If Using the Hard Disk. If you are running *Threshold Competitor* using your hard disk, you need to copy your company data file (CTHR.CTS for *Threshold Competitor Team* or the name you chose when you started the simulation for *Threshold Competitor Solo*) to a floppy disk for safekeeping. Make a backup of your company data file to a back up disk by following the directions for copying files from the hard drive to the company disk under the "Using the Hard Disk" section, above.

TROUBLESHOOTING

The *Threshold Competitor* program has undergone literally hundreds of hours of testing, both inside and outside the classroom. However, it is always wise for you to be prepared for "What do I do if...?" or "What do I do now?" situations.

Complete System Failure

The first thing to remember is that even if the computer system suddenly fails to operate (frequently referred to as a "crash"), the data on your *Threshold Competitor* company disk or on the hard disk will not be destroyed. In this worst-case scenario, restart the *Threshold Competitor* program. Any entries you had already saved will still be on your *Threshold Competitor* company disk or hard disk, depending on which you are using. If you have not yet saved your decisions, you will have to reenter them.

Threshold Competitor Program Failure

If the *Threshold Competitor* program file fails to load, the simplest response is to reload the *Threshold Competitor* program onto your hard disk using the CD in your manual. Before doing this, make sure you have current backup copies of your company data files. Reloading the *Threshold Competitor* program files will not change your company's current data file, but you should make copies to protect yourself in case the program failure is an indicator of problems with your computer's hard disk.

Threshold Competitor Company Disk Failure

Periodically, a sector of a disk becomes worn from high use or damaged by a disk drive as it reads from and writes to the disk. If either the *Threshold Competitor* company disk fails to load because of disk damage, use your backup disk, if you have been keeping it up to date. If you do not have a backup disk, see your administrator for help.

Viruses

The danger of a virus contaminating your *Threshold Competitor* company data file on your company disk or hard disk and disabling the files stored on it is ever present. If your *Threshold Competitor* program will not operate, it may be the result of a virus infection. Run a virus check of your *Threshold Competitor* company disk and your hard disk to see if this has occurred. **If your company disk has a virus on it, do NOT try to use it in another machine without first removing the virus.** If you do not know how to do this, get help! Any continued use of the disk will only spread the virus to more computers.

It is your responsibility to keep your *Threshold Competitor* company disk free of viruses. You would be wise to scan your disk for viruses *every* time you use it and before anytime you turn it in to your administrator. Not doing this leaves you exposed to virus infections. Assume the worst whenever you use a computer that others have used.

Data Entry Errors

If you attempt to make data entries that are outside acceptable limits, you will receive an error message from the *Threshold Competitor* program. Press the [ESC] key to cancel the illegal entry and try again. Remember, you can change your entries as often as you like *before* they are processed. This is discussed in detail in Chapter 6 under the "Sales Forecast Estimate" heading.

A STEP-BY-STEP WALK-THROUGH

You should now be familiar with the mechanics of working with *Threshold Competitor*. Turn to Appendix J and follow its step-by-step directions. Use the *Threshold Competitor Solo* program and enter some decisions and look at the reports resulting from those decisions. Doing this will help you see how you can use the forecasting process to test decision options. It will also show you how your forecasted results will differ from your actual results. Then, go on to Chapter 6. We will discuss the decisions you have available to you to manage your *Threshold Competitor* company.

CHAPTER 6

MAKING DECISIONS

OVERVIEW OF DECISIONS

You need to make and enter decisions in six main areas:
- marketing
- forecasting
- production
- finance
- sales forecasting
- management dilemmas

These six areas of decisions appear on the two decisions screens that you previewed in Chapter 5. In this chapter we will describe each decision for each of those five areas. Refer back to Chapter 5 if you are uncertain how to enter the decisions on the screens. This chapter will discuss the content of the decision, not the process for entering it.

PREPARING FOR DECISIONS: YOUR BUSINESS PLAN

Before making any decisions, you should develop a business plan for your company. This is an important first step to help you cohesively tie together all your decisions. Without this plan, various parts of your business could be working against each other. For example, you might develop a marketing plan designed to sell a high volume of both products. At the same time, you may have developed a production plan with a goal of constraining production to avoid overtime and minimize costs. This could result in stimulating more demand for your products than you had available to sell. This would result in lost sales, which would mean lost income and unhappy customers. Developing a business plan can help you avoid parts of your company working toward conflicting goals. You will use your business plan to guide you in the marketing, operations, and financial decisions you have to make.

Chapter 2 discusses the steps of the planning process: creating a mission statement, and a statement of goals, strategies, and policies. Reread that chapter to guide you in the development of your company's business plan. Once you have made this plan, you are ready to begin to make the specific decisions described in this chapter.

Developing a Business Plan

As discussed in Chapter 2, the first step of the planning process is to develop a mission statement for your company. Let us consider two very different company missions. One would be to meet the customer need for a premier-quality product that is relatively price inelastic. For customers buying this product, quality, not price, drives their decision-making process. The opposite focus would be to meet the customer need for a low-priced product where quality is less important. This does not mean that quality is unimportant, but is a secondary issue after price.

These two different company missions would result in two very different strategies. The high-quality focus would lead to a differentiation strategy, while the low-price focus would lead to a low-cost strategy. Regardless of which strategy you choose to pursue, you will face the same sets of decisions in marketing, operations, and finance. However, the nature of the decisions you make will be very different. For example, you will need to make marketing decisions about price, quality, and promotional support for the sale of your product. A differentiation strategy will naturally lead to high investments in the quality of the product to support the marketing efforts. A cost strategy will of necessity result in efforts to lower the company's cost of operations so that the company can maintain profits even though its product's price is much lower than that of companies with a differentiation strategy. This will make the cost of production a critical concern for companies pursuing the cost strategy. Efficient operations (e.g., plant utilization, worker utilization and productivity, and inventory control), while important to every company, will be a key to achieving success for those companies taking the low-price/low-cost route to the marketplace. Managing your financial requirements to minimize unnecessary financial charges will also be important to pursuers of a cost strategy.

Keep these issues in mind as you read about the different decisions you will make to manage your *Threshold Competitor* company. We will now discuss the six major types of decisions you will make each quarter.

MARKETING DECISIONS

For each quarter, you will have a variety of marketing decisions to make. These decisions will include:
- pricing
- advertising (i.e., TV, newspaper, and magazine)
- market research information (i.e., demand forecasts and competitor activities)

You will enter each of your marketing decisions on the Marketing and Market Research decisions screen (see Exhibit 6.1). We will now discuss each of these decisions in detail.

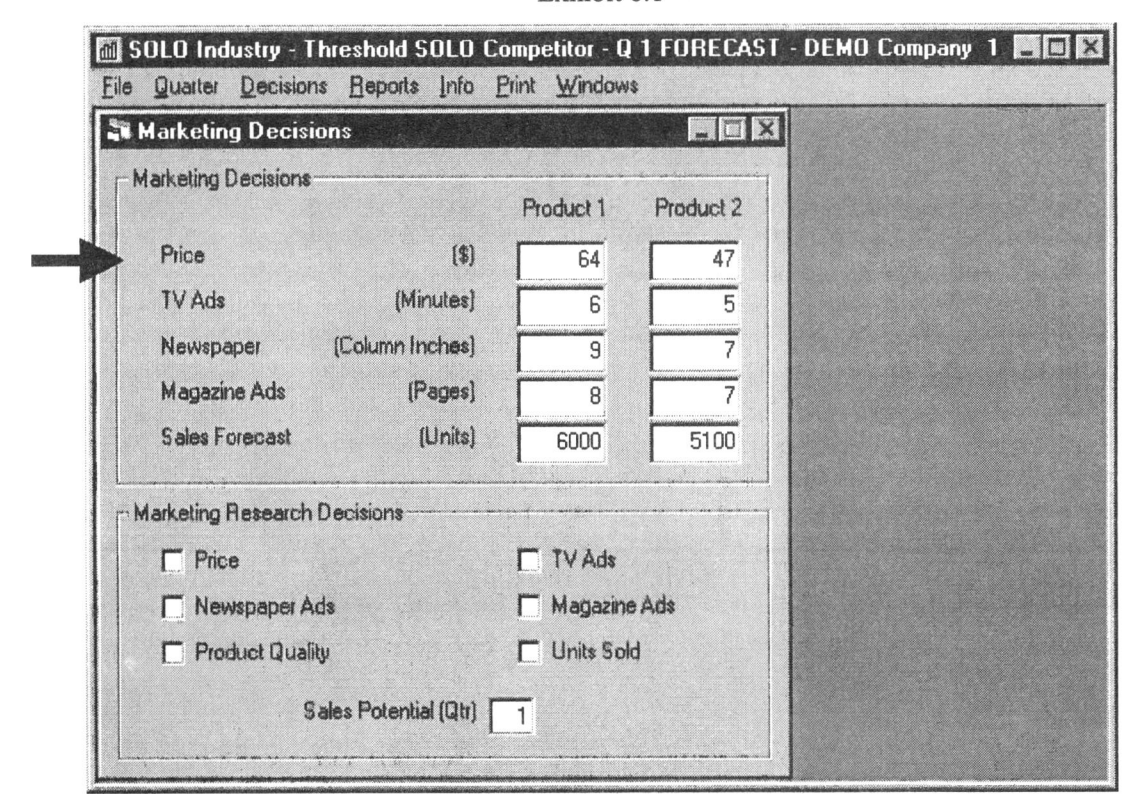

Exhibit 6.1

Marketing Decisions		Product 1	Product 2
Price	($)	64	47
TV Ads	(Minutes)	6	5
Newspaper	(Column Inches)	9	7
Magazine Ads	(Pages)	8	7
Sales Forecast	(Units)	6000	5100

Marketing Research Decisions:
- ☐ Price
- ☐ Newspaper Ads
- ☐ Product Quality
- ☐ TV Ads
- ☐ Magazine Ads
- ☐ Units Sold

Sales Potential (Qtr) 1

Price

In *Threshold Competitor*, companies operate in an oligopoly. This means relatively few companies manufacture the products produced and sold in their industry. In this industry, price is of major importance to the customer. The number of companies offering products for sale makes it easy for potential customers to be aware of price differences in the marketplace. If a company prices its product higher than its competitors', customers will buy the lower-priced product unless they are enticed by stronger marketing efforts, a better quality product, or both.

Effect of Price on Sales. The price of your product affects sales in two ways. One, the price you charge compared to your competitors has the biggest effect on your sales. Considering price alone, a product priced at $70 will sell more than one priced at $71. Two, a change in price from last quarter also has an effect on how much you will sell. All other things being equal, if you just raised your price, you will sell less than if you had kept the price constant from one quarter to the next. If you just lowered your price, you will sell more. The bigger the change in price, the bigger the effect of the price change on demand for your product.

Television Advertisements

A second factor that affects demand for your products is television ads. Each company has the option of purchasing up to 99 minutes of advertising for its products on the local television station. You can also choose to place no TV ads for your products. Enter a number from 0 to 99 for each product. The more minutes of advertising time you purchase *relative to other companies in the industry*, the higher the demand will be for your company's product. However, there is a point of diminishing returns and also a point of saturation. You should not assume that very large amounts of television advertising are necessarily more effective than lesser amounts.

Newspaper Advertisements

Your company can also advertise in a local newspaper. For each quarter of operation, you must decide how many column inches (from 0 to 99) of advertising space you wish to purchase. Each newspaper ad that you purchase will run once a week for the 13 weeks of the quarter. So if you enter a 12 for this decision, it means you have purchased an ad that is 12 column inches in length that will run once each week for the next 13 weeks. Like television advertising, newspaper advertising will tend to increase demand for your product, *to a point*. Determining where these diminishing returns begin to take effect is a puzzle for you to solve. This is also a problem that companies in the real world face. Regardless of whether you are managing General Motors, Kelly's Auto Repairs, or a *Threshold Competitor* company, all companies face the question, "How much advertising is enough and how much is too much?"

Magazine Advertisements

Another factor affecting demand is magazine advertisements. You have the option of purchasing from 0 to 99 full-page ads in popular, general-audience magazines selling in your market area. A point of diminishing returns also exists for this promotional media. A proper advertising campaign used with a market research program should try to identify this point.

Unlike television or newspaper ads, magazine advertisements also have an impact on sales that will carry over to the next quarter. This is because people often save magazines and read them later and because they pass magazines on to others to read. This delayed reading causes a secondary effect on product sales. Thus, demand is affected by the number of magazine ads you purchased this quarter, plus the number of magazine ads placed last quarter.

SALES FORECAST ESTIMATE

In addition to those marketing decisions, you will make sales forecasts of the number of units of Products 1 and 2 that you expect to sell that quarter. The arrow shown in Exhibit 6.2 indicates where you will enter your sales forecasts on the Marketing Decisions screen.

Exhibit 6.2

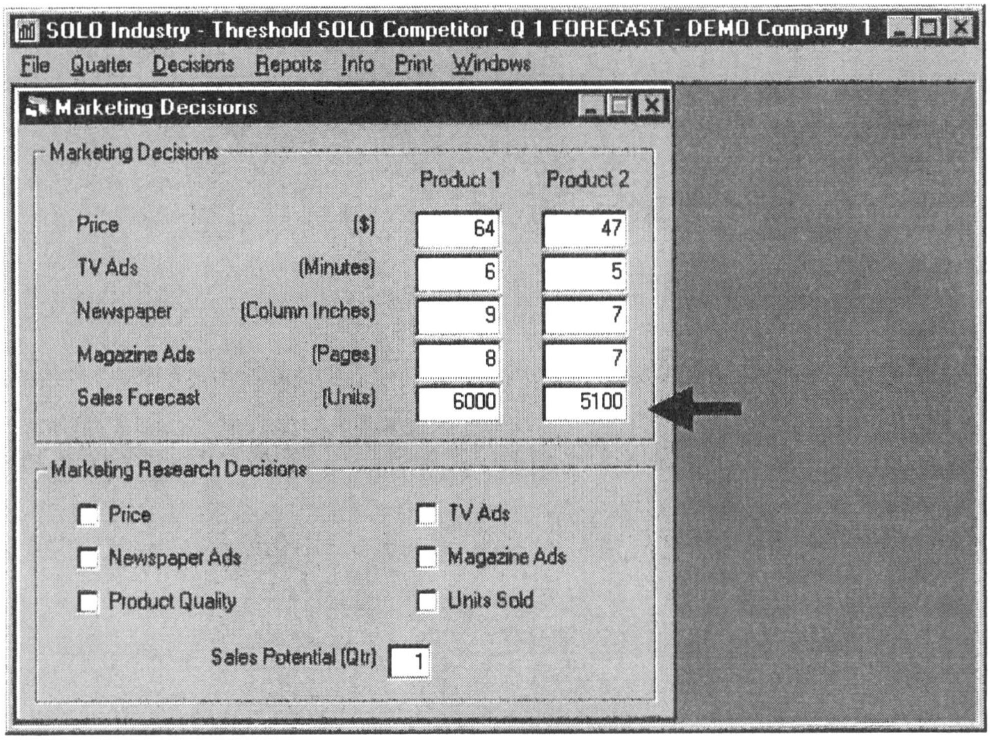

Factors to Consider When Forecasting Sales

Six factors — price, price change, TV ads, newspaper ads, magazine ads, and spending on product quality — combine to determine what portion of the market each company will capture (i.e., its market share). How much you choose to spend on building quality into your products will be discussed later in this chapter under "Production Decisions". The combination of a product's price and quality creates a value to the customer. This value, combined with your promotional efforts (e.g., advertising), will influence sales of your product.

Base your sales forecasts estimate on (a) your decisions regarding the six factors that determine market share, (b) your expectations of your competitors decisions on these factors, and (c) the overall market demand for each of the products. Enter a number between 0 and 99,999 for both Product 1 and Product 2 that is your best estimate of the sales volume you will achieve for each product.

Forecast Reports

Once you enter the forecasts, the *Threshold Competitor* program uses those numbers to generate forecast reports that show what would happen *if you actually sold the amount that you forecasted*. These forecast reports allow you to see what your operating costs and net income would be, whether you need to request a short-term loan, and what your overall picture would be for the quarter. You can also see *forecasts* for your material inventories and the cost of producing your products for that quarter. We discuss each of the reports created by *Threshold Competitor* in detail in Chapter 7.

Take note. These reports are *forecast* reports, and are labeled as forecasts on the report screens and any printouts you generate. They are only as good as your estimate of the demand for your products. No guarantee exists that you will actually sell what you forecast. Actual sales are determined after you have processed your decisions for that quarter and moved on to the next quarter. At that time, the reports are labeled as "actual" reports to distinguish them from the forecasted reports. If you have misjudged your competitors' actions or the general market demand for the two products, your forecasted sales can be considerably different from your actual sales. If this is the case, your forecasted results will not resemble your actual results. This means your ability to plan your actions and predict your results will be highly dependent upon your ability to forecast accurately.

Remember two things about your sales forecasts. One, the sales *forecasts* you enter have no effect on your *actual* sales in a quarter. The *Threshold Competitor* program does not consider sales forecasts when determining actual sales of a product. It only considers the pricing, promotion, quality, and total market demand for a product when allocating sales. Two, *Threshold Competitor* will not warn you if your sales forecasts are unrealistic. It is your responsibility to understand your marketplace, using both quantitative and intuitive skills, and make a reasoned determination of what will be your products' sales volumes.

As was discussed in Chapter 5, you can see these forecast reports by pressing the [PgDn] key, by using one of the "hot" keys after entering all your decisions, or by selecting a desired report from the drop-down options under the Reports menu. After looking at the forecasted reports, you can modify your decision inputs to maximize your company's efficiency and performance. You can make as many modifications to your decision inputs as you wish. The decisions you have entered do not become permanent until you have processed them. You can test any number of possible decision sets to determine which will yield the best results for your company.

Diminishing Returns

As with almost any product, the advertising of your *Threshold Competitor* products can reach a point of diminishing return. As you raise your levels of advertising, more potential customers become aware of your products. Unfortunately, awareness does not guarantee a purchase. At some point, additional expenditures on advertising will result in smaller increases in the number of sales of that product. Determining when you have reached this point is a problem all companies face and will be a continual challenge for your company.

Substitute Products

The issue of diminishing returns does not mean you can avoid promoting your products. If you spend too little on advertising, your efforts may result in few sales because your promotional efforts are overshadowed by your competitors' promotional efforts. Further, if companies in your industry spend little on promotion of the *Threshold Competitor* products, or price them too high, your potential customers will purchase substitute products sold by companies outside your *Threshold Competitor* industry. This would mean neither you nor your *Threshold Competitor* competitors would sell the sales potential forecasted for the industry. This can also occur if the whole industry invests too little in product quality. Your task then is to design a marketing program that is both effective and efficient. For a marketing program to be successful, it must generate the demand you desire at the lowest possible cost.

Marketing Decision Limits

Exhibit 6.3 summarizes the information on marketing decisions and the range of numbers that you can enter for each decision. This information is repeated in Appendix E. You can also access this information through the Info option on the Menu bar or by using "hot" keys (Shift + F1).

Exhibit 6.3

THRESHOLD COMPETITOR MARKETING LIMITS AND TIME LAGS

Decision Variable	Range/ Limits	Lag Before Impact
Price ($)	0 - 99	Immediate
TV Ads (Minutes)	0 - 99	Immediate
Newspaper Ads (Column Inches)	0 - 99	Immediate
Magazine Ads (Pages)	0 - 99	Immediate
Sales Forecasts (Units)	0 - 99,999	No Impact

MARKET RESEARCH DECISIONS

Another set of marketing decisions deals with market research. You will enter these decisions on the Marketing and Market Research screen (See Exhibit 6.4). You tell the computer whether you want to buy a market research report by entering a check mark (✓) for the report you wish to purchase. Do this by clicking on the desired report or by tabbing to the desired report and pressing the space bar.

Exhibit 6.4

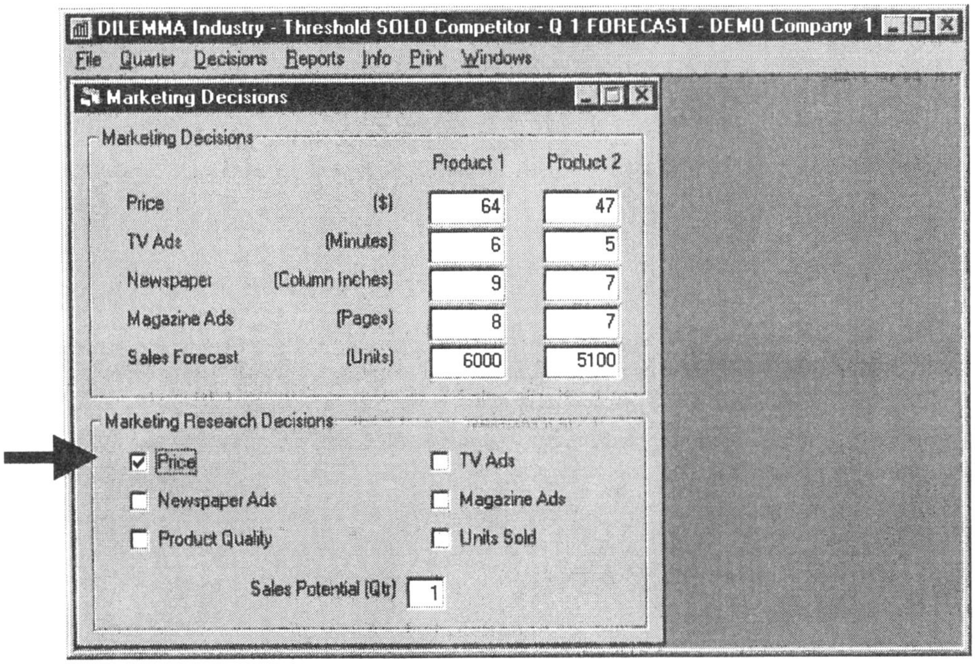

Marketing Decisions		Product 1	Product 2
Price	($)	64	47
TV Ads	(Minutes)	6	5
Newspaper	(Column Inches)	9	7
Magazine Ads	(Pages)	8	7
Sales Forecast	(Units)	6000	5100

Marketing Research Decisions:
- ☑ Price
- ☐ Newspaper Ads
- ☐ Product Quality
- ☐ TV Ads
- ☐ Magazine Ads
- ☐ Units Sold

Sales Potential (Qtr) [1]

Your company may choose to purchase up to seven different market research reports. These allow you to obtain information on your competitors as well as information on demand for the products in your industry. Your company can buy any or all of these reports each *Threshold Competitor* quarter and receive them *after* that quarter is processed. Exhibit 6.5 shows an example of what the Market Research report looks like if you bought all of the market research reports. Next, we will discuss each of the seven different market research reports.

Exhibit 6.5

Co. #	PRICE P1	PRICE P2	TV ADS P1	TV ADS P2	NEWS P1	NEWS P2	MAG P1	MAG P2	QUALITY P1	QUALITY P2	UNITS SOLD P1	UNITS SOLD P2
1	64	47	6	5	9	7	8	7	1.75	3.50	5607	5200
2	63	49	3	3	4	5	8	2	2.93	1.65	5325	2584
3	60	45	4	5	9	5	3	2	4.28	2.34	6000	3761
4	66	47	7	2	9	4	9	4	4.42	4.07	6000	4612
5	63	45	3	3	9	8	7	5	4.87	3.69	6000	5100
6	64	51	5	4	4	2	3	3	5.11	3.21	6000	2603
7	65	50	2	2	4	3	6	6	3.02	3.60	4277	3689
8	61	52	2	4	7	7	9	8	4.62	1.96	6000	3266
9	63	50	6	9	3	8	7	9	3.46	3.57	5744	5100
10	63	49	7	6	5	5	7	3	5.14	3.30	6000	4632
11	67	50	9	6	4	3	3	9	2.77	4.15	4262	5100
12	60	47	4	5	6	5	2	9	3.64	2.09	5130	5027
13	62	45	3	3	5	2	3	3	2.02	3.55	4682	4297
14	62	49	4	8	2	9	6	5	1.43	4.19	3630	5100
15	67	48	7	3	5	4	7	9	4.74	1.42	5237	4180
16	66	47	6	5	9	4	4	3	2.65	4.94	4894	5100

Potential product demands for Quarter 3 are 7000 and 5800 respectively.

Price by Company

The first research report lists the selling price for both products for all companies operating in the industry. Since *Threshold Competitor* industries are oligopolies, the demand for the products is heavily dependent on price. Therefore, this report can prove to be valuable as you assess the results of one quarter and make plans for the next quarter.

Television, Newspaper, Magazine, and Product Quality Reports

These four reports are quite similar. Each report lists the effort expended by each company in your industry for that particular issue. For example, if you purchase the market research on TV advertising, you will receive a report showing the number of minutes of TV advertising purchased that quarter by each company for both of the products. If you purchase the Product Quality Report, you will receive a report showing how much each company invested that quarter on product quality for each product.

Units Sold by Company

You can also purchase a report showing the number of *units* sold of both products by each company. This is different from the sales *revenue* information shown in the Quarter Performance Report you will receive without cost each quarter. We will discuss this report in Chapter 7.

Future Sales Potential

Future demand for a product is of major importance to a company. You can purchase a research report that shows future sales potential for the products up to four quarters in advance of the quarter in which you are operating. You can choose which of the next four quarters you want to buy, but you can buy information for only *one* quarter at a time. Enter the number of the quarter for which you want information on the Marketing and Market Research screen. For example, if you want sales potential information for Quarter 4, enter a "4" on the Sales Potential [Qtr] line. If you enter the number of a quarter that is further out than four quarters, an error message will appear on your screen.

The owners of your company purchased potential market demand for Quarter 1 in Quarter 0. You can see this report when you view the Market Research Report for Quarter 0. The report shows that Quarter 1 demand will be 6,000 units for Product 1 and 5,100 units for Product 2. **These numbers do not represent the guaranteed sales volume for your company in Quarter 1**. They represent the average demand per company for the industry. Depending on your marketing effort relative to that of your competitors, you will sell above or below these levels. The numbers indicate how much each company would sell if the total market potential were divided equally among all companies in your industry. You can determine the total sales potential for a product by multiplying the number given in the research report by the number of companies in your industry. For example, if the number of companies is 16, then the total demand for Product 1 in Quarter 1 will be 96,000 units (i.e., 6,000 units * 16 companies). If one of your goals is to achieve a 10% share of the market for Product 1, your sales goal for Product 1 in Quarter 1 would be 9,600 units (96,000 * .10 = 9,600). This goal is greater than the average demand of 6,000 shown in the report, so to sell this amount requires a marketing effort greater than that of at least some of your competitors. Put simply, the more you want to sell above the average demand for a product, the greater effort you will have to put in to marketing your product relative to your competition. Remember, at some point the cost of this marketing effort will outweigh the benefits that come from the increased sales volume.

Cost of Market Research

The cost for each of the marketing research reports in Quarter 0 is shown in Exhibit 6.6 and in Appendix D. Costs for market information and other cost items are subject to change during the simulation. The *Threshold Competitor* program stores current cost information on your company disk. You can access this information through the Info option on the Menu bar or by pressing the F3 "hot" key. You would be wise to check regularly the costs for your *Threshold Competitor* company for any changes that may have occurred as you move from one quarter to the next. Any cost changes that occur will affect the next quarter of operation, not the quarter for which you are currently making decisions.

62 Chapter 6, Making Decisions

Exhibit 6.6

THRESHOLD COMPETITOR MARKET RESEARCH COSTS		
Market Research Information	Range/ Limits	Cost
Price ($)	By Company and Product	5,000
TV Ads (Minutes)	By Company and Product	5,000
Newspaper Ads (Column Inches)	By Company and Product	3,000
Magazine Ads (Pages)	By Company and Product	4,000
Product Quality ($)	By Company and Product	2,000
Sales (Units)	By Company and Product	5,000
Sales Potential	By Quarter and Product	10,000

You will have to decide what market research information is and is not valuable for managing your company. Careful use of this information can provide you with clues to the relative efficiency of your marketing efforts. You may also glean information about your competitors' strategies from these reports and use them to update your strategies or to make decisions that preempt their competitive actions.

PRODUCTION DECISIONS

The production decisions you must make each quarter are entered on the Production and Finance screen. See the decisions between the two arrows in Exhibit 6.7.

Exhibit 6.7

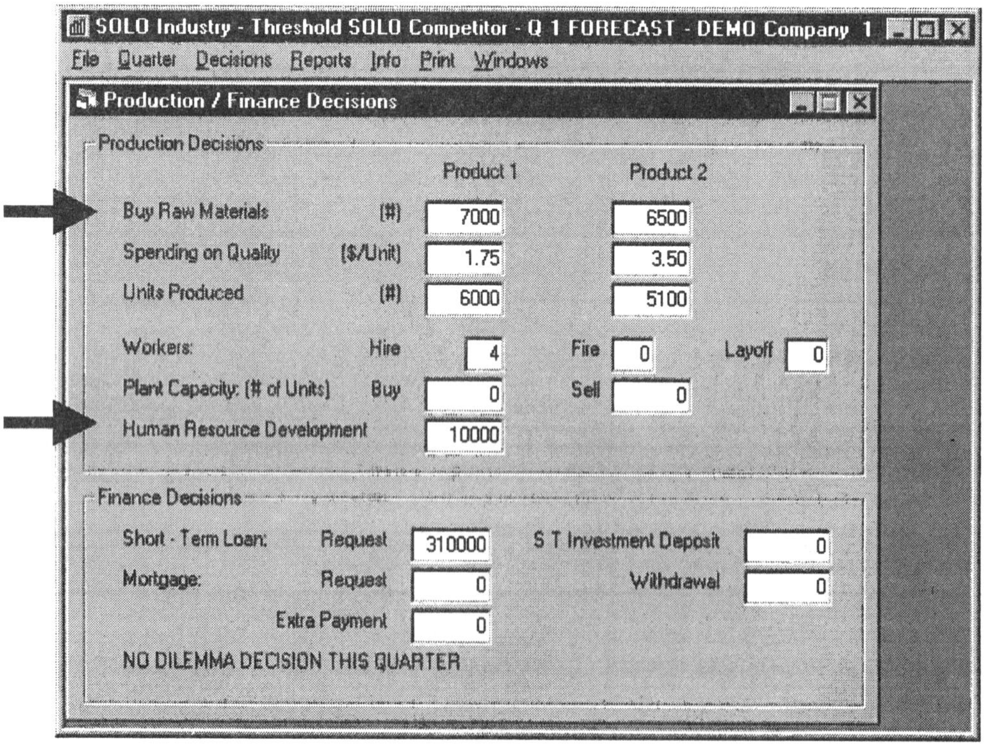

```
SOLO Industry - Threshold SOLO Competitor - Q 1 FORECAST - DEMO Company 1
File  Quarter  Decisions  Reports  Info  Print  Windows

Production / Finance Decisions

Production Decisions
                                        Product 1         Product 2
  Buy Raw Materials        (#)            7000              6500
  Spending on Quality      ($/Unit)       1.75              3.50
  Units Produced           (#)            6000              5100

  Workers:              Hire    4       Fire    0      Layoff   0
  Plant Capacity: (# of Units)  Buy  0    Sell    0
→ Human Resource Development        10000

Finance Decisions
  Short - Term Loan:   Request   310000   S T Investment Deposit   0
  Mortgage:            Request        0   Withdrawal               0
                       Extra Payment    0
  NO DILEMMA DECISION THIS QUARTER
```

There are a number of production decisions you will make in order to operate your business. One of the major decisions will be to decide how much to invest in maintaining or enhancing the quality of your products. The quality decision is a key decision, as it affects both the cost of your product and its position in the marketplace relative to your competitors. Another major production decision you will make is whether to expand your production capacity (i.e., plant capacity). Deciding whether to add to your production capacity will impact the cost structure of your company and its ability to capture market share in the industry. The fit between your production capacity and your marketing strategy will significantly affect the success of your business.

Besides spending on quality, there are a number of additional production decisions you will have to make. These are:
- Ordering raw material for each product.
- How many units of each product to make.
- The number of production workers to hire, fire, or lay off.
- How many dollars to invest in human resource development.

We will now describe each of the production decisions you will make each quarter in detail.

Buy Raw Materials

Your company's products require one unit of the correct raw material for each unit of finished good produced and available for sale. Product 1 requires one kind of raw material and Product 2 another. Companies must purchase the necessary raw materials for their production department. Enter the number of raw material units you wish to purchase for each product. Your purchasing department and your supplier require one full quarter to order and receive the material. This means you must purchase raw materials the quarter *before* you need them. Check the Cost screen to determine the current price.

Raw Material Order Shortages. There is no guarantee you will receive all the raw materials you order. There is a small chance that only 75% of an order for each raw material will actually arrive at your company's plant. Further, material costs may remain stable, decrease, or increase, reflecting a changing economy. This degree of risk forces advance planning.

Quantity Discounts. If you order 15,000 units or more of a particular raw material, you will receive a quantity discount of 15% on the total cost of the materials purchased. The required volume applies to each product, independently. You cannot receive the discount by combining the orders for both products. So you cannot receive the discount by ordering 10,000 units of one product and 5,000 units of the other product. You would have to order 15,000 units of a product to receive the discount for that product.

Warehousing Costs. You cannot warehouse materials (either raw or finished goods) without cost. You incur a carrying charge for every unit of raw material remaining in inventory after the quarter's operations are completed. You will pay these carrying costs the next quarter. This means in Quarter 1 you will pay carrying charges for raw materials based on the inventory you had remaining at the end of Quarter 0. One problem you will face is the need to balance the cost of raw material delivery uncertainties against the cost of carrying an inventory of raw material as a safety stock. Your raw material policy should deal with these issues. The total cost of materials used in the production process will be the cost of the materials plus the cost of carrying any raw materials in inventory.

Spending on Product Quality

Each quarter, you must choose how much money to spend to produce a quality product. Money spent on product quality will build elements of quality into your product that are important to the customer, such as durability and appearance. These features will serve to differentiate your product from your competitors' and make them more attractive to potential customers. So, depending on how your pricing and advertising efforts compare with your competitors', improving the quality of your products will help increase the demand for them.

Your quality investment decision entries reflect the amount *per unit produced that quarter* that you choose to invest in the quality of your product. So, if you enter $2.00 as your quality decision for Product 1 and produce 6,000 units of that product, you will have spent a total of $12,000 on quality for Product 1 that quarter. This cost will be reflected on the Cost of Production report for that quarter. We will discuss this report in detail in Chapter 7.

Money spent on product quality will also increase the cost of producing your products. This means you must increase the price of your product to recover the money spent on producing a quality product. Otherwise, you must increase your sales volume sufficiently to make your investment in product quality worthwhile. Determining the proper mix of price, quality, and sales volume will be a continuing conundrum for your company to resolve.

Effect of Quality on Sales. Potential buyers are only influenced by this quarter's per unit expenditure on quality. They do not consider the differences in per unit quality between products you produced this quarter and those you produced last quarter. This means that in Quarter 2, customers will make their purchase decision based on the money spent on producing a quality product in Quarter 2 and are not swayed by the quality of the product produced in Quarter 1. Diminishing returns also can occur with product quality. At some point, the customer is satisfied with the quality of your product compared to your competitors' products and more dollars spent in this area may not be cost-effective. Remember, your customers will always be comparing the quality and the price of your product to that of your competition to see where they can get the "best buy." This means that even if you have spent money on product quality, your competition may sell more.

Enter a dollar figure from 0 to 20.00 for each of the two products for the amount you choose to spend on producing a quality product. This entry can be in dollars and cents (e.g., 1.75).

Number of Units to Produce

Three factors limit how much your plant can produce. You must have:
- The necessary raw materials available to produce a particular product,
- The plant capacity necessary to handle the combined production level of Product P1 and Product 2 that you desire, and
- Enough workers available to run the production equipment to produce the number of products you desire.

Raw Materials. You must decide how many units of each product you want to produce and enter the number (0 to 99,999) on the Production and Finance screen. Since one unit of raw material makes one finished product, this is one factor controlling the volume that you can produce. Companies cannot produce more units of a product than they have of that product's type of raw material. If a company requests production in excess of raw material available, *Threshold Competitor* will set production at the total of available raw materials. For example, if you enter a production level of 6,000 units for Product 1 with only a 5,000-unit inventory of raw material for Product 1 available, then you can produce only 5,000 units of Product 1. You cannot substitute the raw materials for one of the two products for the other product. So, while you may have a large raw material inventory of Product 2, if you only have 5,000 units of raw material of Product 1 on hand, you cannot produce more than 5,000 units of finished goods of Product 1.

Plant Capacity. Assuming you have the necessary number of raw materials available, you can produce more than plant capacity by working at overtime. The simulation limits overtime production to 150% of plant capacity. For example, with 11,100 units of plant capacity, maximum production allowed using maximum overtime is 16,650 units (11,100 * 150%). You pay an overtime charge for any units you produce at overtime. You will need to balance the cost of producing at overtime against the costs of lost sales because you did not produce enough to meet demand. This will help you to determine whether to purchase additional plant capacity (discussed earlier). Determining the cost of overtime is discussed later in a separate section.

Workers Available. The number of workers you have available and the current productivity levels of those workers limits how many units of each product you can produce. Your Labor Report (discussed in Chapter 7) will show how many workers you have available in the current quarter to manufacture Products 1 and 2. The Labor Report also shows the current productivity levels of your workers. Determining whether you have too many or too few workers for the volume you want to produce is discussed in the "Workers to Hire, Fire, or Lay Off" section that follows.

Overtime. *Threshold Competitor* program automatically calculates when your workers must work overtime to produce the volume you chose. Your company will be assessed overtime charges whenever you either (a) exceed 120% of your plant's capacity or (b) exceed the output your workers can produce *at their current productivity levels*. This means that even if you have enough capacity to produce 12,000 units, if your workers are capable of producing only 10,000 units at their current productivity rates, you will receive an overtime charge for all production above 10,000 units. The reverse of this also holds true. Your workers may be capable of producing 10,000 units, but if your current plant capacity is only 8,000 units, you will be assessed an overtime charge for all units produced above 9,600 units (8,000 * 120%). Notice that if you have enough workers, you can produce 20% above your plant's capacity without incurring overtime charges.

Threshold Competitor pays the workers the equivalent of *double time* for every unit they produce at overtime. To calculate your overtime rate, you must first calculate the average labor cost per unit *for each product*. Then determine the average of those two averages.

The following is an example of how to calculate the cost of producing at overtime in Quarter 1.
Given:
- Initial salary per worker per quarter is $4,000
- Initial worker productivity is 250 units for Product 1
- Initial worker productivity is 300 units for Product 2

Then:
- Average labor cost of Product 1 = $4000/250 = $16.00/unit
- Average labor cost of Product 2 = $4000/300 = $13.33/unit
- Average labor cost of Products 1 and 2 = ($16.00 + 13.33)/2 = $14.66/unit

Since overtime is charged at double normal rates, the cost per unit of overtime production is (14.66 * 2) or $29.32 per unit. Therefore, if you choose to produce 1,000 units at overtime, you will be assessed an overtime charge of $29,320 for those units.

You are not required to produce at plant capacity every quarter. Nor are you required to continue to produce both products. However, you will still incur the costs associated with the plant that you own even if it is not in use. These costs are the depreciation charges that reflect the aging of your plant and equipment. These costs are assigned to your cost of producing the two products in the same proportion that the two products are utilizing the plant. For example, if you produced 4,000 units of Product 1 and

6,000 units of Product 2, then 40% (4,000/[4,000 + 6,000]) of the plant's depreciation costs would be assigned to Product 1. You can see your quarterly depreciation charges on your company's Cost of Production Report. We will discuss this report in some detail in Chapter 7. You will have to decide what production volume is best for your company.

Workers to Hire, Fire, or Lay Off

<u>Hire Workers</u>. To manufacture a product, you must have the proper number of workers available to operate the equipment. Each quarter you will have to decide how many production workers to hire, fire, or lay off in order to maintain the number of workers you desire. Since it takes one quarter to hire and train the workers (discussed below), you will need to do some advance planning, or you could end up without the workers you need to produce your products. Enter the number of each on the Production and Finance screen. Each *Threshold Competitor* company will begin operation with 41 workers.

Each worker can initially produce 250 units of Product 1 or 300 units of Product 2. *Threshold Competitor* will assign these workers to try to produce the number of each product that you request. For example, the current workforce could produce 6,000 units of Product 1 (24 workers * 250 units/worker) and 5,100 units of Product 2 (17 workers * 300 units/worker) per quarter. These production levels would make 100% use of existing capacity (11,100 units) and utilize all the available workers, without incurring any overtime charges.

However, if you asked these same workers to produce 8,000 units of Product 1 and 3,100 units of Product 2 you would be charged overtime for the production of 400 units. This is because you need 32 of your 41 workers to produce the 8,000 units of Product 1 (8,000/250 = 32), leaving 9 workers to produce Product 2. Unfortunately, these 9 workers can produce only 2,700 units of Product 2 (9 workers * 300/worker). This means you need to produce the last 400 units (3,100 – 2,700) at overtime rates. As you can see from this example, workers are first assigned to produce Product 1 and then Product 2, to determine if overtime is needed to meet the desired production level.

You must hire production workers one quarter before you need them. Your human resources department requires one quarter to hire and train a worker at a cost of $2,000. **You need to plan for worker turnover.** Production workers can quit without notice. Historically you have lost 10% of your workforce to turnover each quarter. Beyond this, there is a small random probability of losing an additional worker. Therefore, your company must develop a staffing strategy. The unplanned loss of workers can create a series of problems for your company. You should develop contingency plans to cope with this uncertainty.

<u>Fire Workers</u>. You may choose to fire or lay off production workers. When you fire production workers, they are not available the quarter you discharge them. For example, a worker that you fire in Quarter 4 is discharged at the very beginning of the quarter and is not available to produce any product in Quarter 4. There is no charge for terminating production workers.

<u>Lay Off Workers</u>. You may also decide to lay off workers for one quarter. A laid-off worker leaves at the beginning of the quarter and will return automatically at the beginning of the next quarter. The current cost attached to this method of workforce management is $500 for each worker laid off that quarter. A company must balance the cost of keeping a worker on layoff status against the cost of firing a worker and rehiring a new person.

Buy or Sell Plant Capacity

Buy Plant Capacity. You have the option of purchasing additional plant capacity. This allows you to change the productive capacity of your physical plant. Additions to capacity are currently available for $45 per unit of production capacity. Enter the number of units of production capacity you want to buy on the Production and Finance screen. For example, for $45,000, you could increase capacity 1,000 units to 12,100 units per quarter. Planning the expansion is important because it will take one quarter before you can manufacture any additional products. If you order a plant in Quarter 1, you will bring it on-line and use it in Quarter 2. Remember that you may also need to hire production workers and order raw materials to use the added plant capacity. If you choose to buy additional plant capacity, you must purchase a minimum of 1,000 units. The maximum number of units you can buy in one quarter is 10,000 units.

Sell Plant Capacity. You can choose to sell capacity you no longer need. You sell plant capacity at book value (original cost minus accumulated depreciation). You can use the plant capacity the quarter you make the decision to sell it. The units are removed from the production process at the beginning of the next quarter. Collection of the money from the sale of the plant capacity also occurs at the beginning of the next quarter. For example, a request to sell 1,000 units of capacity in Quarter 2 will result in a 1,000 unit reduction in capacity at the beginning of Quarter 3. You can still use those 1,000 units for production in Quarter 2. You will receive the cash from this sale of plant in Quarter 3.

All capacity depreciates on a straight-line basis over 25 quarters. Therefore, depreciation expenses for any given quarter are 4% of the original cost of the capacity you own. This means the book value (i.e., sale price) of any plant you sell will be its purchase price minus 4% times the number of quarters it has been in operation. For example, if you sell plant that originally cost $100,000 and which has been used for five quarters, you would receive $80,000 (100,000 - [5 * .04 * 100,000] = 80,000).

You will always sell off your oldest plant first. This means if you added 1,000 units of plant capacity in Quarter 2 and then decided to sell 1,000 units in Quarter 5, you would be selling a plant that had been in use since Quarter 0, not the 1,000 units you just purchased in Quarter 2. Enter the number of units of production capacity you want to sell on the Production and Finance screen. You cannot sell more than 4,000 units or 50% of your existing plant capacity in one quarter, whichever is less.

Human Resource Development

Investment in Human Resource Development is money spent in an effort to improve the productivity of your production workers. It includes training programs designed to improve employee skills and morale and increase the amount of finished goods each worker can produce in a quarter. If this occurs, it can effectively lower the company's worker payroll costs. There is no guarantee that money spent in this area will translate into productivity increases. Nor is there a guarantee of how much the workers' productivity will increase, if an increase does occur. All that can be said for certain is that this investment may improve worker productivity. However, it is expected that the larger your investment in HR Development, the greater the likelihood that the productivity of your workers will increase. Similarly, little or no investment in Human Resource Development will most likely lead to lower worker productivity. This is because workers can become less efficient if there are no training programs to improve, or at least maintain, their skills. Workers also can become less motivated to produce up to their ability if they think management is not concerned about productivity.

To the extent that investments in Human Resource Development (HRD) do influence worker productivity, the effect occurs in the quarter *following* the one in which you made the investments. In addition, any investment in productivity lasts for only *one* quarter. For example, an investment in Human

Resource Development in Quarter 1 may improve worker productivity in Quarter 2. Assuming that productivity increased to a new level, it will stay at that level, increase, or decrease in Quarter 3 depending on the amount of money invested in HRD in Quarter 2. Remember, there is no guarantee that a similar investment will result in a similar increase in productivity in subsequent quarters. However, history is often a good predictor of the future. Your company's policies and philosophy will affect your decision about how much your company will choose to invest in Human Resource Development. Enter a dollar figure from 0 to 99,999 as your decision.

Exhibit 6.8 and Appendix E show the ranges within which your production decisions must occur and the time dimensions associated with each decision. Notice that for many of these decisions, there is a one-quarter lag before the decisions take effect. For example, when you order raw materials for your products this quarter, you will not actually receive the materials until next quarter. This means you will need to plan ahead for items that have a time lag associated with them. Note that the Quarter 0 Reports in Appendix B show the results of a number of decisions made by your company's owners prior to Quarter 0 so that production could occur in Quarter 0. These included hiring production workers (45) and ordering raw materials (6,500 units for Product 1 and 5,500 units for Product 2).

Exhibit 6.8

THRESHOLD COMPETITOR LIMITS AND TIME LAGS
PRODUCTION

Decision Variable	Range/ Limits	Lag Before Impact
Buy Raw Material (#) (Products 1 & 2)	0 – 99,999	1 Quarter
Invest in Product Quality ($)	0 – 20.00	Immediate
Units Produced (#) (Products 1 & 2)	0 – 99,999	Immediate
Workers Hired for Next Quarter (#)	0 – 99	1 Quarter
Workers Fired This Quarter (#)	0 – 99	Immediate
Workers Laid Off This Quarter (#)	0 – 99	Immediate
Purchase Plant Capacity (# of Units)	0 – 10,000	1 Quarter
Sell Plant Capacity (# of Units)	0 – 4,000	1 Quarter
Human Resource Development ($)	0 – 99,999	1 Quarter

FINANCE DECISIONS

You must make three types of financial decisions:
- short-term loan requests to finance your current operations,
- long-term mortgages to finance purchases of plant capacity, and
- short-term investment deposits of cash from operations or withdrawals from prior short-term investments.

The finance decisions you must make each quarter are entered on the Production and Finance screen. See the decisions between the two arrows in Exhibit 6.9.

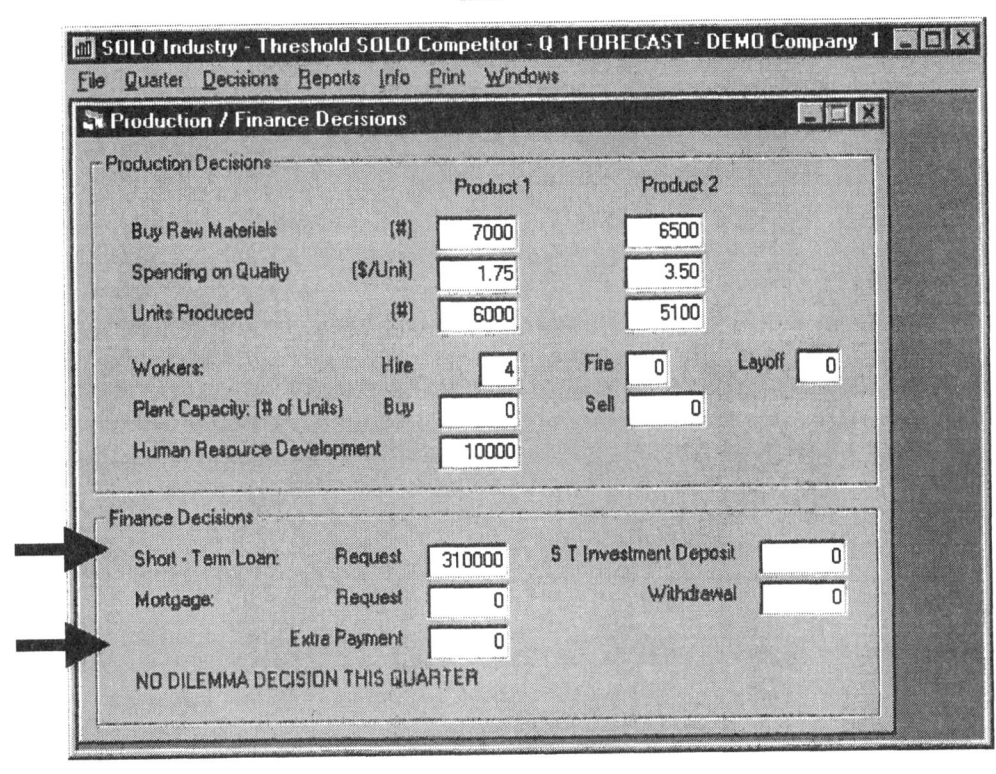

Exhibit 6.9

[Screenshot of SOLO Industry - Threshold SOLO Competitor - Q 1 FORECAST - DEMO Company 1, showing Production/Finance Decisions window]

Production Decisions:

		Product 1	Product 2
Buy Raw Materials	(#)	7000	6500
Spending on Quality	($/Unit)	1.75	3.50
Units Produced	(#)	6000	5100

Workers: Hire 4 Fire 0 Layoff 0
Plant Capacity: (# of Units) Buy 0 Sell 0
Human Resource Development: 10000

Finance Decisions:
→ Short - Term Loan: Request 310000   S T Investment Deposit 0
   Mortgage: Request 0   Withdrawal 0
→ Extra Payment 0
NO DILEMMA DECISION THIS QUARTER

Short-Term Loans

Your company must perform some basic financial activities to conduct the operation of its business. Short-term financing is available to cover cash shortages you might encounter in your normal business operations. This is money you need to cover the costs of the marketing and production decisions you make. Enter the dollar figure of the short-term loan you want. You must forecast your need for money and plan for these shortages. No *Threshold Competitor* company is allowed to operate with a negative cash balance. If you do not forecast cash accurately and end the quarter with a negative cash balance, the *Threshold Competitor* bank will automatically provide your company with an emergency loan for the amount of money necessary to bring the company up to a zero balance. The penalty for this service is double the normal short-term interest rates on the total amount of loan needed for that quarter. This means if you needed $50,000 to finance operations in a quarter, but requested a short-term loan of only $40,000, the interest penalty would be charged on the $50,000 needed, **not** on the $10,000 you were short in your request. Companies who accurately forecast cash will not be subject to this interest penalty. This means you do not want to request a short-term loan that is likely to fall short of your actual cash needs after your decisions have been processed. At the same time, you do not want to request a short-term loan far in excess of your actual cash needs either. If you do, you will end up paying interest charges on money that is sitting idle in your cash account and not working to generate profits for your company. Your goal should always be to have the expenses associated with borrowing money (i.e., interest expenses) be less than the profits generated by the use of that money. Money sitting idle in your cash account neither earns any interest income nor generates any profits for your company.

Any short-term loan money you borrow at the end of a quarter must be completely repaid during the next quarter of operation. This means the $310,000 short-term loan borrowed in Quarter 0 will be repaid in Quarter 1. There is a limit on how much you can borrow short-term in any quarter. The most your *Threshold Competitor* banker will lend you on a short-term basis is $700,000.

Long-Term Mortgages

Request. To gain funds for capital investments, such as plant additions, companies typically use long-term mortgages. You must finance normal operating expenses (i.e., advertising costs or labor costs) through short-term loan requests. The *Threshold Competitor* bank requires you to repay all long-term mortgages in equal installments over 25 quarters. You may request new mortgage loans in addition to any you presently have outstanding. Interest rates on these mortgages will be the prevailing rate set by the bank. Check your Cost screen to determine the current interest rate. Any funds approved in response to a request for a new mortgage will be added to the outstanding balance of any existing mortgage.

Extra Payment. If you so choose, you can make extra payments to reduce the outstanding balance on your mortgage. Reducing the amount of your mortgage will reduce the interest charges associated with it. You will have to determine whether to use any of the extra cash your company has generated to pay down your mortgage balance or for some other purpose.

Short-Term Investments

Deposits. You may forecast that your company will end up with excess cash after paying this quarter's bills. If so, you may choose to invest that money in short-term marketable securities. The company's owners have dictated that you purchase only the most stable securities. Consequently, earnings are relatively low compared to interest rates for higher risk alternatives. Enter the amount of the short-term investment you wish to make on the Production and Finance screen. This amount can range from 0 to 999,999 as your decision.

The timing of this investment is immediate: Any money deposited into short-term investments is immediately deducted from your cash account. If you over-estimate the cash you will have at the end of the quarter and deposit so much into short-term investments that you end up needing cash, you will be forced to take an emergency loan at double the current short-term loan rates. This is because (as discussed earlier) *Threshold Competitor* does not allow you to have a negative cash balance at the end of a quarter's operations. Although you may have funds in your investment account, the marketable securities require that you formally request a withdrawal before any funds can be released and transferred to your cash account at your bank. Funds from your investment account will not be transferred automatically if your cash position is negative. So be careful! You need to forecast cash accurately even when you are cash rich. Investing more money than you have in your cash account can mean receiving a *Threshold Competitor* bank loan at rates much higher than your investment rates, which is not a prudent financial decision.

The bank pays you interest for any money you have invested the quarter after you make a short-term investment. Earnings from investments reduce the overall interest expenses of the company. This means interest income you earn from investments is credited against interest expense you owe for money you have borrowed. This will be reflected in the "Net Interest" line on your Income Statement and the "Net Short-Term Interest" line on your Cash Flow Statement.

If your interest income exceeds your interest expense, your net interest figure will show as a negative number. This will have the effect of adding to the company's operating profit rather than subtracting from it. It will also reduce the total cash payments figure on the company's Cash Flow Statement.

Withdrawals. You can withdraw money you have previously invested in short-term marketable securities. As noted earlier, you must formally request the withdrawal of funds from your investment account before the securities are deposited as cash in your bank account. While this precludes the use of short-term investments to prevent emergency loans, any funds withdrawn will arrive in your cash account in sufficient time to be used as part of the cash available to meet that quarter's expenses.

Exhibit 6.10 and Appendix E show the financial decisions you have to make and the fact that all of the financial decisions take effect immediately.

Exhibit 6.10

THRESHOLD COMPETITOR LIMITS AND TIME LAGS
FINANCE

Decision Variable		Range/Limits	Lag Before Impact
Short-Term Loan:	Requested ($)	0 – 700,000	Immediate
Mortgage:	Request ($)	0 – 9,999,999	Immediate
	Extra Payment ($)	0 – 999,999	Immediate
Short-Term Investment:	Deposit ($)	0 – 999,999	Immediate
	Withdrawal ($)	0 – 999,999	Immediate

MANAGEMENT DILEMMAS

The *Threshold Competitor* simulation may force you to make some difficult decisions concerning your workers and your relationship with the local community. Appendix G presents the dilemmas that you may face. Issues include employee theft, incompetence, bribery, alcohol abuse, and union relations. If no dilemma decision is necessary, the last line on the bottom the Production and Finance screen will read "No Dilemma Decision This Quarter." If you need to make a dilemma decision, that line will tell you the number of the dilemma that is in effect and there will be a cell open for you to enter your decision. The arrow in Exhibit 6.11 points to this line looks like when you need to make a dilemma decision.

Exhibit 6.11

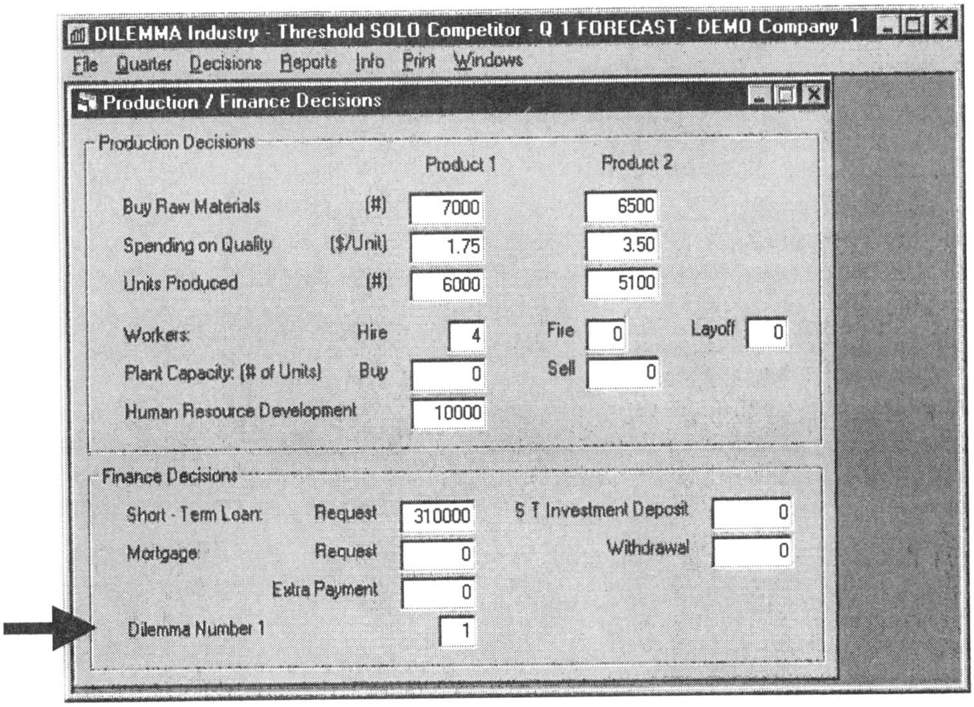

For each dilemma, there are several numbered options shown in Appendix G. Select from among these options, given your perception of the situation you are facing and the possible consequences for your company. There is not only one necessarily correct response, just different ones. In fact, you could select the same option as another company, yet face different consequences from that decision. When dealing with human behavior, different people respond differently to the same actions. The ability to make good decisions where there are no clear answers is one of the critical skills needed by all managers. The consequences of your decisions can affect worker productivity, sales, cost of raw materials, or interest rates. The default choice is "1". If you do not enter a different option, that will be the option entered for your company. Enter your decision on the bottom of the Production and Finance screen.

If your company is confronted with a dilemma in a particular quarter, you will receive feedback on the results of your dilemma decision in the Bulletin for that quarter, *after the quarter has been processed*. Any costs incurred as a consequence of your dilemma decision may affect the current quarter or the upcoming quarter. For example, if you made the dilemma decision in Quarter 3, the costs incurred could affect your Quarter 3 results or your Quarter 4 results. Read the appropriate dilemma in Appendix G for guidance on this. Often the costs incurred from a dilemma are reflected in the Office Expense line of the S & A Costs Report.

COST PARAMETERS REPORT

Appendix D lists the costs and productivity figures for your Quarter 0 decisions. You can also find these costs on the Menu bar under the Info heading or by pressing the F3 "hot" key. You will receive a printout of these costs whenever you request a printout of all pages of your company reports. You can do this by selecting the All Pages option under Print on the Menu bar. You can also choose to print just the Cost screen using the Selected Screens option on the Print menu. You should check your company's cost parameters regularly for any changes. Any of the costs can change during the course of the *Threshold Competitor* exercise. Get in the habit of checking your current costs every quarter. It is up to you to be knowledgeable regarding your company's costs. Not recognizing which costs have changed will be detrimental to your ability to manage you company efficiently. Exhibit shows an example of this

Exhibit 6.12

	Product 1	Product 2
Raw Material	8.00	12.00
Raw Material Warehouse	1.00	2.00
Finished Goods Warehouse	2.50	1.50
Worker Productivity	250	300

Television Ad Minutes	5000	Mkt Research-Product Price	5000
Newspaper Ad Column Inches	1000	Mkt Research-TV Ads Minutes	5000
Magazine Ad Pages	3000	Mkt Research-Newspaper Ads	3000
Workers' Quarterly Wages	4000	Mkt Research-Magazine Ads	4000
Hiring Costs per Worker	2000	Mkt Research-Product Quality	2000
Layoff Costs per Worker	500	Mkt Research-Unit Sales	5000
Administrative Expenses	12000	Mkt Research-Market Demand	10000
New Plant Cost per Unit	45	Manufacturing Overhead Rate	50.0
Short-Term Loan Rate	10.0	Mortgage Interest Rate	9.0
Short-Term Investment Rate	5.0		

DECISIONS FLOW CHART

Appendix I provides a flow chart of the decisions you will make and how they lead to the forecast and actual reports you will use to manage your *Threshold Competitor* company. In the next chapter, we will discuss in some detail each of the reports available in *Threshold Competitor* that you will use to assess your company's performance and determine what future actions you wish to take in the managing of your *Threshold Competitor* company.

SOME DECISION GUIDELINES

Some of the most common problems participants face in *Threshold Competitor* is that they simply don't pay attention to what they are doing, or examine closely what is going on in their industry. For example, they may forget to hire to replace workers lost to turnover or purchase market research information but then not examine it. Here are some reminders as you compete in *Threshold Competitor*.

1. Do your decisions reflect your strategy? Are they consistent with each other? (Do your sales forecasts reflect the production decisions you made? Are you forecasting lost sales?)
2. Have you analyzed your competitors' performances and strategies?
3. Do you have confidence in your sales forecasts? Do your forecasts reflect (a) your present sales level, (b) expected changes in sales due to anticipated actions by your competitors and trends in industry demand, (c) changes in your marketing mix for the quarter, *and* (d) your historical forecasting accuracy? *Remember*: Wishing for high sales does not make them happen.
4. Before submitting your decision for a quarter, did you examine your forecasted income statement? Does it show you making the profits you have planned? *If not, why submit the decision?* What do you have to do to achieve your desired profit level? **Remember:** The accuracy of your forecasted income statement depends on the accuracy of the sales forecasts you submit!
5. Do you have the *information* you need to make intelligent decisions? What reports hold this information?
6. Are you actually doing what you intend to do? (Do you *really have* the lowest price in the industry or are your decisions based on ill-founded assumptions?)
7. What marketing tools seem to be most effective in your industry? Have you carefully considered how much you're spending on each of your promotion tools? (Is your spending insufficient and/or ineffective? Are you on past the point of diminishing returns and throwing money away?)
8. Are your production costs under control? Have you done everything you can to minimize these costs? What is the quarterly trend of your unit costs as shown on the Cost of Production Report?
9. Is your Gross Profit insufficient to cover your other costs and still achieve a profit for the quarter? (If it is less than 25% of sales, it will be difficult to achieve a profit.)
10. Did you order enough raw material for each product for the quarter *after this one*? Remember, for the current quarter (say Q3) you can only produce the raw material inventory on hand. The quantity you order on your Q3 decision form is not received until Q4. Thus, in Q3 you must forecast ahead and anticipate how much you plan to produce in Q4. Stocking out may be more expensive than the cost of carrying inventory into next period.
11. Did you check your cash flow statement and request a large enough loan so that you don't have to pay high emergency loan interest rates?
12. Did you check to be certain you aren't submitting some of last quarter's decisions unintentionally?

74 Chapter 7, *Threshold Competitor* Reports

CHAPTER 7

THRESHOLD COMPETITOR REPORTS

After you process each set of decisions, you will receive a number of reports that will show, in detail, the results of those decisions. You can view these reports and those of previous quarters using the Select Quarter option under File on the Main Menu. See Chapter 5 for a discussion of the process for viewing and printing reports. Remember, when you load up the *Threshold Competitor* program, it automatically loads up the *next* quarter's decision screens and associated reports. If you want to access the quarter that was just processed, you will have to use the Select Quarter option or the Quarter option to move back to those reports.

In Chapter 7 we will provide a description of each *Threshold Competitor* report that you can access on your company disk. Appendix B contains the Quarter 0 reports for the start of the simulation. In this chapter we will discuss the *Threshold Competitor* actual reports from a sample Quarter 1 processed using *Competitor Solo* program. As discussed in Chapter 6, *actual* reports are the same as *forecast* reports except that the numbers in the actual reports reflect the actual number of units sold after a quarter has been processed versus numbers generated based on your forecast of the number of units that might be sold. The reports include:
- Decisions reports
    - Marketing decisions report
    - Production / Finance decisions report
- Operations reports
    - Inventory report
    - Labor report
    - Cost of Production report
- Marketing reports
    - Selling and administrative expense report
    - Marketing research report
- Financial reports
    - Income statement
    - Balance sheet
    - Cash flow statement
- Industry performance reports

DECISIONS REPORTS

The decisions reports show the final decisions that you made during the forecasting process. These reports are the same as the Marketing and Production/Finance decision screens where you entered your decisions with a few key differences. We will point out these differences and how they affect the other *Threshold Competitor* reports as we discuss the reports.

Marketing Decisions Report

The Marketing Decisions Report shows the last set of pricing, promotion, sales forecast, and marketing research decisions you entered before processing these decisions. The difference on the *actual* Marketing Decisions report from the *forecast* report is the addition of the "Actual Demand (Units)" line. The arrow in Exhibit 7.1 points to this line. Actual Demand is the number of units of sales generated by the company's marketing efforts that quarter. This will be the number of units of the product you sold *IF* you had sufficient finished goods inventory on hand to meet the demand generated. Your Inventory Report will show the number of units of each product that you sold, plus any sales lost because the actual demand was greater than the number of units available for sale that quarter.

Exhibit 7.1

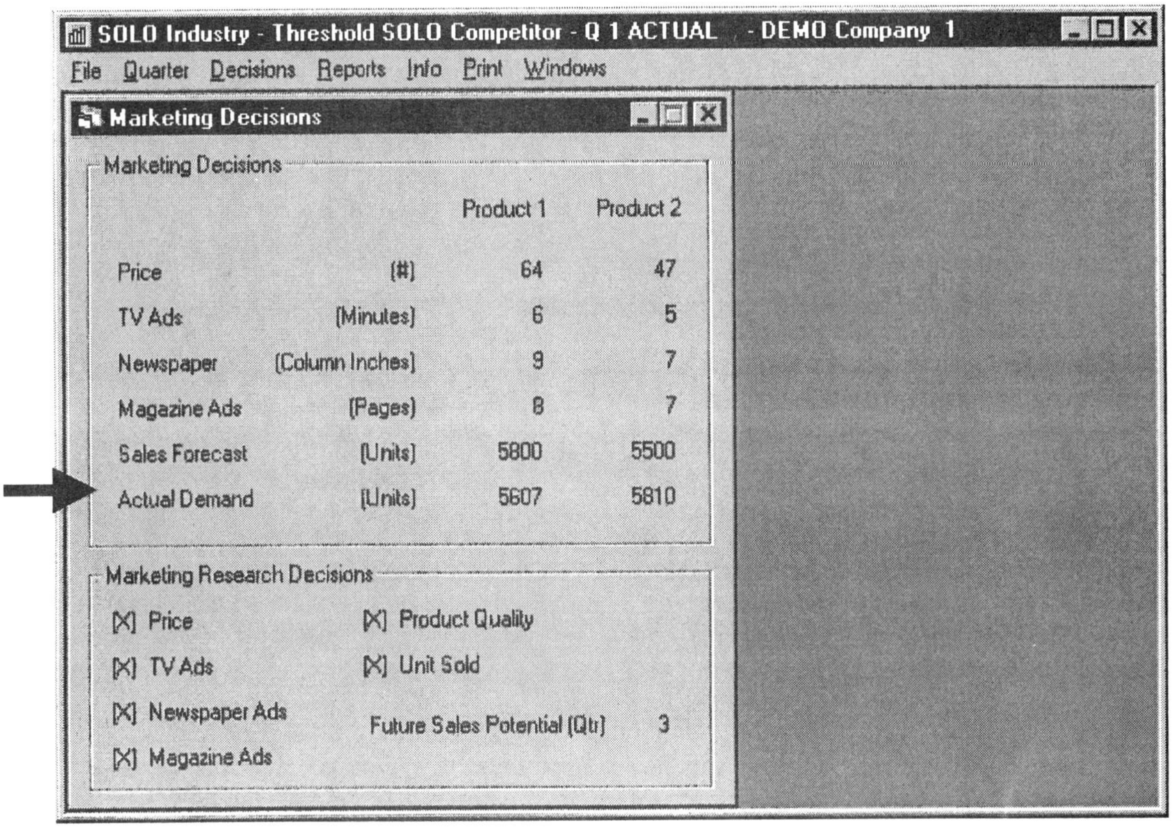

SOLO Industry - Threshold SOLO Competitor - Q 1 ACTUAL - DEMO Company 1

File Quarter Decisions Reports Info Print Windows

Marketing Decisions

		Product 1	Product 2
Price	(#)	64	47
TV Ads	(Minutes)	6	5
Newspaper	(Column Inches)	9	7
Magazine Ads	(Pages)	8	7
Sales Forecast	(Units)	5800	5500
Actual Demand	(Units)	5607	5810

Marketing Research Decisions

[X] Price   [X] Product Quality
[X] TV Ads   [X] Unit Sold
[X] Newspaper Ads
[X] Magazine Ads   Future Sales Potential (Qtr)   3

Production / Finance Decisions Report

The Production/Finance Report shows the last set of production operations and finance decisions you entered before processing these decisions, with one *possible* exception. The difference that may occur relates to the Short-Term Loan Request entry. The arrow in Exhibit 7.2 points to this line. The number displayed on this report will be the same as the entry you made if you requested sufficient cash to finance your company's cash needs during the quarter. However, if your company ended up short of cash because your *actual* cash needs were greater than what you forecasted, or you forgot to request a short-term loan, the *Threshold Competitor* bank will have given you an emergency loan to cover your cash needs. If this happened, the Short-Term Loan Request number displayed on your Production/Finance Decisions Report will be the amount of that emergency loan. We discuss in detail this circumstance, and its consequences, when we get to the Cash Flow Report later in this chapter.

Exhibit 7.2

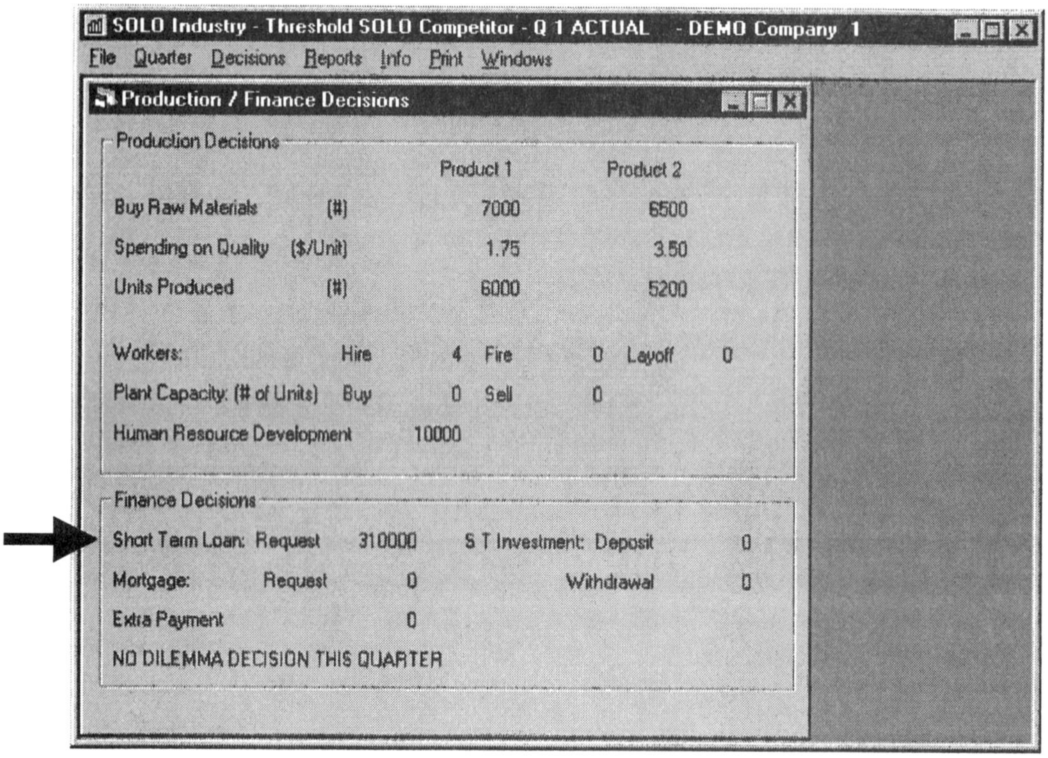

```
SOLO Industry - Threshold SOLO Competitor - Q 1 ACTUAL   - DEMO Company 1
File  Quarter  Decisions  Reports  Info  Print  Windows

Production / Finance Decisions
┌─Production Decisions─────────────────────────────────────┐
│                                Product 1      Product 2  │
│  Buy Raw Materials     (#)      7000           6500      │
│  Spending on Quality   ($/Unit) 1.75           3.50      │
│  Units Produced        (#)      6000           5200      │
│                                                          │
│  Workers:          Hire    4    Fire    0   Layoff   0   │
│  Plant Capacity: (# of Units)  Buy  0   Sell    0        │
│  Human Resource Development    10000                     │
└──────────────────────────────────────────────────────────┘
┌─Finance Decisions────────────────────────────────────────┐
│  Short Term Loan: Request   310000   S T Investment: Deposit   0 │
│  Mortgage:        Request   0                Withdrawal        0 │
│  Extra Payment              0                                    │
│  NO DILEMMA DECISION THIS QUARTER                                │
└──────────────────────────────────────────────────────────┘
```

OPERATIONS REPORTS

Three of the *Threshold Competitor* reports show the current status of your manufacturing operations. These reports show the cost of manufacturing finished products that you made available for sale to your prospective customers.

Inventory Report

The first operations report shows the inventory levels for Products 1 and 2, respectively. The top of the Inventory Report shows the Raw Materials inventory levels for Products 1 and 2 (see Exhibit 7.3). The bottom of the Inventory Report shows the Finished Goods inventory levels for the two products. This report also shows the product and inventory costs of the two products.

Raw Material Inventory. The report for Quarter 1 shows a Beginning Balance of 500 units for Product 1 and 400 units for Product 2. These are the number of units of raw material for each product available from last quarter's operations at the start of Quarter 1. This line also shows the total dollar value for these units. The second line of the report shows how many units of raw materials were received in Quarter 1 and their total dollar value. The Units Received combined with the units in the Beginning Balance yield the Total Available raw materials. This is shown in both units and total dollar value. This shows the number of units that can be used to produce finished goods. A total of 7,000 units of raw materials were received in Quarter 1 for Product 1 and 6,500 for Product 2. Adding the beginning balance for both of the products results in total available raw material of 7,500 units worth $56,000 for Product 1 and 6,900 units worth $82,800 for Product 2. The first arrow in Exhibit 7.3 points to this line of the Inventory Report. *This is the **maximum** number of units a company can produce in that quarter*, because any units purchased a quarter (e.g., Q3) are not received until the following quarter (e.g., Q4).

The fourth line shows the number of units of raw material that were used in the production process that quarter and their dollar value. Reports for Quarter 1 show production of 6,000 of Product 1 units valued at $48,000. That leaves a raw material Ending Balance of 1,500 units valued at $12,000.

The Raw Material Warehouse Costs reflect the cost of carrying units of raw material in inventory from one quarter to the next. The 500 units shown as the beginning balance for Product 1 are the raw material units that remained in inventory at the end of Quarter 0. It cost $500 to hold these units in inventory from Quarter 0 to Quarter 1.

Exhibit 7.3
Inventory Report

RAW MATERIAL

INVENTORY REPORT	Product 1 Units	Product 1 Value	Product 2 Units	Product 2 Value
Beginning Balance	500	4000	400	4800
Units Received	7000	56000	6500	78000
Total Available	7500	60000	6900	82800
Used in Production	6000	48000	5200	62400
Ending Balance	1500	12000	1700	20400
Raw Matl Warehouse Costs	500	500	400	800
Total Product Cost		48500		63200

FINISHED GOODS

INVENTORY REPORT	Product 1 Units	$/Unit	Value	Product 2 Units	$/Unit	Value
Beginning Balance	0	0.00	0	0	0.00	0
Production	6000	37.77	226620	5200	40.61	211160
Units to Sell	6000	37.77	226620	5200	40.61	211160
Units Sold	5607	37.77	211776	5200	40.61	211160
Ending Balance	393	37.77	14844	0	0.00	0
FG Warehouse	0	2.50	0	0	1.50	0
Lost Sales	0	64.00	0	610	47.00	28670

The last line of the Raw Materials section of the Inventory Report shows the Total Cost of the raw materials for Product 1 that were put into the production process. This figure includes the cost of the material itself ($48,000), plus the cost of carrying raw materials in inventory ($500). The total cost of raw materials charged to the production process for Product 1 equaled $48,500.

Finished Goods Inventory. The lower half of the Inventory Report shows the Finished Goods warehouse operations for both products. The columns show the number of units, the per unit cost, and the total value of that item. The first line shows the Beginning Balance of finished goods remaining in inventory from last quarter. This line shows the number of units not sold last quarter that are available for sale this quarter. At the beginning of Quarter 1, no finished goods remained in inventory.

The next line, Production, indicates the number of units you chose to produce when you made your entry on the Production/Finance decision screen. This number also reflects the number of units of raw material that were converted into finished goods. The per unit cost reflects all the costs of manufacturing Products 1 and 2 (i.e., the cost of materials, labor, overhead, etc.) to make them ready for sale to prospective customers. In Quarter 1, 6,000 units of raw material for Product 1 were converted into finished products at a cost of $37.77 per unit. The cost elements that go into that $37.77 will be discussed in the Cost of Production Report below. The second arrow in Exhibit 7.3 points to this line of the Inventory Report.

The next line, Units to Sell, shows the number of finished units available for sale over the course of the quarter. This is the combination of the beginning balance and the units produced for the quarter. The line also shows the per unit cost and the total value of these finished units.

The number of units that were sold during the quarter are shown next. The Ending Balance line shows the number of units remaining in finished goods inventory after that quarter's sales have been made. In Quarter 1 a total of 5,607 units of Product 1were sold. This left an Ending Balance of 393 units of finished goods (6,000 – 5,607 = 393) at the end of the quarter.

The FG Warehouse line shows the warehouse costs associated with carrying finished goods in inventory from one quarter to the next. In Quarter 0 no warehouse costs were charged for finished goods for either product because no inventory was carried over from last quarter.

The last line shows the sales units lost because of a lack of sufficient goods available for sale. This line also reflects the additional sales revenue you could have had during the quarter if you had sufficient goods available for sale. Exhibit 7.3 shows that Product 2 had Lost Sales of 610 units which would have yielded sales revenue of $28,670 (610 * $47 = 28,670) if there had been sufficient finished goods available to meet the demand generated by the company's marketing efforts.

Losing sales because you have an insufficient number of finished goods in stock does not just mean the loss of sales revenues for this quarter. It also creates a negative goodwill with potential customers in the next quarter. As word spreads that you do not always have the products that you advertised available, potential customers discount your advertising claims and look elsewhere to satisfy their needs. So your challenge is to keep inventories low to avoid excessive warehouse costs, while avoiding the "costs" of stocking out and having lost sales.

Labor Report

This report gives you information on the production workforce used to convert raw materials into finished products. Exhibit 7.4 is an example of this report for Quarter 1. It shows the total number of workers employed at the beginning of the quarter, plus the number of workers hired the previous quarter (i.e., Quarter 0) that went through your training program and were capable of working this quarter. It also shows how many workers quit (i.e., current quarter turnover), and how many workers you laid off, or fired during this period of operation. The Total Available Workers shows the number of workers that were available to operate your production equipment after all these actions were considered. In Quarter 1, you have 41 workers available to produce Products 1 and 2.

The next two lines show the productivity levels of your workers for each of the products for that quarter. Remember, worker productivity can increase, decrease, or remain the same from one quarter to the next depending on the amount of spending on human resource development the prior quarter. As we discussed in Chapter 6, worker productivity affects how many units you can produce, and whether you will incur overtime charges. So remember to monitor your worker productivity each quarter. Failure to do this can result in unexpected overtime charges, driving up the manufacturing cost of your products. The first arrow in Exhibit 7.4 points to this line of the Labor Report.

The Labor Report also shows what the cost of maintaining this workforce was during Quarter 1. You can find these costs on the Cost Parameters screen (press the F3 "hot" key). In our example, it cost $2,000 to hire and train a worker and $500 to lay off a worker. The first line under Personnel Costs shows the total cost of hiring for the quarter. The report shows that four workers were hired in Quarter 1, so the total hiring cost was $8,000.

The remaining lines show the layoff costs, the dollars spent on employee training programs to improve worker productivity (i.e., the investment in Human Resource Development), regular wages, and any overtime wages you have to pay. The last line gives the total of all these costs. So for our example, your total labor costs were $184,933. The second arrow in Exhibit 7.4 points to this line of the report.

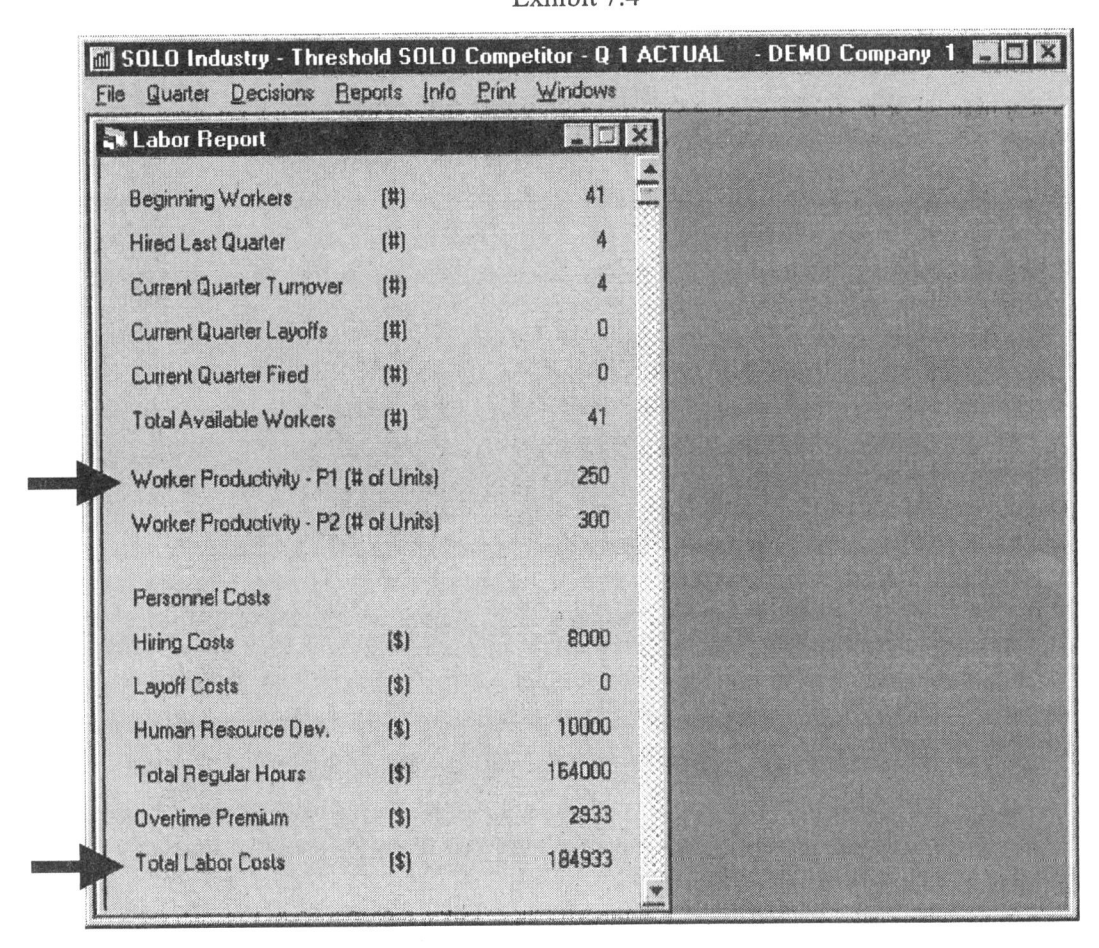

Exhibit 7.4

Labor Report		
Beginning Workers	(#)	41
Hired Last Quarter	(#)	4
Current Quarter Turnover	(#)	4
Current Quarter Layoffs	(#)	0
Current Quarter Fired	(#)	0
Total Available Workers	(#)	41
Worker Productivity - P1 (# of Units)		250
Worker Productivity - P2 (# of Units)		300
Personnel Costs		
Hiring Costs	($)	8000
Layoff Costs	($)	0
Human Resource Dev.	($)	10000
Total Regular Hours	($)	164000
Overtime Premium	($)	2933
Total Labor Costs	($)	184933

Cost of Production Report

The Cost of Production Report (Exhibit 7.5) provides key information on how much it cost you to produce a finished product. This is often referred to as Manufacturing Cost of Goods Sold or Mfg COGS. This includes just the production costs, not the cost of marketing the product or financing the business. This report provides you with information regarding:
- The cost of raw materials used in the production process.
- The cost of labor used to convert raw material into finished goods.
- Overhead costs associated with running the manufacturing operations.
- The cost of improvements in quality made to the product.
- Depreciation charges made to reflect the aging of your plant and equipment.

80   Chapter 7, *Threshold Competitor* Reports

The costs for each element are shown for each product that you manufacture. For example, in Quarter 1 the raw material costs for Product 1 were $48,500, the labor costs were $107,381, and the amount spent on improvements in the quality of your product was $10,500. The report also shows the total for all of these costs. For our example, in Quarter 1 the total costs to manufacture Product 1 were $226,620. The first arrow in Exhibit 7.5 points to this line of the Cost of Production Report.

Exhibit 7.5

	Prod 1	Prod 2	Total
Raw Material	48500	63200	111700
Labor Costs	107381	77553	184933
Overhead	49536	42931	92467
Spending on Quality	10500	18200	28700
Depreciation	10704	9276	19980
Total Costs	226620	211160	437780
Production (#)	6000	5200	11200
Unit Costs ($)	37.77	40.61	39.09
Plant Capacity (Units)		11100	

SOLO Industry - Threshold SOLO Competitor - Q 1 ACTUAL - DEMO Company 1
Cost of Production Report

You sometimes may notice that the Total Costs line does not equal the total costs of the lines being added together. This is caused by the decimal rounding performed by the *Threshold Competitor* program. These rounding "errors" are small (usually only a dollar or two) compared to the total costs of operating your company and are not a cause for concern. You may experience these rounding errors on any of the *Threshold Competitor* reports.

Because the manufacturing process is fairly simple, all production of raw material into a finished product is completed at the end of each workday. This means there is no "work in process" inventory. An item in inventory is either raw material or a finished good.

Costs Per Unit. Just below the listing of the costs associated with producing your products, the Cost of Production Report shows the per unit cost to manufacture each product. These costs are calculated by dividing the number of units produced into the total cost for that production process. For our example, a total of $226,620 was spent to produce 6,000 units of Product 1 in your plant. This resulted in a per unit cost of $37.77 (226,620 / 6,000). Notice how this per unit cost ties back to the per-unit cost for Product 1 on the Finished Goods section of the Inventory Report. The second arrow in Exhibit 7.5 points to this line of the Cost of Production Report.

Learning how to control your manufacturing costs is a key to your company's success. If your cost of manufacturing each unit of a product rises too high, you will be unable to price the product competitively and still be able to make a profit selling that product. You need to have a sufficient margin between the price you charge for your product and the cost of making that product to be able to pay for the cost of marketing and financing the product and still have money left (i.e., a profit). Continual failure to achieve a margin that will cover all your costs will lead to the failure of your company!

Cost Breakdown of Mfg COGS. It is important to recognize sources of production costs so that you can evaluate the contribution individual parts make to the total. Divide each of the individual costs for a product (e.g., raw material costs, labor costs, etc.) by the number of units of that product that were produced that quarter to get a per-unit breakdown of production costs. An example of a per-unit cost breakdown for Product 1 follows in Exhibit 7.6.

Exhibit 7.6

Cost Breakdown for Product 1

Source of Cost	Cost / Production Volume		Per-Unit Cost	Percent
Raw Material	$ 48,500 / 6,000	=	$ 8.08	21.4%
Labor Costs	107,381 / 6,000	=	17.90	47.4%
Overhead	49,536 / 6,000	=	8.26	21.9%
Quality	10,500 / 6,000	=	1.75	4.6%
Depreciation	10,704 / 6,000	=	1.78	4.7%
Total Costs	$ 226,620 / 6,000		$ 37.77	100.0%

Knowing how much of your per-unit cost of goods sold is caused by labor costs versus material costs will help your company to better control these costs. For example, a cost breakdown could indicate whether your problems stem from poor management of your production workforce or from the costs of raw materials.

The Cost of Production Report also includes the plant capacity available for production during the quarter. This shows the volume of production that you can maintain without incurring any overtime cost because your production decision exceeded 120% of your plant's capacity. Remember, you can also incur overtime charges if you do not have enough production workers available to handle your production volume *at their current productivity levels* on a regular-time basis.

MARKETING REPORTS

Selling and Administrative Costs Report

This report shows the cost of advertising your two products to prospective customers. This includes the cost of television, newspaper, and magazine advertising, plus the cost of market research information you purchased this quarter. This report also shows the Office Expense cost for the administrative staff in your company offices. The Office Expense line also will include charges related to dilemma decisions your company made and can increase if you purchase additional plant capacity.

The S & A Costs Report also shows any fines assessed your company by the simulation administrator for actions on your part such as turning in late decisions. Finally, it also shows any refunds given to your company. Exhibit 7.7 gives an example of this report for Quarter 1.

As shown in Exhibit 7.7, the total cost of sales and administration for Product 1 in Quarter 1 was $87,643. Of this total, $30,000 was spent on television advertisements, $9,000 for newspaper ads, and $24,000 for magazine ads.

Exhibit 7.7

SELLING	Prod 1	Prod 2	Totals
TV Ads	30000	25000	55000
Newspaper Ads	9000	7000	16000
Magazine Ads	24000	21000	45000
Subtotal	63000	53000	116000
ADMINISTRATION			
Office Expense	6429	5571	12000
Market Info	18214	15786	34000
Fines	0	0	0
Refunds	0	0	0
TOTAL	87643	74357	162000

The remaining promotional costs were administrative costs. Office expenses for the quarter were $12,000. This is the cost for both of your product lines. It is split between the two products based on the sales volume of each. In Quarter 1, sales of Product 1 were 51.9% of the company's total sales (5,607/[5607+5200] = 51.9%). Therefore, the office cost for Product 1 in Quarter 1 was 51.9% of $12,000 or $6,429. The cost for conducting market research is also split between the two products based on sales volume. This means the market research costs assigned to Product 1 in Quarter 1 were $18,214. The arrow in Exhibit 7.7 points to this line of the S&A Costs Report.

The operations reports (i.e., Inventory, Labor, and Cost of Production) and the Sales and Administrative Costs Report can help you assess the efficiency of your company. If you are falling short of profit goals, you need to know where the problem lies. Is the cause poor control of manufacturing costs or ineffective use of promotional dollars? By analyzing these reports, you should be able to get some sense of how to attack your problem.

Market Research Report

The Market Research Report shows information you purchased regarding your competitors' actions and estimates of potential sales (i.e., market demand) in future quarters. Exhibit 7.8 and Appendix C show examples of this report. To access a particular market research report, you must select the quarter in which you purchased the information. You cannot view this report in a quarter that has not yet been processed (i.e., a quarter in which you are *forecasting* results versus viewing *actual* reports). For example, if you purchased the information in Quarter 1, you must select Quarter 1 option from the Quarter menu to be able to view the report. Remember, after Quarter 1 has been processed the program will automatically load and open your company's files to forecast reports for Quarter 2. So you will have to first change to the *actual* reports for Quarter 1 to view the Market Research Report.

It is important to remember two things as you view this report. One, the Units Sold figures show how many units each company sold that quarter. That number does *not* reflect any lost sales the company incurred because demand for its products exceeded the units they had available for sale. Two, the Potential Product Demands (see the arrow in Exhibit 7.8) reported for a quarter is *not* a guarantee of how many units each company will sell in that quarter. Reread the section on Future Potential Sales in Chapter 6 to ensure you understand what these two numbers mean.

Exhibit 7.8

SOLO Industry - Threshold SOLO Competitor - Q 1 ACTUAL - DEMO Company 1

Market Research

Co. #	PRICE P1	PRICE P2	TV ADS P1	TV ADS P2	NEWS P1	NEWS P2	MAG P1	MAG P2	QUALITY P1	QUALITY P2	UNITS SOLD P1	UNITS SOLD P2
1	64	47	6	5	9	7	8	7	1.75	3.50	5607	5200
2	63	49	3	3	4	5	8	2	2.93	1.65	5325	2584
3	60	45	4	5	9	5	3	2	4.28	2.34	6000	3761
4	66	47	7	2	9	4	9	4	4.42	4.07	6000	4612
5	63	45	3	3	9	8	7	5	4.87	3.69	6000	5100
6	64	51	5	4	4	2	3	3	5.11	3.21	6000	2603
7	65	50	2	2	4	3	6	6	3.02	3.60	4277	3689
8	61	52	2	4	7	7	9	8	4.62	1.96	6000	3266
9	63	50	6	9	3	8	7	9	3.46	3.57	5744	5100
10	63	49	7	6	5	5	7	3	5.14	3.30	6000	4632
11	67	50	9	6	4	3	3	9	2.77	4.15	4262	5100
12	60	47	4	5	6	5	2	9	3.64	2.09	5130	5027
13	62	45	3	3	5	2	3	3	2.02	3.55	4682	4297
14	62	49	4	8	2	9	6	5	1.43	4.19	3630	5100
15	67	48	7	3	5	4	7	9	4.74	1.42	5237	4180
16	66	47	6	5	9	4	4	3	2.65	4.94	4894	5100

→ Potential product demands for Quarter 3 are 7000 and 6800 respectively.

INCOME STATEMENT

The purpose of the Income Statement for any quarter is to show the amount of profit or loss that occurred as a result of your company's operations that quarter. Exhibit 7.9 shows the Income Statement for our example of Quarter 1 operations. On the Income Statement, the first two lines show the sales revenue of Products 1 and 2 for the quarter. The next line gives the total sales revenues generated by the two products.

The various costs of running the business that quarter are then subtracted from the total sales revenues. The Manufacturing COGS is the first item subtracted. It is the addition of the dollar value numbers for the two products reported on the Units Sold line of the Inventory Report. (As shown in Exhibit 7.3, these values are ($211,776 for Product 1 and $211,160 for Product 2). This figure, $422,936 for Quarter 1, reflects the cost of producing finished goods that quarter. (See the first arrow in Exhibit 7.9) It includes depreciation charges that reflect the "wear and tear" on your plant and equipment during the production process. These costs are not cash payments made by your company, but are bookkeeping charges determined by accounting practices to show the true cost of doing business. Cash payments, alone, do not reflect all the costs of operating a business during any one period of time. For example, if you drove a car from New York City to Boston, the cost of the trip is not just the cash you paid for gasoline. You should also include non-cash costs such as tire wear and engine wear. Both of these are very real costs of your trip, even though your cash payouts for these costs would occur after your trip was completed.

Exhibit 7.9

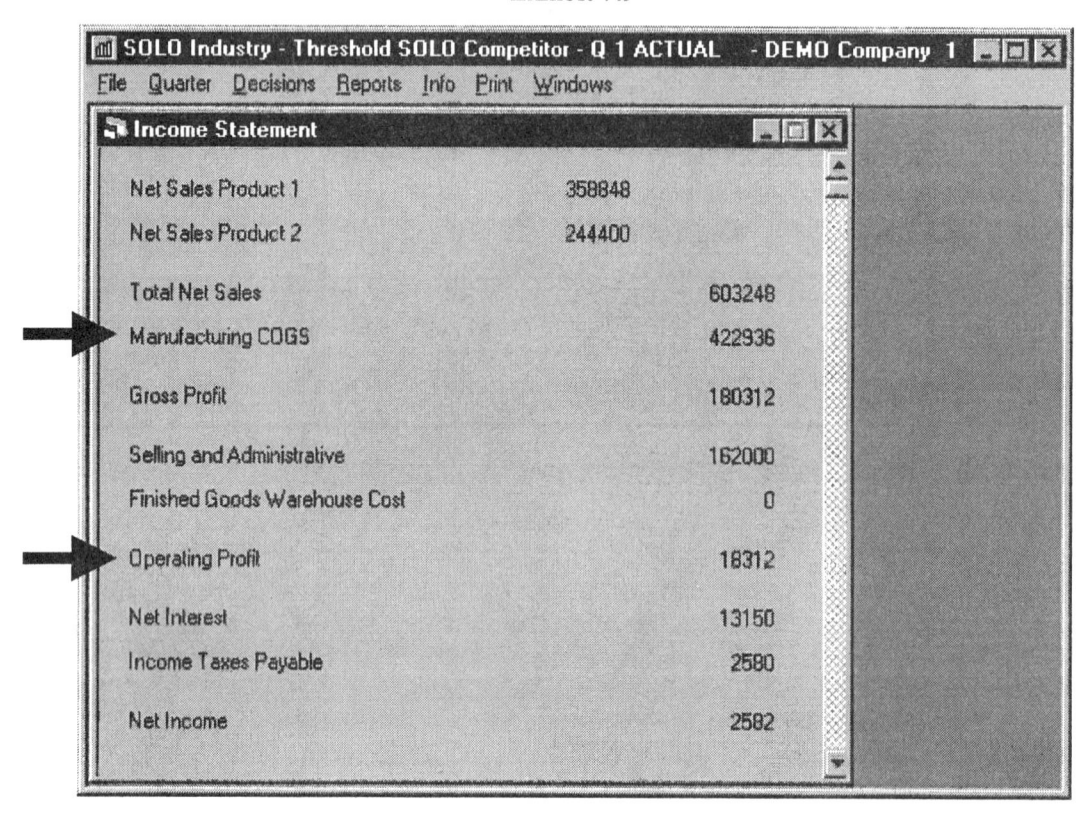

```
SOLO Industry - Threshold SOLO Competitor - Q 1 ACTUAL    - DEMO Company 1
File  Quarter  Decisions  Reports  Info  Print  Windows

Income Statement

Net Sales Product 1                    358848
Net Sales Product 2                    244400

Total Net Sales                        603248
→ Manufacturing COGS                   422936

Gross Profit                           180312

Selling and Administrative             162000
Finished Goods Warehouse Cost               0

→ Operating Profit                      18312

Net Interest                            13150
Income Taxes Payable                     2580

Net Income                               2582
```

Running a manufacturing process also has immediate and delayed cash payouts that are connected to its operations. You did not pay out any cash to replace plant and equipment that quarter, but you did use up some of the useful life remaining for these items. The "wear and tear" on these items needs to be reflected in your Income Statement. That way, any profit or loss shown includes all the costs of doing business.

Including these depreciation charges in the Income Statement reduces the profit you show for the quarter. This allows you to pay less tax. These tax savings can then be used to help pay for new equipment when the current equipment completely wears out. The differences between cash payments and accounting charges will be discussed in more detail under the section on the Cash Flow Statement.

The Gross Profit line shows whether your manufacturing operation generated a profit during the quarter. This is the money left after subtracting manufacturing costs (Mfg. COGS) from your sales revenues. Gross profit does not reflect all the costs of running your company because it excludes such costs as marketing and financing. It reflects just the costs of making the products and how much money your company had left after making the products. Gross profit shows the money you have left to pay for the marketing, administrative, and warehouse costs associated with running your company and promoting your products. In our example, Gross Profit was $180,312 in Quarter 1.

The charges for Selling and Administrative expenses and Finished Goods Warehouse Costs are taken directly from the Selling and Administrative Costs Report and the Finished Goods Warehouse Costs line of the Inventory Report. In Quarter 1 the total S&A costs were $162,000. There were no charges for

Finished Goods Warehouse Costs since there was no finished goods inventory at the end of the prior quarter (i.e., Quarter 0) to be charged to this quarters operations.

After deducting costs for Selling and Administrative expenses and Finished Goods Warehouse Costs, the Income Statement shows the profit resulting from operating your business. Your operating profits do not include the cost of financing your business. In Quarter 1, the company generated $18,312 in operating profits. The second arrow in Exhibit 7.9 points to this line of the Income Statement.

Deductions for interest payments reflect the cost of borrowing money to run the company. This includes interest for short-term loans as well as interest on any mortgages you have outstanding, less any interest income you received from your short-term investments. By keeping the costs of financing your business out of the Operating Profit calculation, you can more readily see whether problems that develop originate in how you operate your business or the financing of these operations. It is not uncommon for a business to be profitable in the making and selling of its product, but to end up losing money because it borrowed large sums to develop the business. Knowing the cause of your problem is the first step in being able to solve it. Exhibit 7.9 shows that the company paid $13,150 in interest charges for the quarter.

The Income Taxes Payable line shows the taxes you must pay on any profits you earned that quarter. The current tax rate you must pay is 50%. If you lose money in a quarter, you will not have to pay any taxes for that quarter. Further, those losses will serve as a tax shelter to counter taxes owed on profits generated in later quarters. The calculation of whether you are due any tax refunds because of losses you incurred earlier is done in the last quarter of each year. Your company's tax year runs on a calendar year (i.e., January through December) Since Quarter 1 represents the first quarter of the year (January – March), any year-end tax reconciliations will occur in Quarters 4, 8, 12, 16, etc. In our example, a total of $2,580 was owed for taxes at the end of Quarter 1.

After paying all expenses and any taxes due, this leaves the Net Income your company earned for the quarter. In our example, in Quarter 1 the company's Net Income was $2,582. Note that the taxes payable may not always be exactly 50% of profits due to rounding. In our example, the taxes payable was rounded *down* to $2,580, which resulted in a net profit of $2,582 due to a figure that was rounded *up* as a consequence of how the program handled a number with many decimal places that do not get displayed.

BALANCE SHEET

The next report is the Balance Sheet (Exhibit 7.10). It shows the financial status of your company at the end of the quarter. The Balance Sheet is a snapshot summary indicating the Assets and Liabilities of the company at the end of that accounting period. Through it you can determine whether investments made in plant and equipment or equity investments are receiving a good rate of return.

The Balance Sheet also shows the net value (i.e., net worth) of your company. This is the liquidated value of the business if it "closed-up shop" and sold everything of value to pay for everything the business owed. Whether the owners would actually collect this amount of money would depend on whether they could sell their assets for "book value" (i.e., the value of the assets shown on the Balance Sheet). The owners might end up selling the company's assets for more or less than their stated book value. This is similar to selling a used car. How much the potential buyer wants the car and what shape it is in will affect whether the car is sold at, above, or below a car dealer's "Blue Book" price. The same kind of situation holds for the seller of assets of a business. The only asset that is worth exactly what is shown on the Balance Sheet is Cash. And even this account can become open to bargaining if the company does business outside the United States and has to deal with changing rates of exchange for the dollar. This is not the case for your *Threshold Competitor* companies. All your revenues are from domestic sales.

Exhibit 7.10

```
┌─────────────────────────────────────────────────────────────────────┐
│ SOLO Industry - Threshold SOLO Competitor - Q 1 ACTUAL - DEMO Company 1 │
│ File  Quarter  Decisions  Reports  Info  Print  Windows             │
│ ┌─ Balance Sheet ──────────────────────────────────────────────┐    │
│ │                                                              │    │
│ │ ASSETS                        LIABILITIES AND OWNERS EQUITY  │    │
│ │                                                              │    │
│ │ Current Assets:               Current Liabilities            │    │
│ │  Cash                 11027    Short-Term Payable   310000   │    │
│ │  Accounts Receivable 301624    Taxes Payable          2580   │    │
│ │  Investments              0    Total Curr. Liabilities 312580│    │
│ │  Raw Materials        32400                                  │    │
│ │  Finished Goods       14844   Long-Term Liabilities          │    │
│ │  Total Current Assets 359895   Mortgages Payable    230000   │    │
│ │                                                              │    │
│ │ Long-Term Assets:              Total Liabilities    542580   │    │
│ │                                                              │    │
│ │  Plant and Equipment  499500  Owners Equity         276855   │    │
│ │   Less Acc. Depreciation 39960                               │    │
│ │  Total Long-Term Assets 459540  TOTAL LIABILITIES & 819435   │    │
│ │  TOTAL ASSETS         819435    OWNERS EQUITY                │    │
│ └──────────────────────────────────────────────────────────────┘    │
└─────────────────────────────────────────────────────────────────────┘
```

Assets

The assets shown on the left side of the Balance Sheet are divided between Current Assets and Long-Term Assets. The Current Assets include cash and those assets that can be converted into cash within the next business period. (In *Threshold Competitor*, the next business period is the next quarter of operation.) Accounts Receivable shown here are different from those shown on the Cash Flow Statement (discussed in the next section). Accounts Receivable on the Balance Sheet show all the money owed by customers who have bought your product but who have not yet paid. In our example in Exhibit 7.10 the Accounts Receivable total $301,624 at the end of Quarter 1. The first arrow on the left of in Exhibit 7.10 points to this line of the Balance Sheet.

The other Current Assets show the value of investments you have made in short-term investments such as money market funds, and the value of inventories of Raw Materials and Finished Goods of the company as of the date of the Balance Sheet. For example, as shown in Exhibit 7.10 the company's Raw Materials inventory was valued at $32,400 at the end of Quarter 1.

The Long-Term Assets show the original cost of the Plant and Equipment of the company and the charges that have been assessed for depreciation of those assets. Subtracting depreciation charges from the original cost of Plant and Equipment gives the current value for those assets. In our example this equaled $459,500 at the end of Quarter 1. The left arrow on the left of in Exhibit 7.10 points to this line of the Balance Sheet.

Adding the Current Assets and the Long-Term Assets gives the Total Assets of the company. In Quarter 1, the Total Assets of your company were valued at $819,435.

Liabilities

The Liabilities shown on the Balance Sheet reflect the money the company owes others with which it does business. They are divided into Current Liabilities and Long-Term Liabilities.

Current Liabilities are those you will have to pay during the next quarter of business operations. These include short-term loan payments you have to make to your bank, and taxes you have to pay to the government. In Quarter 1, you owed $310,000 in short-term loans and $2,580 in taxes. Total Current Liabilities that you will have to pay in Quarter 2 are $312,580 (310,000 + 2,580). The first arrow on the right of in Exhibit 7.10 points to this line of the Balance Sheet.

Long-Term Liabilities on the Balance Sheet show the amount you owe the bank for mortgages you have taken out in past quarters of operations. At the end of Quarter 1, you owed $230,000 for mortgages you had taken out with your bank. Each quarter, this balance will be reduced by the quarterly payment you are required to make. The Total Liabilities account summarizes all of the money you owe to others.

Owners' Equity

Subtracting Total Liabilities from Total Assets shows the amount of equity the owners have accumulated in the business. Owners' Equity reflects what the company would be worth to the owners if the company stopped operating the business, sold off all its assets at book value and paid off all its liabilities, leaving the remainder (i.e., the Owners' Equity) for the owners of the company. At the end of Quarter 1, Exhibit 7.10 shows that the company had an Owners' Equity value of $276,855. (The second arrow on the right of in Exhibit 7.10 points to this line of the Balance Sheet.) Remember, as discussed at the beginning of this section on the Balance Sheet, the owners might not collect this exact amount. Much would depend on how much the buyers of the company's assets would be willing to actually pay for them.

CASH FLOW STATEMENT

The Cash Flow Statement provides information on the cash your company received and paid out this quarter. Exhibit 7.11 shows the impact of decisions made in Quarter 1 on your company's cash flow for that quarter.

The Cash Flow Statement differs from the Income Statement, which shows the dollar value of products you sold and the profits you earned during the quarter. The Cash Flow Statement shows the *actual* cash you received this quarter. This includes money you collected from Accounts Receivable. The Accounts Receivable on the Cash Flow Statement shows the amount of cash that was received from the accounts owing the company money for sales made in the prior quarter.

Cash Receipts

Your cash receipts will typically include Cash on Hand remaining from the last quarter's operations and the Collection of Accounts Receivable. You may also periodically add to your cash receipts by requesting a mortgage from the *Threshold Competitor* bank. The remaining cash receipts will come from money received if you decide to sell some of your plant capacity, interest on funds you previously deposited in your short-term investment account, or from money you withdraw from this account.

Threshold Competitor companies sell their products on credit. Normal terms are net 90 days, but some customers will pay cash for the products. For any given quarter, 50% of the sales will be collected immediately, with the remaining 50% collected in the next quarter. This means the receivables from last quarter (i.e., 50% of last quarter's sales) are added to 50% of this quarter's sales to produce the cash inflow from sales for this quarter. In Quarter 1, your company collected $613,474 of your outstanding Accounts Receivable. (See the first arrow on the left in Exhibit 7.11) Because of this delayed collection of sales revenues, managing your cash flow requires planning.

Exhibit 7.11

CASH RECEIPTS:		CASH PAYMENTS:	
Cash On Hand	48875	Purchase Raw Materials	135300
Collection of A/R	613474	Labor and Overhead	277400
Investment Interest	0	Product Quality	28700
Mortgage	0	Total Warehouse Costs	0
Sale of Plant	0	Selling & Administrative	162000
ST Investment Withdrawal	0	Short-Term Interest Expense	7750
TOTAL CASH RECEIPTS	662349	Short - Term Loan Payment	310000
		Mortgage Interest	5400
		Mortgage Retirement	10000
NET CASH FLOW	-298973	Income Taxes Paid	24772
ST LOAN GRANTED	310000	Investment Deposit	0
NET CASH BALANCE	11027	Purchase Plant Capacity	0
		TOTAL CASH PAYMENTS	961322

Having this delay between when the company sells its products and when it receives the cash for these sales is typical for almost every business. Just think of how often you pay for your purchases with a credit card. You leave the store with the merchandise and all the store has is a slip of paper that says the credit card company will send the cash later, usually months later. Yet the storeowner has had to pay out *cash* for employee wages and advertising before you even entered the store. Consequently, learning how to manage your cash flow can be a key to achieving success for any organization.

Cash Payments

Cash Payments reflect the payments your company made during the quarter. The first line under cash payments shows the payment made for raw materials received that quarter. Raw materials are paid on a cash-on-delivery basis. This means you pay for materials in the quarter you receive them, not when you order them. For example, Exhibit 7.11 shows the cash payment made for raw material purchases made in Quarter 0. At that time, the owners purchased 7,000 units of Product 1 raw materials worth $56,000 and 6,500 units of Product 2 raw materials worth $78,000. You received these materials in Quarter 1 (see Exhibit 7.3) and paid the supplier $134,000 (i.e., $56,000 + $78,000).

Labor and Overhead costs are taken from the second and third lines of the Cost of Production Report. In Quarter 1 you paid a total of $184,933 in labor costs and $92,467 in overhead costs (50% of total labor costs), for a grand total of $277,400 for these two costs (see Exhibit 7.5). The first arrow on the right in Exhibit 7.11 shows this line.

Product Quality payments shows the money spent improving the quality of your products. This figure is taken from the fourth line of the Cost of Production Report. A total of $28,700 was spent on product quality in our Quarter 1 example.

The next line shows the total dollars spent to warehouse both the raw materials and the finished goods inventories. This cost is taken from the Inventory Report for Product 1 and Product 2. The warehouse costs for raw materials left in inventory at the end of the prior quarter (i.e., Quarter 0) totaled $1,300. As shown on the Inventory Report in Exhibit 7.3, this included $500 for Product 1 and $800 for Product 2. Because no finished goods inventory was carried over from Quarter 0, no finished goods carrying costs were incurred. This resulted in a total of $1,300 paid for warehouse costs for the quarter.

Selling and Administrative payments are taken from the Selling and Administrative Expense Report to show the marketing and staff costs for the quarter. In our example for Quarter 1, this totaled $138,000.

Net Short-Term Interest shows the interest payment made for money borrowed last quarter. In our Quarter 1 example the company paid $7,750 in interest for the $310,000 it borrowed in Quarter 0. The Short-Term Loan Payment line shows the amount repaid on any short-term loans you have outstanding. In Quarter 0 the company received a $310,000 short-term loan. This loan was repaid in Quarter 1.

The Mortgage Interest line shows the interest paid on mortgages the bank has issued your company. In Quarter 1 you paid $5,400 in Mortgage Interest. Payments to retire (i.e., pay off) your mortgages are shown on the following line. You are presently paying $10,000 per quarter on the mortgage you have with the *Threshold Competitor* bank.

The Income Taxes Paid line shows the taxes you had to pay out. This is different from Income Taxes Payable on the Income Statement because those are not paid out in cash until the next quarter of operation. In Quarter 1 the company paid $24,772 in taxes on profits earned in Quarter 0. The second arrow on the right in Exhibit 7.11 shows this line.

The Investments Deposit line shows any investments you made in short-term money markets this quarter. No short-term investments were made in Quarter 1.

The last cash payment item shows payments made to purchase additional plant capacity. *Threshold Competitor* requires that all plant capacity purchases be paid in cash the day that the capacity is ready for use. Plant purchased this quarter is not usable until next quarter, so the payment for it is due next quarter. This payment schedule means you do not have to arrange financing for the purchase of plant capacity until the quarter following the purchase. Remember, you receive any money you borrow the same quarter you request it.

The last line of the Cash Payments column shows the total of the cash payments made that quarter. In our Quarter 1 example, this totaled $961,322.

Net Cash Flow and Short-Term Loan

The last three lines on the left side of the Cash Flow Statement are Net Cash Flow, Short-Term Loan Granted, and Net Cash Balance. Net Cash Flow is the result of subtracting Total Cash Payments from Cash Receipts. The second arrow on the left in Exhibit 7.11 shows this line.

Net Cash Flow reflects the cash generated by this quarter's operations or, if a minus figure, the cash needed to finance the operations. If you need a short-term loan to cover a cash shortfall, you must be sure to determine accurately the amount of your cash needs and request that amount. *Threshold Competitor* places a premium on cash planning. Any time your company does not have a combination of cash receipts and a short-term loan request sufficient to cover your cash payments, you will receive an automatic emergency loan from your bank to bring your cash balance up to zero. The interest rate for an emergency loan will be double the normal rate for short-term loans. This emergency loan will be at higher than normal interest rates to cover the cost of making the loan on such short notice. Remember, as explained in Chapter 6 under the Short-Term Loans section, the *Threshold Competitor* bank charges you this higher interest on the total loan granted, not just on the difference between the amount you requested and amount actually needed.

The Net Cash Balance shows the total of your Net Cash Flow and Short-Term Loan. If your Net Cash Balance is zero, it probably means you did not request a short-term loan large enough to cover all your cash needs for the quarter. Either that, or you were incredibly lucky and had requested the precise amount of cash you needed when you processed the quarter's decisions. Remember, as was discussed in Chapter 6, you need to request a short term loan that balances the risk of falling short of actual cash needs and incurring an emergency loan, with the expense of paying interest charges on money not really needed. Remember as you do your cash planning that 50% of the cash you will collect for accounts receivable comes from sales this quarter. So if your sales forecast is optimistic, the *actual* collection of accounts receivable for the quarter will be less than what you *forecasted*.

INDUSTRY PERFORMANCE REPORTS

In addition to reports on the performance of your individual company, you will also receive two industry performance reports. Both reports will provide you with information for all companies in your *Threshold Competitor* industry on four factors: sales, income, return on assets (ROA), and the accuracy of each company's sales forecasts. One of the industry performance reports shows the performance of all the companies on these four factors for the current quarter. The other report shows a game-to-date summary on these factors. Appendix H provides an example of both of these reports.

Exhibit 7.12 shows an example of just the Quarter Performance Report. We will use this example to discuss each of the four performance factors and explain how the *Threshold Competitor* program calculates the points assigned to each company in the PTS AWRD columns.

Exhibit 7.12

COMP	SALES	PTS AWRD	INCOME	PTS AWRD	ROA	PTS AWRD	FORECAST ERRORS	PTS AWRD	OVERALL PTS	RANK
1	603248	16	2581	6	0.32	3	503	14*	38	6
2	462091	12	11536	26	1.32	11	3101	2	52	3
3	526245	14	4270	10	0.50	4	4016	2	29	8
4	607458	16	5950	14	0.67	6	1614	4	39	5
5	607500	16	-6236	-14	-0.71	-6	1915	4	-1	10
6	516753	13	21564	49*	2.47	21*	3159	2	86	1
7	458472	12	14064	32	1.65	14	3134	2	60	2
8	531199	14	-7911	-18	-0.89	-8	4427	2	-10	11
9	616872	16*	-36793	-49	-4.16	-21	1321	5	-49	13
10	602652	16	-20458	-46	-2.31	-20	2127	3	-47	12
11	535873	14	-21489	-49	-2.46	-21	1476	5	-51	14
12	544069	14	-31580	-49	-3.68	-21	1453	5	-51	15
13	479160	12	9456	21	1.13	10	2121	3	47	4
14	472410	12	-32961	-49	-3.98	-21	3684	2	-56	16
15	551519	14	2873	7	0.33	3	1773	4	28	9
16	560257	15	4093	9	0.47	4	1534	5	32	7

The Four Performance Factors

For each of the four factors, the report shows each company's performance, plus a ranking and evaluation of that performance. The column under each heading — Sales, Income, etc. — shows what each company achieved for that factor in that quarter. Figures shown for the sales, income, and return on assets factors indicate each company's actual performance. For example, Company 1 had sales revenues for Quarter 1 of $603,248 and net income of $2,581. Both of these figures are taken from the company's Income Statement for the quarter. Company 1's ROA (i.e., return on assets) was 0.32, which indicates the company's net income represents a 0.32% return on the total assets of the company, as listed on its Balance Sheet. To calculate your company's ROA, divide your net income by the total assets of your company.

For the sales forecast factor, the figure shows the *absolute* difference in unit sales between the *actual demand* generated by a company's marketing efforts and the sales *forecast* made by that company. The report does not make any distinction on whether the sales forecast was high or low. It is only concerned with how inaccurate the forecast was from the actual demand generated for a company's products. Notice that it is actual demand, not actual sales, that is used to determine this factor. This means any sales lost due to stockouts will be included in determining the accuracy of a company's sales forecasting. The actual demand for each of your products is shown on the Marketing Decisions Report (see Exhibit 7.1). For this factor the smallest error indicates the best performance. In Exhibit 7.10, Company 1 had combined total unit sales forecast errors for both products of 503 for Quarter 1.

Calculation of Points Awarded

The Points Awarded (Pts Awrd) columns show the number of points awarded based on each company's performance on the four factors. The points awarded to each company for their performance on a particular factor are calculated based on (a) that company's performance relative to the company that achieved the best performance on that factor and (b) the maximum possible points that could be achieved for that factor. (The maximum points awarded for a factor to the team(s) with the best performance on that factor is indicated by a * next to the number.) For example, Exhibit 7.12 shows that Company 1 was awarded 6 points of a maximum 49 points for the Net Income factor. This was calculated by dividing Company 1's income for the quarter by Company 6's quarterly income and then multiplying that by 49 ([2,581/21,564] * 49). In this example, Company 1's income was 12.0% (2,581/21,564) of the company which achieved the best income for the quarter (Company 6). Consequently, Company 1 received 12.0% of the maximum possible points (49) that could be achieved for that factor. This resulted in a Pts Awrd of 6 (12.0% * 49). In our example, Company 1 was awarded a total of 38 points for its performance in Quarter 1. It received 16 points for sales revenues, 6 points for income, 3 points for its ROA, and 14 points for its forecasting errors. This performance earned Company 1 a ranking of number 6 in the industry for that quarter.

As with the Quarter Performance Report, the Game-to-Date summary shows the total points awarded to a company based on the number of points it received on each of the four performance factors. For the Game-to-Date Report, these calculations are based on all quarters of operation. For the sales, net income, and sales forecast factors, the Game-to-Date Report is an *accumulation* of the combined total of all quarters of operation. For the ROA factor, this report shows the *average* for all quarters of operation, rather than the total of the quarters. This allows a better comparison of game-to-date performance with current-quarter performance. The Game-to-Date summary also shows the rank of each company based on the total points it had been awarded.

The administrator determines the maximum possible points for each of the four factors. The points allocated to a company for each individual factor can range from -99 to 99, but the total of all starred points (the maximum points for an individual factor) for the four factors must equal exactly 100. This means that at points must be allocated to at least two factors. Usually at least a few points are allocated to each factor.

INFORMATION REPORTS

You can also receive four reports that are listed under the Information menu option. These are the Marketing/Finance Limits report, the Production Limits report, the Cost Parameters report, and the Bulletin. The first two of these reports list the limits to the decision entries and the time lag before the decisions take effect. The Cost report shows the current costs affecting your company's operations. These costs can change from quarter to quarter, so it is important that you monitor this report each quarter. The Cost report for Quarter 0 is shown in Appendix D. The Marketing/Finance Limits report and the Production Limits report are shown in Appendix E.

The Bulletin may have a message from your administrator. This can be a note about an upcoming assignment or it might include a comment about changes affecting all companies in the industry. It will also include information about the consequences of any dilemmas that you might face during the quarter you manage your company.

A FINAL COMMENT

You should now have a basic understanding of each of the *Threshold Competitor* reports that you will work with throughout the simulation exercise. The more you work with them, the greater your confidence should become in using them to manage your company. While these reports are simplistic compared to those of large, complex organizations, the principles for using the reports to gain insight into how to manage any company are similar. Learning how to analyze where your costs are coming from, and how to control these costs, is a key to working within any company. We hope and believe the challenges you face in this simulation experience will aid you in that process.

Good luck.

APPENDICES

APPENDIX A
QUARTER 0 DECISIONS

Marketing Decisions

		Product 1	Product 2
Price	(#)	64	47
TV Ads	(Minutes)	6	5
Newspaper	(Column Inches)	9	7
Magazine Ads	(Pages)	8	7
Sales Forecast	(Units)	6000	5100
Actual Demand	(Units)	6000	5100

Marketing Research Decisions

[ ] Price   [ ] Product Quality
[ ] TV Ads   [ ] Unit Sold
[ ] Newspaper Ads
[ ] Magazine Ads   Future Sales Potential (Qtr)   1

Production / Finance Decisions

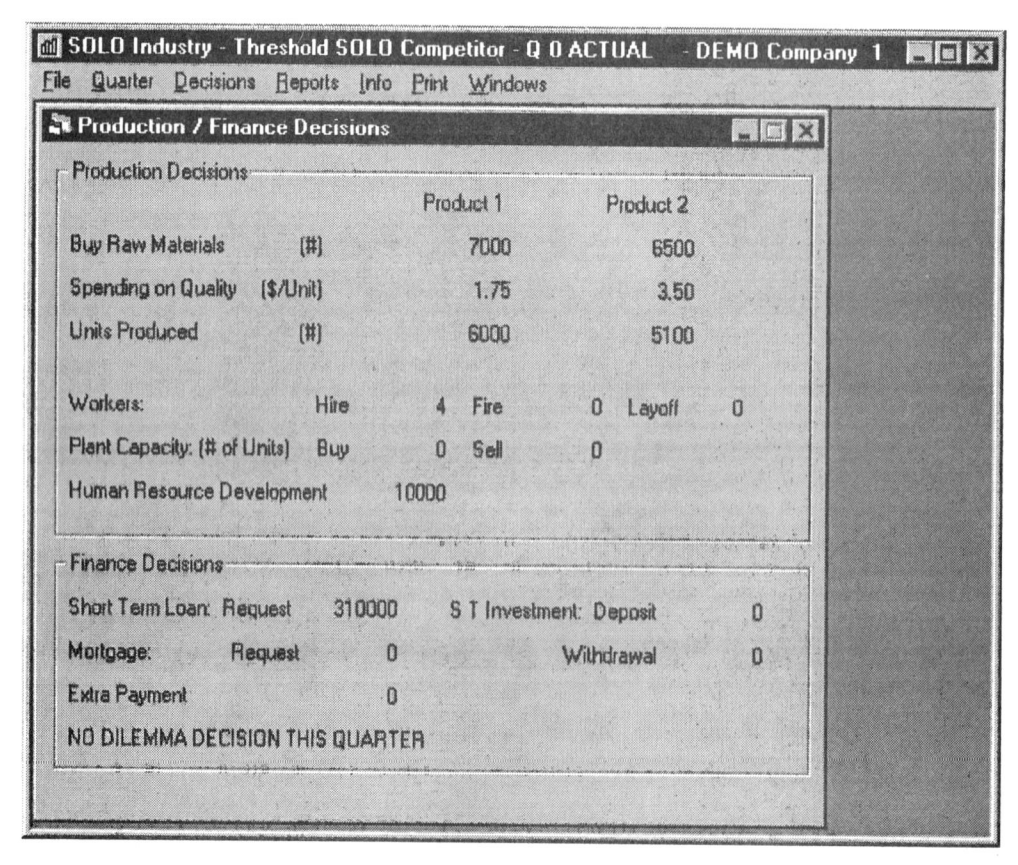

Production Decisions

		Product 1	Product 2
Buy Raw Materials	(#)	7000	6500
Spending on Quality	($/Unit)	1.75	3.50
Units Produced	(#)	6000	5100

Workers: Hire 4   Fire 0   Layoff 0
Plant Capacity: (# of Units) Buy 0   Sell 0
Human Resource Development   10000

Finance Decisions

Short Term Loan: Request 310000   S T Investment: Deposit 0
Mortgage: Request 0   Withdrawal 0
Extra Payment   0

NO DILEMMA DECISION THIS QUARTER

APPENDIX B
QUARTER 0 REPORTS

Marketing Decisions

		Product 1	Product 2
Price	(#)	64	47
TV Ads	(Minutes)	6	5
Newspaper	(Column Inches)	9	7
Magazine Ads	(Pages)	8	7
Sales Forecast	(Units)	6000	5100
Actual Demand	(Units)	6000	5100

Marketing Research Decisions

[ ] Price   [ ] Product Quality
[ ] TV Ads   [ ] Unit Sold
[ ] Newspaper Ads   Future Sales Potential (Qtr) 1
[ ] Magazine Ads

Production / Finance Decisions

Production Decisions

		Product 1	Product 2
Buy Raw Materials	(#)	7000	6500
Spending on Quality	($/Unit)	1.75	3.50
Units Produced	(#)	6000	5100

Workers: Hire 4 Fire 0 Layoff 0
Plant Capacity: (# of Units) Buy 0 Sell 0
Human Resource Development 10000

Finance Decisions

Short Term Loan: Request 310000   S T Investment: Deposit 0
Mortgage: Request 0   Withdrawal 0
Extra Payment 0
NO DILEMMA DECISION THIS QUARTER

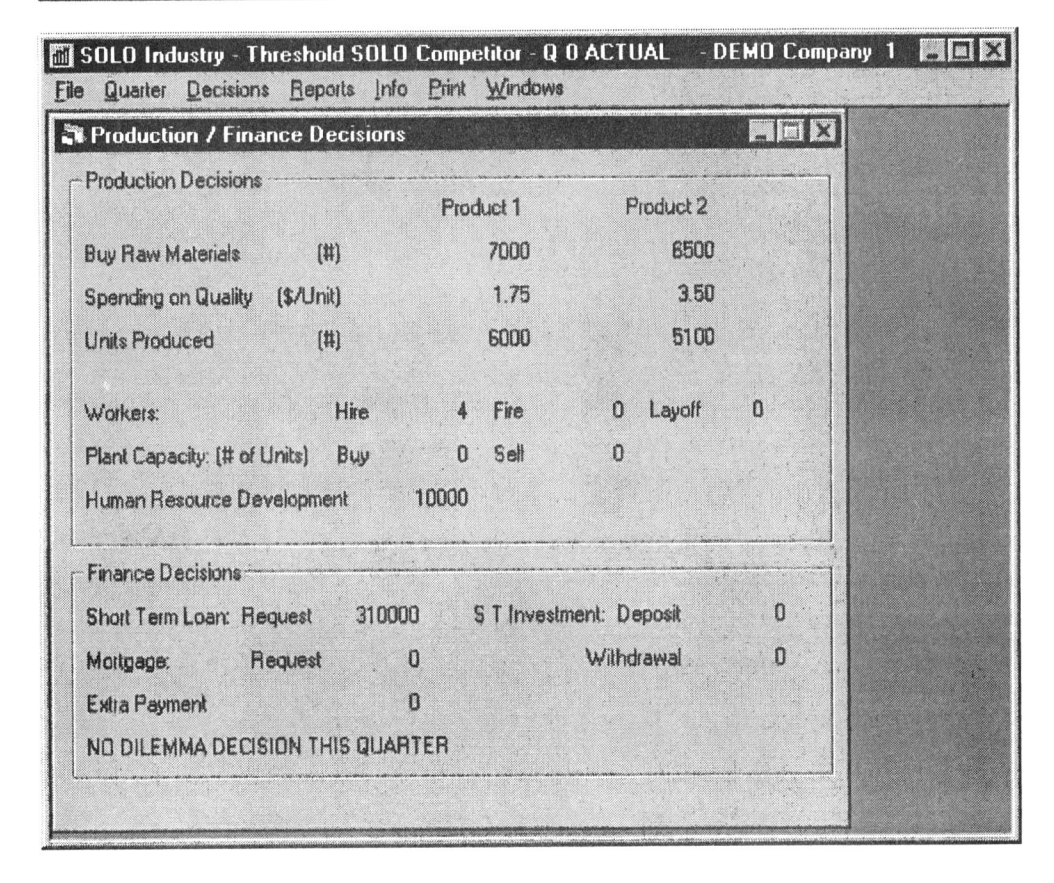

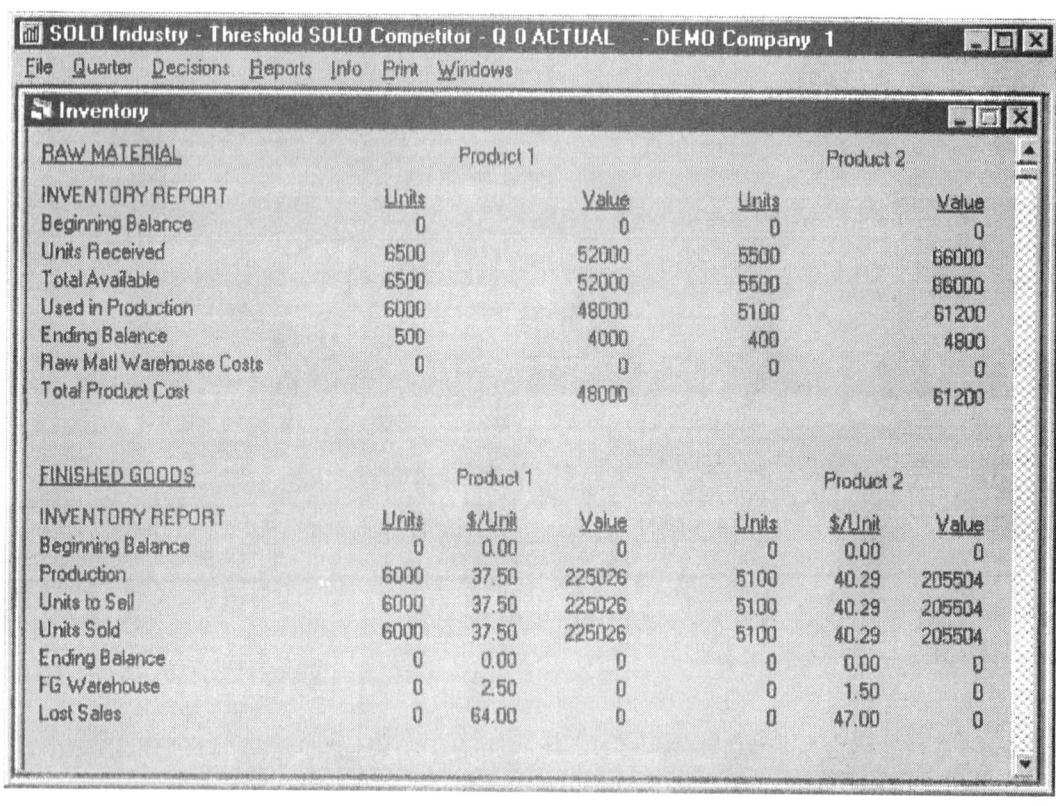

Appendix B, Quarter 0 Reports

Inventory

RAW MATERIAL

INVENTORY REPORT	Product 1 Units	Value	Product 2 Units	Value
Beginning Balance	0	0	0	0
Units Received	6500	52000	5500	66000
Total Available	6500	52000	5500	66000
Used in Production	6000	48000	5100	61200
Ending Balance	500	4000	400	4800
Raw Matl Warehouse Costs	0	0	0	0
Total Product Cost		48000		61200

FINISHED GOODS

INVENTORY REPORT	Product 1 Units	$/Unit	Value	Product 2 Units	$/Unit	Value
Beginning Balance	0	0.00	0	0	0.00	0
Production	6000	37.50	225026	5100	40.29	205504
Units to Sell	6000	37.50	225026	5100	40.29	205504
Units Sold	6000	37.50	225026	5100	40.29	205504
Ending Balance	0	0.00	0	0	0.00	0
FG Warehouse	0	2.50	0	0	1.50	0
Lost Sales	0	64.00	0	0	47.00	0

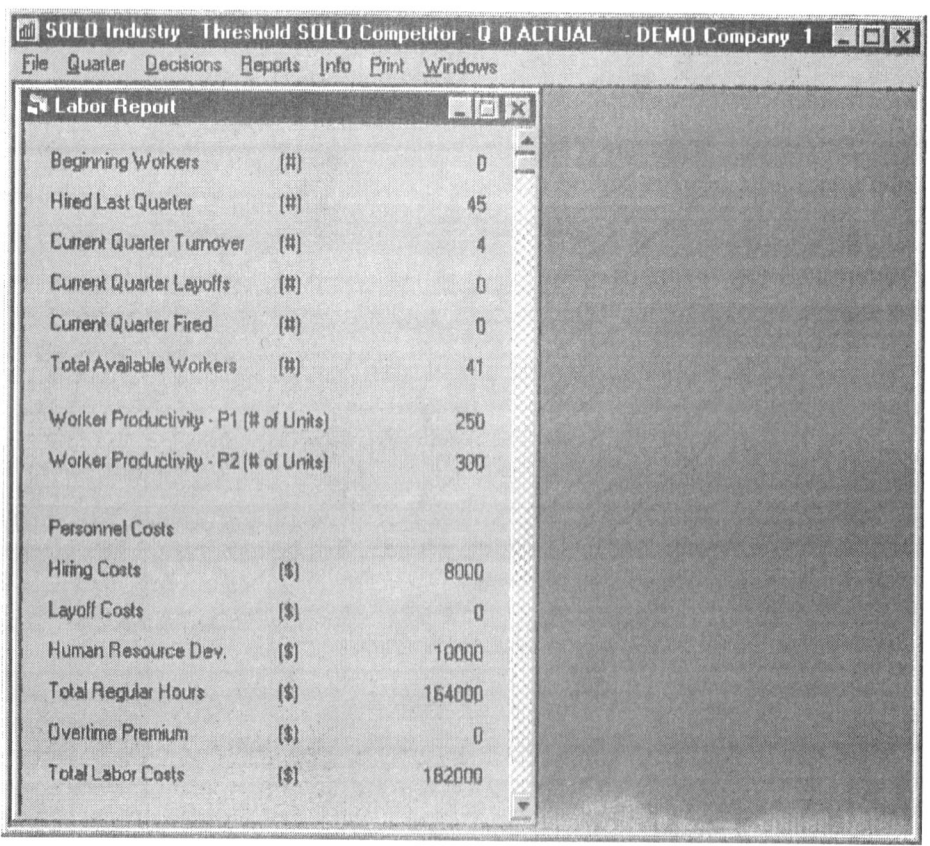

Labor Report

Beginning Workers	(#)	0
Hired Last Quarter	(#)	45
Current Quarter Turnover	(#)	4
Current Quarter Layoffs	(#)	0
Current Quarter Fired	(#)	0
Total Available Workers	(#)	41
Worker Productivity - P1 (# of Units)		250
Worker Productivity - P2 (# of Units)		300
Personnel Costs		
Hiring Costs	($)	8000
Layoff Costs	($)	0
Human Resource Dev.	($)	10000
Total Regular Hours	($)	164000
Overtime Premium	($)	0
Total Labor Costs	($)	182000

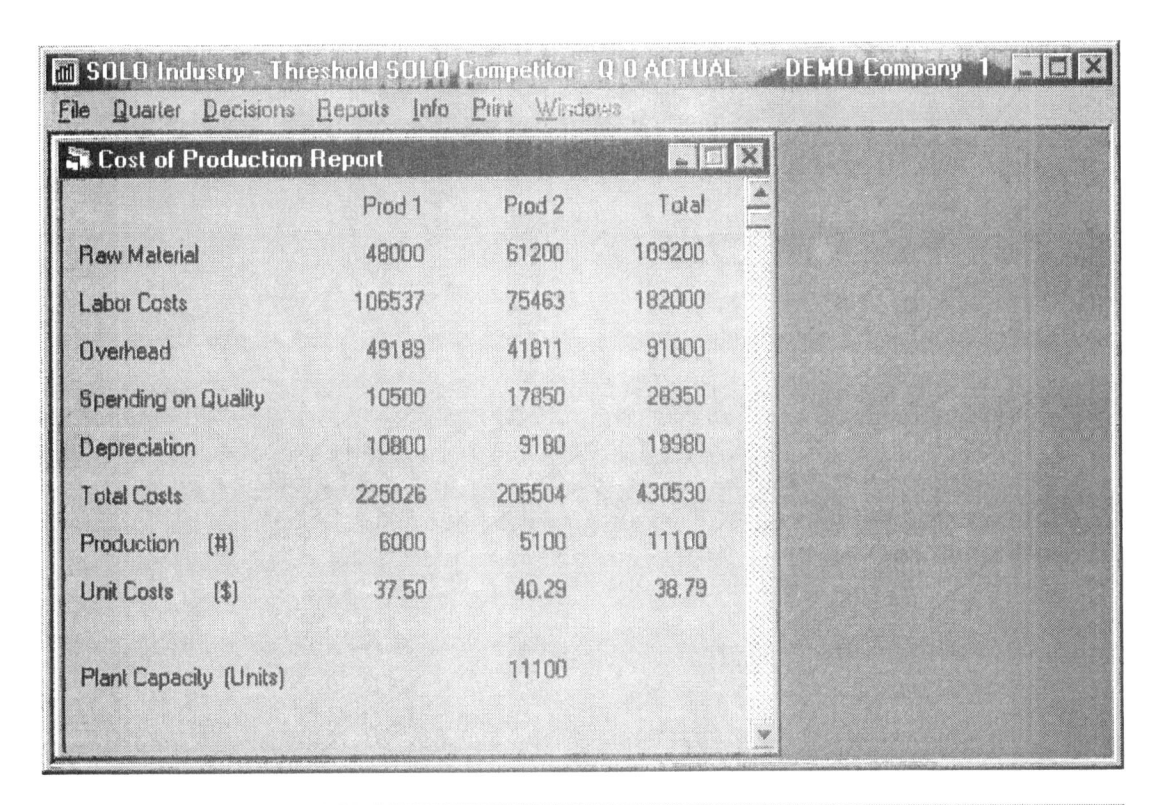

Cost of Production Report

	Prod 1	Prod 2	Total
Raw Material	48000	61200	109200
Labor Costs	106537	75463	182000
Overhead	49189	41811	91000
Spending on Quality	10500	17850	28350
Depreciation	10800	9180	19980
Total Costs	225026	205504	430530
Production (#)	6000	5100	11100
Unit Costs ($)	37.50	40.29	38.79
Plant Capacity (Units)		11100	

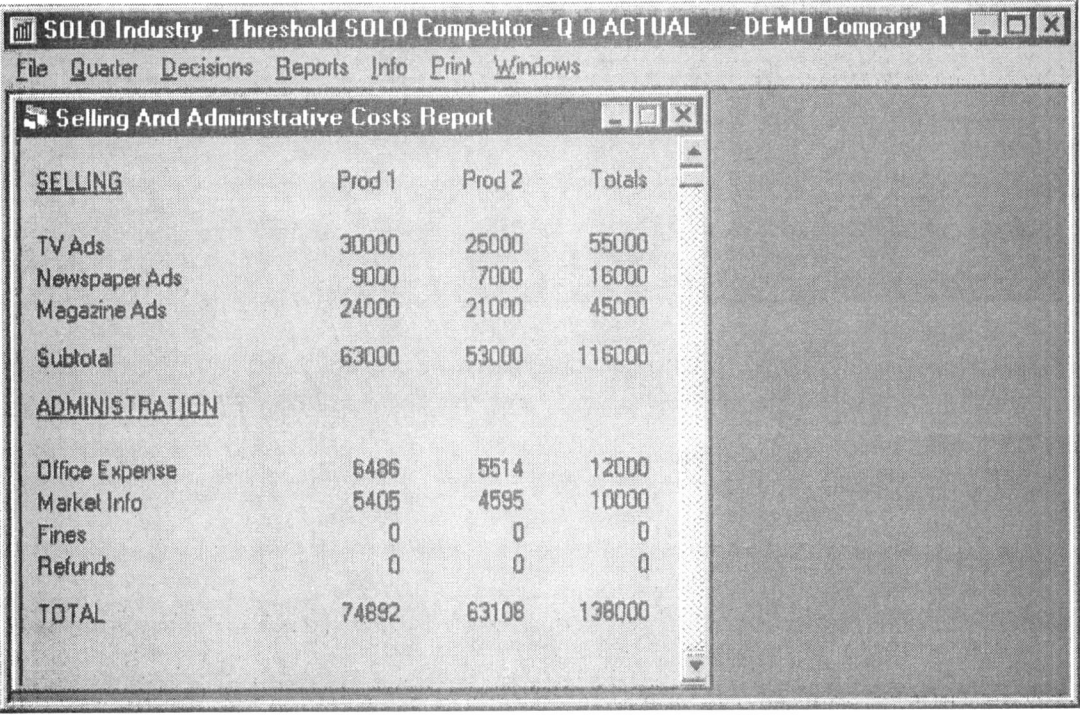

Selling And Administrative Costs Report

SELLING	Prod 1	Prod 2	Totals
TV Ads	30000	25000	55000
Newspaper Ads	9000	7000	16000
Magazine Ads	24000	21000	45000
Subtotal	63000	53000	116000
ADMINISTRATION			
Office Expense	6486	5514	12000
Market Info	5405	4595	10000
Fines	0	0	0
Refunds	0	0	0
TOTAL	74892	63108	138000

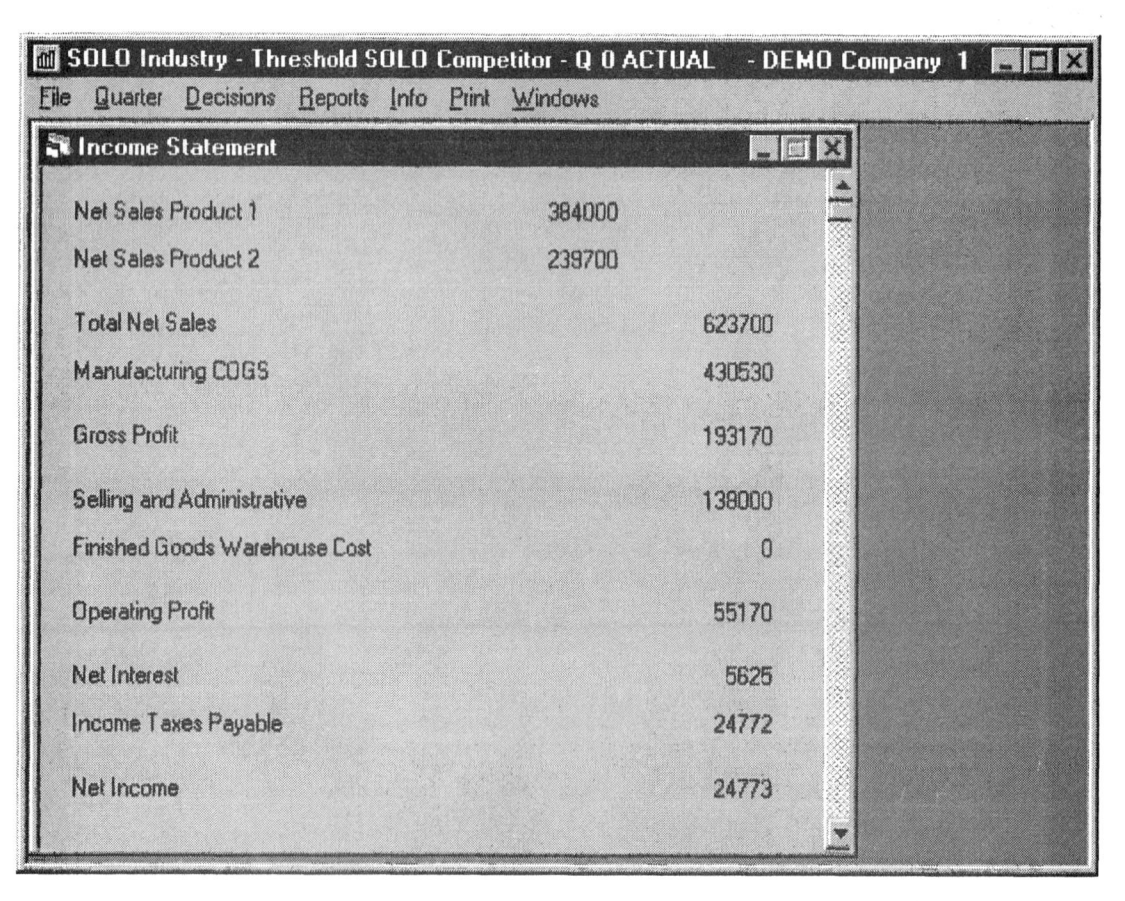

Appendix B, Quarter 0 Reports

SOLO Industry - Threshold SOLO Competitor - Q 0 ACTUAL - DEMO Company 1

Income Statement

Net Sales Product 1	384000
Net Sales Product 2	239700
Total Net Sales	623700
Manufacturing COGS	430530
Gross Profit	193170
Selling and Administrative	138000
Finished Goods Warehouse Cost	0
Operating Profit	55170
Net Interest	5625
Income Taxes Payable	24772
Net Income	24773

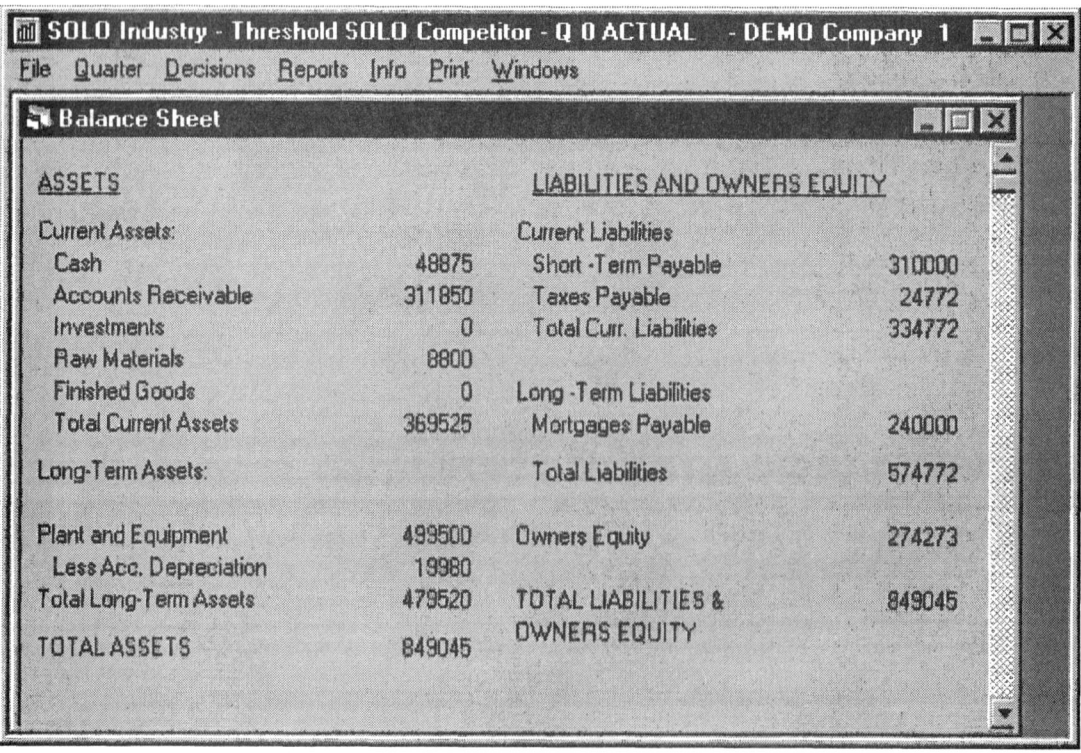

SOLO Industry - Threshold SOLO Competitor - Q 0 ACTUAL - DEMO Company 1

Balance Sheet

ASSETS		LIABILITIES AND OWNERS EQUITY	
Current Assets:		Current Liabilities	
Cash	48875	Short-Term Payable	310000
Accounts Receivable	311850	Taxes Payable	24772
Investments	0	Total Curr. Liabilities	334772
Raw Materials	8800		
Finished Goods	0	Long-Term Liabilities	
Total Current Assets	369525	Mortgages Payable	240000
Long-Term Assets:		Total Liabilities	574772
Plant and Equipment	499500	Owners Equity	274273
Less Acc. Depreciation	19980		
Total Long-Term Assets	479520	TOTAL LIABILITIES & OWNERS EQUITY	849045
TOTAL ASSETS	849045		

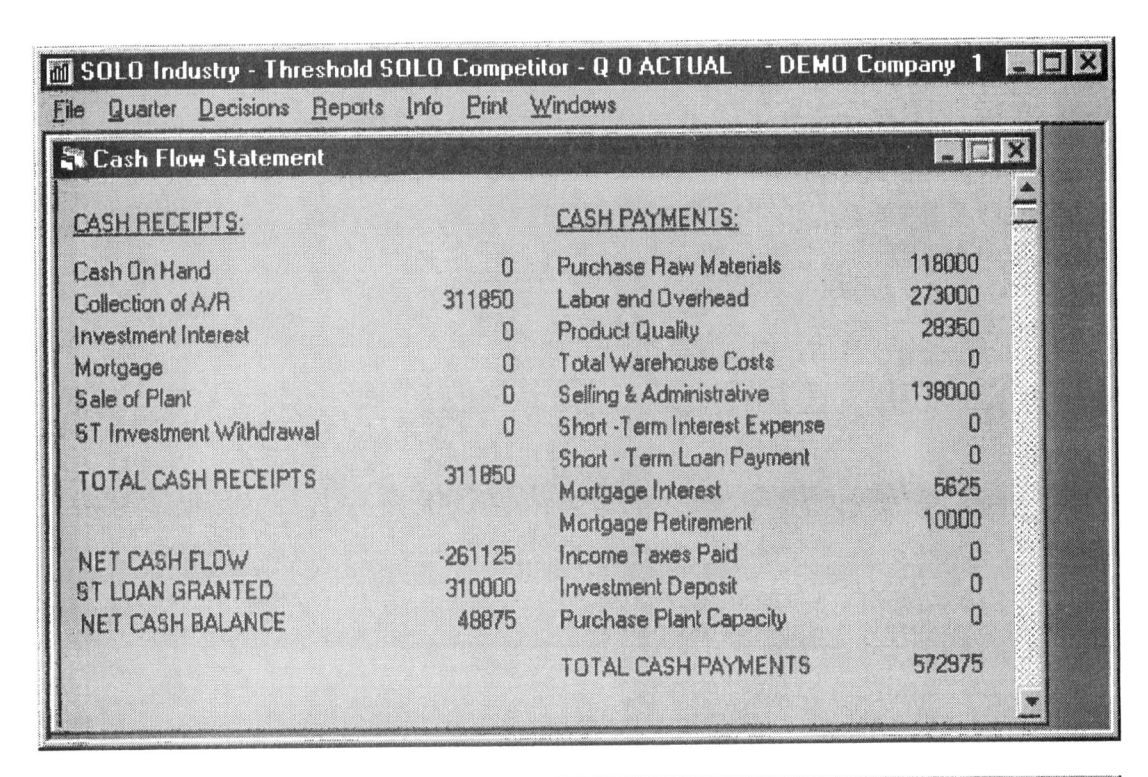

Cash Flow Statement

CASH RECEIPTS:		CASH PAYMENTS:	
Cash On Hand	0	Purchase Raw Materials	118000
Collection of A/R	311850	Labor and Overhead	273000
Investment Interest	0	Product Quality	28350
Mortgage	0	Total Warehouse Costs	0
Sale of Plant	0	Selling & Administrative	138000
ST Investment Withdrawal	0	Short-Term Interest Expense	0
		Short-Term Loan Payment	0
TOTAL CASH RECEIPTS	311850	Mortgage Interest	5625
		Mortgage Retirement	10000
NET CASH FLOW	-261125	Income Taxes Paid	0
ST LOAN GRANTED	310000	Investment Deposit	0
NET CASH BALANCE	48875	Purchase Plant Capacity	0
		TOTAL CASH PAYMENTS	572975

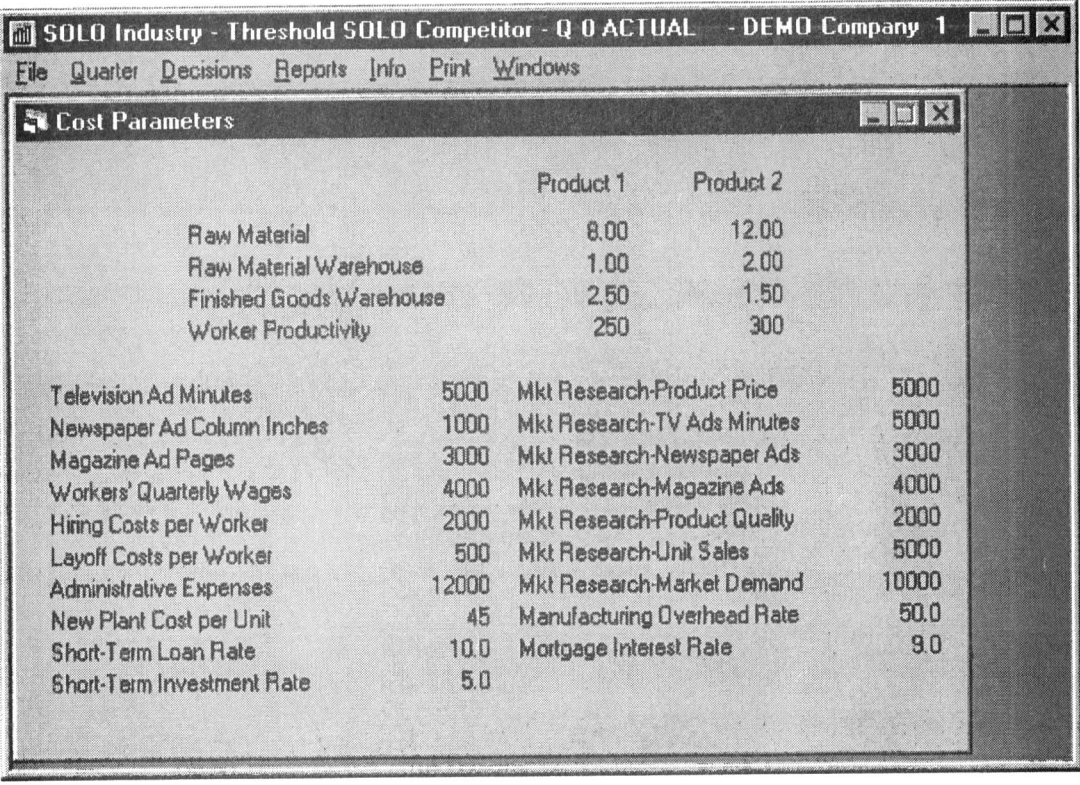

Cost Parameters

	Product 1	Product 2
Raw Material	8.00	12.00
Raw Material Warehouse	1.00	2.00
Finished Goods Warehouse	2.50	1.50
Worker Productivity	250	300

Television Ad Minutes	5000	Mkt Research-Product Price	5000
Newspaper Ad Column Inches	1000	Mkt Research-TV Ads Minutes	5000
Magazine Ad Pages	3000	Mkt Research-Newspaper Ads	3000
Workers' Quarterly Wages	4000	Mkt Research-Magazine Ads	4000
Hiring Costs per Worker	2000	Mkt Research-Product Quality	2000
Layoff Costs per Worker	500	Mkt Research-Unit Sales	5000
Administrative Expenses	12000	Mkt Research-Market Demand	10000
New Plant Cost per Unit	45	Manufacturing Overhead Rate	50.0
Short-Term Loan Rate	10.0	Mortgage Interest Rate	9.0
Short-Term Investment Rate	5.0		

APPENDIX C
SAMPLE MARKET RESEARCH REPORT

SOLO Industry - Threshold SOLO Competitor - Q 1 ACTUAL - DEMO Company 1

File Quarter Decisions Reports Info Print Windows

Market Research

Co. #	PRICE P1	PRICE P2	TV ADS P1	TV ADS P2	NEWS P1	NEWS P2	MAG P1	MAG P2	QUALITY P1	QUALITY P2	UNITS SOLD P1	UNITS SOLD P2
1	64	47	6	5	9	7	8	7	1.75	3.50	5607	5200
2	63	49	3	3	4	5	8	2	2.93	1.65	5325	2584
3	60	45	4	5	9	5	3	2	4.28	2.34	6000	3761
4	66	47	7	2	9	4	9	4	4.42	4.07	6000	4612
5	63	45	3	3	9	8	7	5	4.87	3.69	6000	5100
6	64	51	5	4	4	2	3	3	5.11	3.21	6000	2603
7	65	50	2	2	4	3	6	6	3.02	3.60	4277	3689
8	61	52	2	4	7	7	9	8	4.62	1.96	6000	3266
9	63	50	6	9	3	8	7	9	3.46	3.57	5744	5100
10	63	49	7	6	5	5	7	3	5.14	3.30	6000	4632
11	67	50	9	6	4	3	3	9	2.77	4.15	4262	5100
12	60	47	4	5	6	5	2	9	3.64	2.09	5130	5027
13	62	45	3	3	5	2	3	3	2.02	3.55	4682	4297
14	62	49	4	8	2	9	6	5	1.43	4.19	3630	5100
15	67	48	7	3	5	4	7	9	4.74	1.42	5237	4180
16	66	47	6	5	9	4	4	3	2.65	4.94	4894	5100

Potential product demands for Quarter 3 are 7000 and 6800 respectively.

APPENDIX D
INITIAL COST PARAMETERS

	Product 1	Product 2
Raw Material	8.00	12.00
Raw Material Warehouse	1.00	2.00
Finished Goods Warehouse	2.50	1.50
Worker Productivity	250	300

Television Ad Minutes	5000	Mkt Research-Product Price	5000
Newspaper Ad Column Inches	1000	Mkt Research-TV Ads Minutes	5000
Magazine Ad Pages	3000	Mkt Research-Newspaper Ads	3000
Workers' Quarterly Wages	4000	Mkt Research-Magazine Ads	4000
Hiring Costs per Worker	2000	Mkt Research-Product Quality	2000
Layoff Costs per Worker	500	Mkt Research-Unit Sales	5000
Administrative Expenses	12000	Mkt Research-Market Demand	10000
New Plant Cost per Unit	45	Manufacturing Overhead Rate	50.0
Short-Term Loan Rate	10.0	Mortgage Interest Rate	9.0
Short-Term Investment Rate	5.0		

APPENDIX E
THRESHOLD COMPETITOR LIMITS AND TIME LAGS

Marketing & Finance Limits and Time Lags

Decision Variable		Range / Limits	Lag Before Impact
Product Decisions - Product 1 and Product 2			
Price	($)	0 - 99	Immediate
TV Ads	(Minutes)	0 - 99	Immediate
Newspaper Ads	(Column Inches)	0 - 99	Immediate
Magazine Ads	(Pages)	0 - 99	Immediate
Product Quality	($)	0 - 99,999	Immediate
Sales Forecast - Product 1 & 2	(#)	0 - 99,999	No Impact
Short-Term Loan Requested	($)	0 - 9,999,999	Immediate
Mortgage Request	($)	0 - 9,999,999	Immediate
Short-Term Investment	($)	0 - 999,999	Immediate
Short-Term Withdrawal	($)	0 - 999,999	Immediate
Extra Payment	($)	0 - 999,999	No Impact

Production Limits and Time Lags

Decision Variable		Range / Limits	Lag Before Impact
Human Resource Development	($)	0 - 99,999	1 Quarter
Workers Hired for Next Quarter	(#)	0 - 99	1 Quarter
Workers Fired This Quarter	(#)	0 - 99	Immediate
Workers Laid Off This Quarter	(#)	0 - 99	Immediate
Purchase Plant Capacity	(# of Units)	1,000 - 10,000	1 Quarter
Sell Plant Capacity (# of Units) (Maximum of 50% of current capacity)		0 - 4,000	1 Quarter
Product 1 or Product 2:			
Purchase Raw Material	(#)	0 - 99,999	1 Quarter
Production Volume	(#)	0 - 99,999	Immediate

APPENDIX F
THRESHOLD COMPETITOR "HOT" KEYS

Screen	"Hot" Key(s)
To see	**Press**
Decisions	
Marketing and Market Research	F1
Production and Finance	F2
Reports	
Marketing Decisions	CTRL + F1
Production Decisions	CTRL + F2
Inventory	CTRL + V
Labor	CTRL + L
Production Costs	CTRL + P
Selling and Administration	CTRL + S
Income Statement	CTRL + I
Balance Sheet	CTRL + B
Cash Flow	CTRL + C
Market Research	CTRL + R
Quarter Performance	CTRL + Q
Game-to-Date Performance	CTRL + G
Info	
Marketing Limits	SHIFT + F1
Production Limits	SHIFT + F2
Costs	F3
Bulletin	F4

Appendix G

Management Dilemmas

MANAGEMENT DILEMMA 1
WHY DOES IT HAVE TO BE EMILY?

"... and whichever of the decisions you choose to make on this matter is totally up to you." The door closes behind you as you walk out of David Anderscott's office. Just what you need, another smoldering fire that might burst into flames no matter what you do. You stop and chat with several office workers on your way back to your office. But your mind is really on this new situation concerning Emily Bergmeier.

Emily is your purchasing agent and has been a trusted employee in Anderscott organizations for many years. She has a business degree from one of the better schools and has used her knowledge to keep your total purchasing expenditures among the lowest in the industry. Anderscott has just informed you that Emily has been accepting payments from one of your suppliers. For every $100 of goods she buys from the supplier, she receives a payment of $1 in the form of merchandise or cash mailed to her home. Information obtained by Anderscott indicates that no cost to the company can be traced to her actions. In fact, her performance has made her a highly recruited professional.

You must decide what to do about this embarrassing, if not illegal, situation. Your options, as spelled out by Anderscott, are to:

1. Do nothing since Emily is performing well and your costs are among the lowest in the industry.

    The effect of this action could result in a $25,000 fine by industry governmental regulators. If you are fined, it will be paid next quarter.

2. Terminate Emily immediately. Call the supplier and tell them of the problem. Inform your new purchasing agent not to purchase from that supplier in the future.

    The effect of this action could cause raw material costs to increase by 40% next quarter.

3. Terminate Emily immediately. Call the supplier and tell them of the problem. Inform your new purchasing agent not to accept payments from any of your suppliers.

    The effect of this action could cause raw material costs to increase by 25% next quarter.

4. Discipline Emily immediately. Call the supplier and tell them of the problem. Inform Emily not to accept payments from the supplier.

    The effect of this action could cause raw material costs to increase by 10% next quarter.

5. Appoint a committee of supervisors to investigate the accusations and report back to you with their findings and recommendations.

    The effect of this action could result in a $20,000 fine by industry governmental regulators if no corrective action seems likely. You would pay this fine next quarter.

Enter the number of your decision on the Production and Finance screen.

MANAGEMENT DILEMMA 2
CAN YOU STEAL GARBAGE?

Glancing up at the clock you realize that it's almost 11:30 p.m. You put away the papers you've been working on, pick up your coat, and walk out of your office into the empty plant. A flash of light catches your eye as you look down the alleyway lined with company trash carts. You see the outline of a pickup truck and a person loading items into the back of it. Strange, you think as you walk over and turn on the alley lights, no one should be here at this time. You see one of your production workers, Miles Molbeck.

"Hey, Miles!" you call. "What's going on here?"

"Uh, oh... Hello, boss. What brings you here at this hour?" Miles asks you as you continue to walk closer.

"I haven't been home yet," you say, "but what are you doing here? You know the plant is off-limits after working hours."

"Oh..., uh... I'm just here collecting these corrugated cartons that contained our raw materials. You know my wife's been sick and I need a few extra bucks. I learned a high-school buddy uses discarded corrugated paper in his business, and he pays seventy cents for a hundred pounds of crushed boxes. I take these home, smash them, and then sell them to him. I'm not getting rich on it. It just helps pay the bills. Anyway, this is garbage. It's not of any value to the company. In fact, you pay to have it hauled away, don't you?"

"That's not the issue," you say. "You know the company policy on theft. Anyone caught stealing company property is subject to immediate discharge and criminal prosecution. Those boxes are company property, and you have no authority to take them. That constitutes theft. Unload those boxes and go home. I want you in my office at nine o'clock tomorrow morning. Now get out of here."

"Yeah, sure. What a rinky-dink outfit. I'm going to be fired for stealing garbage that you're paying to have hauled away to the landfill."

Great, you think. What am I going to do now? You sympathize with Miles, and deep down agree that theft of garbage is a silly charge. But the company policy on theft is very specific and you must be wary of setting a precedent that goes against it. Can you really look the other way? Is Miles any different from any other employee? What if someone else needs money? Is it fair to the other employees? Who determines what is and what isn't garbage?

On the other hand, what happens if you fire Miles? Is employee morale going to be lowered? What about public opinion? Miles is well liked by the workers and popular in the community. Will business suffer because of bad press?

Your options are to:

1. Do nothing.

    If you choose this course of action, employee morale reaction is uncertain. Some of the employees will applaud your actions as humanitarian, while other employees who may also be in financial straits will feel slighted. This could have an effect on worker productivity next quarter. Also of concern is that you don't know what Anderscott will say if he ever hears about the incident.

2. Fire Miles and prosecute him for theft.

    This action will ensure that you have no extraordinary losses because of theft. But this action will probably lower worker productivity beginning next quarter.

3. Discipline Miles by suspending him for one quarter without pay.

    You anticipate this action will prevent losses because of theft, but employee morale will probably suffer. Thus you expect an increase in production costs for several quarters.

4. Subject Miles to minor discipline and a reprimand.

    Little effect on morale and worker productivity is anticipated. However, the minor punishment may encourage other employees to steal. This action could cause an increase in losses of up to $20,000 next quarter.

Enter the number of your decision on the Production and Finance screen.

MANAGEMENT DILEMMA 3
THE OLDER EMPLOYEE

One of your employees in the Marketing Department has not been able to adequately perform his assigned duties. He is a long-standing employee who has been with the company for 19 years. While he was an able employee in the past, the changing demands of the business, along with expanding job requirements for his position, have resulted in performance that is severely lacking. He is 57 years old. In one more year he will receive extra retirement benefits granted to 20-year employees. If you continue to "carry him" (employ him) for that year, you will undoubtedly have to hire an extra employee to "pick up the slack." This could also set a precedent for other employees facing similar circumstances throughout the company. On the other hand, firing him could affect the morale and loyalty of other employees. You also worry that if you fire him he will sue claiming age discrimination. Your assessment of the situation leads you to the following options with the following consequences.

1. Carry the employee for one year until his retirement benefits are in full force.

   This would necessitate hiring an additional employee to perform many of the duties this employee should be performing, but is not able to handle. The full cost of this employee (i.e., wages, benefits, office space, etc.) would be $40,000. The owners have said you would have to set aside $40,000 next quarter to pay for this action.

   There is a debate among your legal advisors whether this sets a precedence that would require similar treatment of other "older" employees. If similar treatment is required, you will have to pay an additional $50,000 into an escrow account next quarter.

2. Fire the employee.

   This will cost your company $27,000 as a severance payment to the employee (one-half of one year's salary). This will be paid next quarter.

   If a lawsuit is filed, company lawyers estimate the total cost, regardless of who wins the suit, to be $100,000. These costs would be paid next quarter.

3. Offer the employee early retirement with full benefits of a 20-year employee.

   This will cost the company an additional (i.e., beyond current retirement benefit costs) $50,000 in retirement benefits costs. This would be paid into an escrow account next quarter. You know the employee prefers to continue to work until he is 62 years old. Even with the benefits offered, his annual income will drop considerably.

   If other "older" employees demand equal treatment, you estimate the company would have to pay an additional $50,000 into its retirement fund to pay for these costs. This payment would be made next quarter. Your human resource people think there is little chance of this demand for equal treatment occurring.

4. Spend an additional $65,000 in training for a special program to improve the productivity of your older workers.

   The $65,000 must be paid next quarter. Your human resource people believe the productivity of the older workers could be improved to a level so that no additional action would have to be taken.

Enter the number of your decision on the Production and Finance screen.

MANAGEMENT DILEMMA 4
THE ALCOHOLIC EMPLOYEE

One of your employees has returned from lunch in various stages of drunkenness many times over the past three weeks. Without question, his drinking affects his performance as well as that of those around him. You are concerned that this could be a problem throughout the company. Rather than treat this as an isolated case concerning one employee, you are considering the possibility of instituting company-wide policies and programs.

Your options are to:

1. Do nothing and hope things get better.

   There is no direct cost to this, but other workers may get upset having to work with this person and quit without warning. There is also the chance this worker could be injured on the job because of the effects of the intoxication. Your liability because of your inaction could cost you up to $20,000.

2. Require the employee to attend a chemical-abuse program.

   This is a residence program that lasts for three months. You will pay the employee's salary while he is on leave, plus the cost of the program. The total cost will be $10,000.

   If he refuses to attend, he will be terminated. The costs associated with this would be $3,000. If he attends the program, but quits before its completion, the cost would be $15,000.

3. Institute a company-wide Chemical Abuse Awareness Program.

   The cost of this program would be $24,000. Your expectation is that productivity would be improved. This would mean higher crew productivity on the shop floor. The extent of these gains is unpredictable given the lack of experience the company has with this type of program. While only temporary, your Human Resources manager estimates it could range anywhere from 3% to 8%.

4. Put the employee on notice that repeating this behavior will result in termination.

   There is no cost if the employee mends his ways. Termination costs will be $3,000 if he comes in drunk again. Chances are this is likely to occur. Other workers may react negatively to your lack of a positive approach.

Enter the number of your decision on the Production and Finance screen.

MANAGEMENT DILEMMA 5
WILDCAT STRIKE

Several of your production employees are dissatisfied with the shop rules. They are also upset with their pay levels given the prevailing wage rates in their community for their type of work. In addition, they claim their fringe-benefit package is inadequate. They have been promoting the idea of a wildcat strike among the rest of the production workers as a means to get immediate attention to their concerns rather than wait for the current contract to expire. It is unlikely that the whole production workforce would join in a strike, but a significant portion could. Conceding to some or all of their demands would effect the chances of a strike occurring, but could also have an impact on future contract negotiations.

If a strike or walkout occurs, it will not take affect until the next quarter of operations. For example, if you make this dilemma decision in Quarter 4, any workers participating in the walkout would not report for work in Quarter 5. These workers would remain on the job in Quarter 4.

Your options are to:

1. Do nothing and hope that calmer heads on the shop floor will prevail.

    If a strike occurs it could mean up to 20% of your production workers would join the walkout. It would take the union leadership one quarter to get the workers to return to their jobs.

2. Offer a bonus of $10,000 as recognition of the legitimacy of their concerns.

    This would significantly reduce the chance of a strike occurring, but not guarantee it.

3. Offer a bonus that would cost a total of $20,000.

    This would make the likelihood of a strike small.

4. Offer a bonus that would cost a total of $50,000.

    No strike would occur.

5. Fire the workers involved. These workers represent about 10% of your current workforce.

    Chances of a walkout for one quarter by 25% of the production workforce would be 50/50.

Enter the number of your decision on the Production and Finance screen.

MANAGEMENT DILEMMA 6
SUBSTITUTE RAW MATERIALS

You have a chance to acquire a supply of substitute raw materials for Product 1. A large salvage company is accepting closed bids for a type of plastic slightly different from the raw material you presently use. A materials consultant thinks that this material would be an adequate substitute. Nothing appeared wrong with the sample material he inspected. Your production manager, Sylvia Wainright, is concerned that not all the material would meet your quality standards. She estimates that up to 30% of the material might not be usable. She also believes that your bid will affect the quality of the raw materials you receive. The higher the bid, the higher the quality of the materials received.

The salvage company has decided to sell the materials in lot sizes of 20,000 units. It will not sell more than one lot of 20,000 to any one company.

Since this is a closed bid, you will not know how much others are bidding for the materials. You will be allowed to make only one bid. How much you bid will affect the likelihood of successfully getting the material.

Anderscott has authorized you to make a bid on these materials, if you choose to do so. However, he has made it clear that the decision on whether to make a bid, or how much to bid, is yours to make. If you bid for the materials, and win, the number of units you will receive will be *in addition to* whatever volume you purchase from your regular supplier.

Your options are to:

1. Make no bid.

2. Make a bid of 50% of the current price you are paying for raw materials for Product 1.

3. Make a bid of 65% of the current price you are paying for raw materials for Product 1.

4. Make a bid of 80% of the current price you are paying for raw materials for Product 1.

Enter the number of your decision on the Production and Finance screen.

MANAGEMENT DILEMMA 7
WHERE THERE'S SMOKE, THERE'S FIRE

"Remember," says Anderscott, "the new policy is your baby. We're not required to have a smoking policy in this state, but a 1988 survey conducted by the U.S. Department of Health showed 35.6% of the companies in their survey had an employee help program concerning tobacco. The program will cost us money, but the benefits should outweigh the costs. Let me know what you decide to do."

The next day you meet with various employees and talk with other managers you know. After considerable discussion, you identify the following smoking policy alternatives.

Your options are to:

1. Do nothing beyond providing no-smoking sections in the eating areas.

    There are no data that show your firm incurs any costs caused by tobacco. You believe employees should make their own decisions regarding smoking and its health effects.

    There is the chance that nonsmokers will complain to the Health Department about second-hand smoke throughout the company buildings. Costs associated with responding to the Health Department inquiries and tests could cost up to $30,000. This fee would be payable next quarter.

2. Adopt a "smoke free" policy that prohibits tobacco use in the building and on company property.

    The administration costs of the policy are expected to be $20,000 and will be paid into an escrow account next quarter. You estimate that productivity might increase for some workers by up to 4% because of a reduction in sick leave taken.

    You anticipate some resistance because almost 20% of your workforce smokes. The increased level of discontent and problems associated with nicotine withdrawal could result in a loss of productivity for those workers.

3. Adopt a "smoke free" environment in the buildings but allow tobacco use outside and in personal vehicles on the company parking lot.

    The cost of this program is $15,000 with payment into an escrow account next quarter. You estimate that this program may increase productivity by 2%.

    You expect little direct opposition to this program from the workforce but predict the policy will increase the length of coffee breaks and lunches taken by smokers in your company. Nonsmokers are likely to extend their break periods as well.

4. Create a "smoking lounge" where tobacco use is allowed and permit tobacco use outside all buildings.

    The smoking lounge will have special fans and trash receptacles that cost $5,000. This will bring the total cost of the lounge to $8,000 with payment into an escrow account next quarter.

    You expect no resistance from the workforce, but extra trips to the smoking lounge could cause a drop in productivity after this policy goes into effect.

5. Put up "No Smoking" signs in the plant, require smokers to sit in a special area in the canteen, and prohibit smoking in all open offices.

   The cost of this policy is $5,000 with payment into an escrow account next quarter. You expect little worker dissent and benefits will be minimal.

   There is a possibility that nonsmokers may complain to the Health Department about second-hand smoke in the canteen. The costs associated with responding to the Health Department inquiries and tests could cost up to $10,000 and would be payable next quarter.

Enter the number of your decision on the Production and Finance screen.

MANAGEMENT DILEMMA 8
DID YOU HEAR THE ONE ABOUT...?

Lee, your personnel director, is in the process of giving you some disturbing information. You asked her to look into why the turnover for the administrative office staff in your organization is three times the industry average. You initially thought the high turnover rate was because the positions are entry-level, minimum-wage, and clerical. You asked Lee to examine the issue and report back to you. She conducted a number of interviews with the staff as well as exit interviews with individuals who quit during the last month.

"... and I think the exit interview with Rebecca Meeker confirms my diagnosis," says Lee. "We have two employees in the plant whose actions people in administration find unpleasant. Our warehouse coordinator, Butch Pilson, and a clerk in receiving named Tom West are the culprits. They tell off-color stories and jokingly proposition *every* woman in the office, regardless of how attractive the woman is."

"Many see the behavior as harmless bantering, but I think Rebecca's right. Butch and Tom's behavior borders on sexual harassment. Rebecca says she is considering a lawsuit, and there is the chance of a judgment against us. Glad this is your problem to solve."

You look back and see that no one has ever complained about the two men officially before this. Butch and Tom are among your best and most well-liked employees. Most of the employees seem to enjoy the verbal dueling. They accept it in the spirit of fun, not as serious attempts to proposition the women or degrade them.

Still, you cannot ignore the facts. Turnover in one department is three times the industry average. On top of all this, the threat of a sexual harassment lawsuit now hangs over your head. If a lawsuit is filed, you estimate legal costs will be $10,000 even if you win, and up to $50,000 if you lose the case. You will pay any legal expenses associated with this problem next quarter. After much thought, you identify the following alternatives.

Your options are to:

1. Do nothing.

    You feel the evidence you have is not conclusive enough to take any action. If you accuse the individuals of sexual harassment, you might ruin their careers. Without hard proof, the two men could sue the company for defamation of character. But how would the women react to this lack of action on your part?

    You anticipate no direct costs with this action. However, the turnover problem would continue and there would be a relatively large probability of legal action. If a suit is filed, you will almost certainly lose because you took no action to stop the men's behavior.

2. Fire Butch and Tom.

   You feel that a warning would only create a division among employees as each chose a side. Taking a firm stand would reinforce the company's attitude on behavior such as this.

   A cost of $15,000 would be incurred to cover severance pay and pension donations for the two individuals. This action virtually guarantees no legal action will be taken against your company for sexual harassment.

   You expect there is little chance either of the two men will find other employment in the near future. There is a good chance they may sue you for wrongful dismissal. This could cost you up to $40,000 in legal costs.

3. Suspend Butch and Tom for two weeks without pay.

   This action would emphasize the company's displeasure with this type of behavior. You believe this action would send a strong message to all company employees.

   You estimate that costs incurred with this action will be up to $20,000. There is a slight probability that your company will be named in a lawsuit because of your stand. Given the strong action you took, it is unlikely you would lose the case. However, if a suit is filed, your lawyer estimates the legal costs to defend the case would total $35,000.

4. Verbally warn the two men and place a note of reprimand in their personnel files stating any further problem in this area will result in their termination.

   You believe the banter was meant to be harmless. Once Butch and Tom recognize that some people find it unpleasant, they will stop. The two men are valued employees and would be difficult to replace.

   You estimate that costs incurred with this action will be up to $10,000. There is a smaller probability of legal action than for Option 2, but an increased chance you will lose the case if a lawsuit is filed against your company.

5. Informally caution the two men.

   This approach would keep any disciplinary actions out of their personnel files and save the two men from public embarrassment. You are uncomfortable with taking stronger action before giving the men a chance to change their ways.

   You estimate no costs associated with this action. In fact, you think there could be some efficiencies achieved as people spend less time bantering. This could save up to $5,000 this quarter. You see this as only a temporary gain, expecting employees to return to joking around about topics other than sex.

   The lack of visible action will increase the chance of a lawsuit. If a suit is filed, you are likely to lose because you will be unable to show that you took any action to stop the men's behavior.

Enter the number of your decision on the Production and Finance screen.

APPENDIX H
THRESHOLD TEAM COMPETITOR INDUSTRY PERFORMANCE REPORTS

SOLO Industry - Threshold SOLO Competitor - Q 1 ACTUAL - DEMO Company 1
File Quarter Decisions Reports Info Print Windows

Quarter Peformance Report

COMP	SALES	PTS AWRD	INCOME	PTS AWRD	ROA	PTS AWRD	FORECAST ERRORS	PTS AWRD	OVERALL PTS	RANK
1	603248	16	2581	6	0.32	3	503	14*	38	6
2	462091	12	11536	26	1.32	11	3101	2	52	3
3	526245	14	4270	10	0.50	4	4016	2	29	8
4	607458	16	5950	14	0.67	6	1614	4	39	5
5	607500	16	-6236	-14	-0.71	-6	1915	4	-1	10
6	516753	13	21564	49*	2.47	21*	3159	2	86	1
7	458472	12	14064	32	1.65	14	3134	2	60	2
8	531199	14	-7911	-18	-0.89	-8	4427	2	-10	11
9	616872	16*	-36793	-49	-4.16	-21	1321	5	-49	13
10	602652	16	-20458	-46	-2.31	-20	2127	3	-47	12
11	535873	14	-21489	-49	-2.46	-21	1476	5	-51	14
12	544069	14	-31580	-49	-3.68	-21	1453	5	-51	15
13	479160	12	9456	21	1.13	10	2121	3	47	4
14	472410	12	-32961	-49	-3.98	-21	3684	2	-56	16
15	551519	14	2873	7	0.33	3	1773	4	28	9
16	560257	15	4093	9	0.47	4	1534	5	32	7

SOLO Industry - Threshold SOLO Competitor - Q 1 ACTUAL - DEMO Company 1
File Quarter Decisions Reports Info Print Windows

Game to Date Peformance Report

COMP	SALES	PTS AWRD	INCOME	PTS AWRD	AVG ROA	PTS AWRD	FORECAST ERRORS	PTS AWRD	OVERALL PTS	RANK
1	1226948	16	27354	29	0.06	3	503	14*	62	5
2	1085791	14	36309	38	0.23	11	3101	2	66	3
3	1149945	15	29043	31	0.09	4	4016	2	52	8
4	1231158	16	30723	32	0.12	6	1614	4	59	6
5	1231200	16	18537	20	-0.11	-6	1915	4	33	10
6	1140453	15	46337	49*	0.42	21*	3159	2	87	1
7	1082172	14	38837	41	0.28	14	3134	2	71	2
8	1154899	15	16862	18	-0.14	-7	4427	2	27	11
9	1240572	16*	-12020	-13	-0.69	-21	1321	5	-12	15
10	1226352	16	4315	5	-0.38	-19	2127	3	5	12
11	1159573	15	3284	3	-0.40	-20	1476	5	3	13
12	1167769	15	-6807	-7	-0.61	-21	1453	5	-8	14
13	1102860	14	34229	36	0.19	10	2121	3	63	4
14	1096110	14	-8188	-9	-0.66	-21	3684	2	-14	16
15	1175219	15	27646	29	0.06	3	1773	4	51	9
16	1183957	15	28866	31	0.08	4	1534	5	55	7

Appendix I

Threshold Competitor Flow Chart

Decisions Under Your Control   **Decisions Outside Your Control**

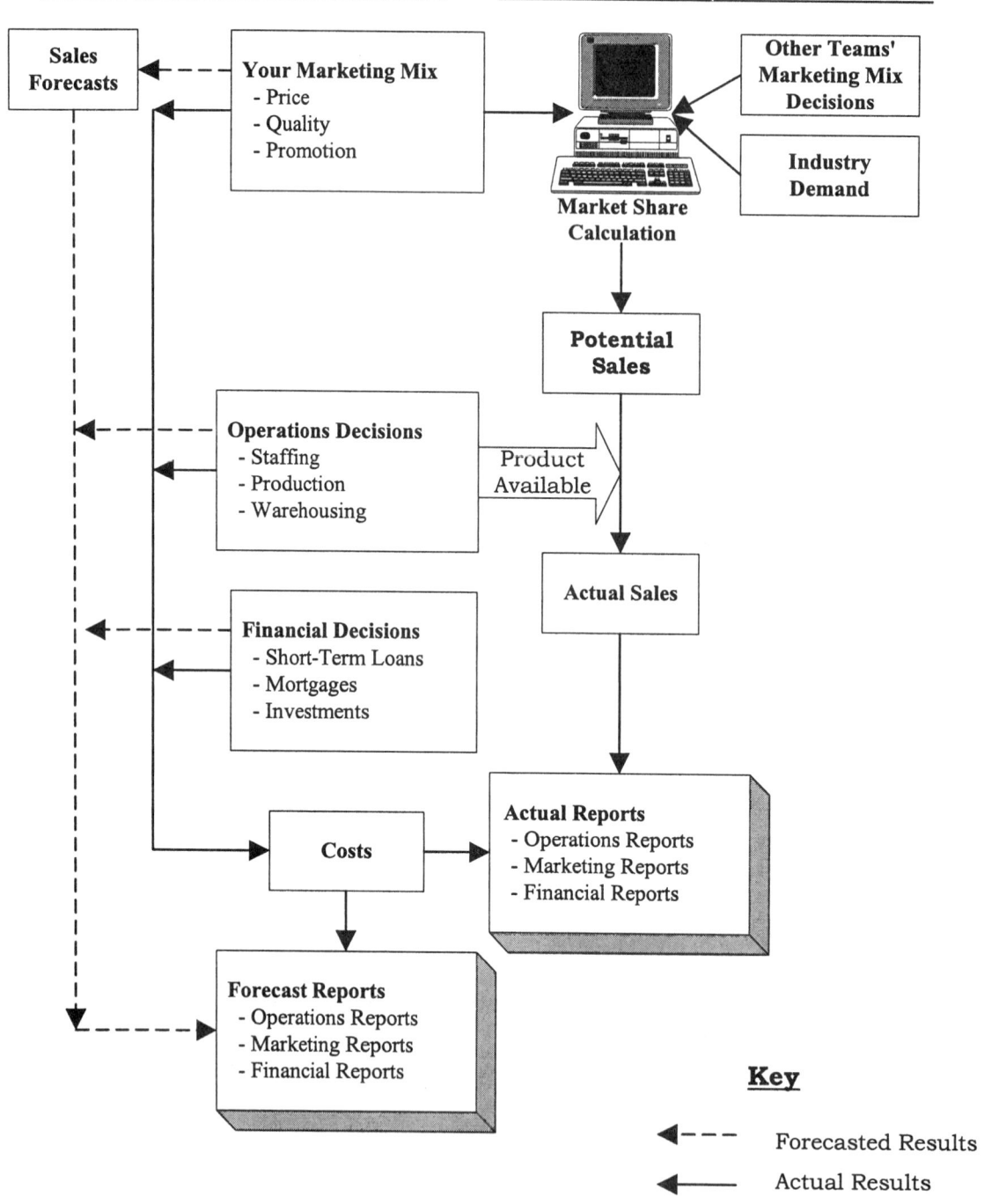

Sales Forecasts

Your Marketing Mix
- Price
- Quality
- Promotion

Other Teams' Marketing Mix Decisions

Industry Demand

Market Share Calculation

Potential Sales

Operations Decisions
- Staffing
- Production
- Warehousing

Product Available

Actual Sales

Financial Decisions
- Short-Term Loans
- Mortgages
- Investments

Costs

Actual Reports
- Operations Reports
- Marketing Reports
- Financial Reports

Forecast Reports
- Operations Reports
- Marketing Reports
- Financial Reports

Key

← - - - Forecasted Results

← Actual Results

APPENDIX J
A STEP-BY-STEP WALK-THROUGH

1. Start the *Threshold Competitor* program.

2. Enter some decisions.
    - Raise price of Product 1 by $2.
    - Buy 10 more TV ads for Product 1.
    - Lower sales forecast for Product 1 by 500 units.
    - Buy Price and Units Sold information under Market Research on bottom half of screen. (Enter a "Y".)

3. Look at the Forecast reports.
    - Use mouse to select the Reports option on the Menu bar.
    - Select the Income Statement.

4. Press the F3 "hot" key to access the Cost screen.
    - Notice the cost of TV ads is $5,000 (listed in the left column, first item).

5. Press the F1 "hot" key to return to the Marketing screen (or select the Decisions option on the Menu bar).

6. Vary the decisions.
    - Lower the TV ads for Product 1 by 5.
    - Lower sales forecast for Product 1 by another 300 units.

7. Look at the Income Statement again (see Point #3).
    - Notice the change in the Net Income from first forecast.

8. Print out selected reports.
    - Select the Print option on the Menu bar.
    - Choose the Selected Screens option.
    - Click on the Income Statement and the Cash Flow options, then click on OK.
    - Click OK when the Printer dialogue box appears.

9. Exit *Threshold Competitor*.
    - Select the File option on the Menu bar and then Exit.

APPENDIX K
Threshold Competitor CompData Excel File

Excel Column	Variable Name	Definition
A	Quarter	Quarter number
B	P1Price	Price – Product #1
C	P2Price	Price – Product #2
D	P1TV	# of TV ads – Product #1
E	P2TV	# of TV ads – Product #2
F	P1News	# of newpaper ads – Product #1
G	P2News	# of newpaper ads – Product #2
H	P1mags	# of magazine ads – Product #1
I	P2mags	# of magazine ads – Product #2
J	P1SlsFcst	Sales Forecast (# of units) – Product #1
K	P2SlsFcst	Sales Forecast (# of units) – Product #2
L	P1SlsAct	Actual # of units sold – Product #1
M	P2SlsAct	Actual # of units sold – Product #2
N	P1FGEndInv	Finished Goods Ending inventory – Product #1
O	P2FGEndInv	Finished Goods Ending inventory – Product #2
P	P1MfgCost	$ Manufacturing Cost, per unit – Product #1
Q	P2MfgCost	$ Manufacturing Cost, per unit – Product #2
R	P1ProdQual	$ amount spent on quality, per unit – Product #1
S	P2ProdQual	$ amount spent on quality, per unit – Product #2
T	P1Revenue	$ Sales Revenue – Product #1
U	P2Revenue	$ Sales Revenue – Product #2
V	NetIncome	$ Net Income
W	ROA	Return on Assets

APPENDIX L
Threshold Competitor **PerfData Excel File**

Excel Column	Variable Name	Definition
A	Quarter	Quarter number
B	Company	Company number
C	QSales$	Quarterly sales ($)
D	QtrInc	Quarterly income ($)
E	QROA	Quarterly return on assets (%)
F	QPoints	Quarterly Performance Points Received (#)
G	CumSales	Cumulative sales ($)
H	CumInc	Cumulative income ($)
I	CumROA	Cumulative return on assets (%)
J	CumPoints	Cumulative Performance Points Received (#)

INDEX

Actual Results 48
Advertising (TV, Newspaper, Magazine) 56
Assets 86

Backup Disk 37, 52
Balance Sheet 85-87
Bulletin 44
Business Plan 54
Buy (Purchase) Plant Capacity 67
Buy (Purchase) Raw Materials 63

Calculation of Points Awarded 92
Capacity: (Manufacturing, Plant) 15, 67
Cash Flow Statement 87-90
Cash Payments 88
Cash Receipts 87
Change Company Name 40
Change Password 24
Company Disk Failure 53
Company Name 39
Company's Products 14
Computer System Requirements vii, 18
Controlling 13
Copying Disks 52
Copying Files Between the Company Disk and the Hard Disk 51
Correcting an Error 32
Cost Breakdown of Mfg. COGS 81
Cost of Market Research 61
Cost Per Unit 80
Cost Parameters Report 43, 72
Cost of Production Report 79-81
Create Backup Company File 37
Create Company Spreadsheet 38
Create New Industry 37
Create Performance Spreadsheet 38
CSS Extension 25
Current Assets 86
Current Liabilities 87
Cursor Movement 32-33

Data Entry Error 53
Data File Storing 22-23
Decisions, Entering 31
Decisions Flow Chart 73
Decision Guidelines 73
Decision Menu 41
Decision Reports 74
Deposit, Short-Term Investment 70

Dilemmas 71
Diminishing Returns 58
Disk Failure 53
Displaying Multiple Screens Simultaneously 48

Entering Company Name 24
Entering Decisions 31-32
Entering Password 24
Effect of Price on Sales 56
Effect of Quality on Sales 64
Equipment Needed vii, 18
Error Correction 32
Exiting the Program 40
Extra Payment, Mortgages 70

Factors to Consider When Forecasting 57
File Menu 36
Finance Decisions 68-71
Finance Decisions Report 75
Finished Goods Inventory 77
Fire Workers 66
Flow Chart, Decisions 73
Forecasting Sales 57
Forecasting Stage 2
Forecast Reports (Results) 47, 58
Four Performance Factors 91
Future Sales Potential - Market Research 61

Goals 10

Hard Disk (Drive) 51
Hire Workers 66
History of the Company 14-15
"Hot" keys 36
Human Resource Development 67-68

Icon to Start Program 20
Industry Performance Report 90-92
Income Statement 83-85
Info Menu 43
Installation 18-20
Internet Connection 18
Inventory Report 76-79
Investment in Product Quality 63
Investments, Short-Term 70

Labor Costs 79
Labor Report 78

Index

Lay Off Workers 66
Leading 12
Liabilities 87
Limits, Marketing/Finance 43
Limits, Production 43
Loading the Software 18-20
Loans, Short-Term 69
Location of *Threshold Competitor* Icons 20
Long-Term Liabilities 87
Lost Sales 78

Management Dilemmas 71
Magazine Ads 56
Magazine Ads – Market Research 60
Manufacturing Cost 79-81
Marketplace of the Company 16-17
Market Research Costs 61
Market Research Decisions 59
Market Research Report 60, 82
Marketing Decisions 55-57
Marketing Decisions Report 74
Marketing/Finance Limits Report 43, 59
Menu Bar 36-37
Mission (Mission Statement) 9-10
Mortgages (Requests, Extra Payment) 70
Moving From Screen to Screen 33
Moving the Cursor 32
Mouse, Using the 33, 34
Multiple Screens, Display Simultaneously 48

Navigating Around Threshold Competitor 21
Net Cash Flow 89
Newspaper Ads 56
Newspaper Ads – Market Research 60

Owners' Equity 87
Opening an Existing Solo Data File 28, 36
Opening an Existing Team Data File 30
Operations Reports 76-81
Organizing 12
Overtime 65
Overview vii, 1, 54

Password 24, 39
Performance Report 90-92
Performance Factors 91
PgUp, PgDn Keys 35
Planning 8-11, 54-55
Plant Capacity 65, 67
Points Awarded (PTS AWRD) 92
Policies 11

Pricing Decision 56
Price – Market Research 60
Print All Pages 47
Print Current Screen 46
Print Decisions 46
Print to File 46
Print Menu 44-47
Print to Printer 45
Print Selected Screens 46
Process the Decisions 37, 48
Process Industry 37
Processing Stage 2-3
Product Quality 63
Product Quality – Market Research 60
Products, *Threshold Competitor* 16-17
Production Costs 79-81
Production Decisions 62-68
Production/Finance Limits Report 43
Production Workers 66
Products 14
Program Failure 53
Purchase Plant Capacity 67
Purchase Raw Material 63

Quality, Product 63
Quality Information - Market Research 60
Quantity Discounts, Raw Materials 63
Quarter Menu 40-42

Raw Material Inventory 64, 76
Raw Material Order Shortages 63
Raw Material, Purchase 63
Reports Menu 42
Report Screens 35
Reprocessing a Quarter 49-51
Request Mortgage 70
Results Stage 3-4
Return on Assets (ROA) 91
Running a Team Company Data File on a
   Floppy Disk 26
Running a Team Company Data File on a Hard
   Disk 27

Sales Forecast 57
Sales Potential - Market Research 61
Saving Decisions 32, 40
Select Quarter 39
Sell Plant Capacity 67
Selling and Administrative Cost Report 81
Setup Instructions (Setting up) 18-22
Short-Term Loan 69, 89

Short-Term Investment (Deposit, Withdrawal) 70
Simultaneous Screen Display 48
Spending on Product Quality 63
Spreadsheets 38
Staffing 12, 66
Starting the *Competitor Solo* Program 23
Starting the *Competitor Team* Program 26
Storing Company Data File 22
Strategy (Strategies) 10-11, 54
Substitute Products 17, 58
System Failure 52

Tab Key 32
Tips on Succeeding with *Threshold Competitor* 5
Total Assets 86
Training (Human Resource Development) 67
Trouble Shooting 52
Turnover, Worker 16, 66
TV Ads 56
TV Ads – Market Research 60

Unit Cost 80
Units Produced 64-65
Units Sold - Market Research 61
Using the Arrow Keys 34
Using the "Hot" Keys 36
Using the Icon to Start the Program 20
Using the Manual 6
Using the Menu Bar 33
Using the Mouse 33, 34
Using the [PgUp] and [PgDn] Keys 35
Using the Tab Key 32

Valid Access Number 18
Viruses 53

Walk-through 53
Warehousing Costs 63
Withdrawals, Short-Term Investment 70
Windows, Using 18-20
Worker Overtime 65
Workers (Hire, Fire, Layoff, Turnover) 66
Workers Available 65